GLENDA FARRELL

Hollywood's Hardboiled Dame

GLENDA FARRELL

Hollywood's Hardboiled Dame

by Scott Allen Nollen

Midnight Marquee Press, Inc.
Baltimore, Maryland, USA; London, UK

for

Kris and Martha Marentette

Contents

Preface

Torchy Blane: model for Superman's Lois Lane. Five-foot-three firecracker. Smart, adventurous blonde. Gimme girl. Wry eyes, pouty kisser. Wicked wisecrack. Sly double take. Fast-talking, no-nonsense, straight-shooting, standup, hardboiled dame.

Anyone for Glenda?

As often as she played a blonde, Glenda Farrell actually had light brown hair and dark gray eyes. And regardless of the hundreds of witty one-liners she tossed off in countless films, she really wasn't hardboiled at all.

In real life, Glenda usually didn't deliberately say things to be funny; she said them to be *honest*. In fact, she was so *unlike* her screen image that she often disappointed eager fans that met her when she wasn't working (which wasn't often during the 1930s).

During the "Golden Age" of Hollywood, Glenda was considered a bit of a rebel. Her dislike for the typical Tinsel Town social scene and refusal to show skin on the screen or in promotional photographs made her a sort of quiet "women's libber" before that mantle was taken up more brazenly by the likes of Miss Bette Davis (and even Bette posed for cheesecake stills).

A 1938 *Hollywood* magazine article by Ruth Rankin presents a contemporary impression of Glenda. (It's almost as if Teresa "Torchy" Blane herself wrote the piece.)

> One of the most important rules in that masterly treatise "How to Win Friends and Influence People" (or "Never Be Yourself") is: "Call attention to people's mistakes indirectly."
>
> Now our little Miss Farrell and this rule have less than practically nothing in common. ("You look terrible—where on Earth did you get that hat—looks like it was dredged out of the harbor," is a stock greeting.) The Farrell type is a frank, open-faced model ... that believes that a straight line is the shortest distance between two points, and hopes you are the same. Expects you to be. This tightrope-balancing act of keeping on the good side and sundry by never having an idea of expressing an opinion is not for the Glenda Farrells of this world. The Glenda Farrells get things done while the others stand around explaining.
>
> Glenda has it all figured out that you can't be on everybody's side at once—which is a pretty rare trait in Hollywood ... And if Glenda is on your side, you've got something there...

Studio portrait

Glenda is the champion "on approval" dame of Hollywood … However, out of all the hats and handbags she has sent out, she keeps enough so that the game seems to be worth it in the long run. Anyway, the stores keep sending them …

One store, you can't blame them, is mad for keeps. Glenda ordered an entire fall wardrobe and sent it *all* back. An acquaintance—not a friend, mind you—went to Glenda with

Studio portrait

a sob story. He was in an awful jam—would she help him out? The sum he needed was rather staggering—enough so that it was a choice between the wardrobe or helping him out. She will never see a cent of the "loan" again. The man is a person of no influence, if that is what the Hollywood-wise are thinking. No, it was an act of pure altruism, perpetuated by one of Hollywood's very, very real altruists.

She's rather swell people, Glenda. If her enemies won't stay that way, it isn't her fault. Heaven knows, she tries.[1]

In her screen work, Glenda primarily called herself a comedian (not "comedienne"). Like many actors, she considered comedy far more difficult to play than drama—and she had great experience in both, including being on the stage for more than four decades. Though she occasionally received the top-billed female role in a film, she didn't think of herself as a "movie star." She was pleased to say that she was a "character person."

This is the first book about Glenda. Thirty years ago, when I first saw her in *I Am a Fugitive from a Chain Gang* (1932), she became my favorite actress. I instantly knew that she wasn't a glamour girl. On the screen, she was a gimme girl—in more ways than one.

Even though she was playing a completely unsympathetic character, Glenda was instantly appealing. I could immediately see how Paul Muni's character, James Allen, could get so easily taken in by her manipulative Marie Woods.

As I began to seek out more of Glenda's classic films, I realized that she always gave her best, regardless of the quality of the vehicle. Between her marriages, from the onset of the Great Depression to the dawn of U.S. involvement in World War II, she worked constantly, first on the stage, then at Warner Bros., relentlessly, and as a freelance film actress.

Glenda was a single mother with serious responsibilities. As her character, Marie Callahan, in *Kansas City Princess* (1935) would say, these required a lot of *money, jack and dough*—and Glenda earned it all herself. During the 1930s, she was fortunate to be able to buy a house for her widowed father, so he could look after her young son, Tommy, who was educated at military school.

And Glenda's generosity went far beyond providing for her father and son. She welcomed friends into her home and spread her good fortune outside of it. In real life, she was a "givey" girl.

Following her very wise move of marrying the well-regarded, gentlemanly Dr. Henry Ross at age 39, Glenda still continued to work, occasionally in films, but more often on the stage and then television. She was a natural-born performer, learned her craft by *doing it* and carried on until ill health finally stopped her.

Today, more than four decades after her passing, her naturalistic performances are as fresh as ever, while the work of many of her star contemporaries seems overly stylized and theatrical by comparison. And, if comedy truly is more difficult to play than drama, then Glenda may have been an even better actor than she realized. Her comic timing, particularly in her films with Joan Blondell, is exquisite; and she makes it look so effortless.

Glenda's career in films, television, radio and on stage is covered in these pages. Although few major primary research sources exist (Glenda's son, friends and colleagues are no longer with us), her personal life, including her attitudes, interests, hobbies and activities (particularly her charity work before and during World War II), is also given serious attention. Fortunately, the 1930s press covered Glenda's social life and career extensively.

Glenda loved people and truly enjoyed taking part in sincere social and community events. Her best friends from her Warner Bros. contract days were Mary Brian and frequent costar Joan Blondell. She also palled around with fellow Warner Bros. "stock company" actors Allen Jenkins and Hugh Herbert. During the 1930s and early 1940s, two of her close theatrical colleagues were Lyle Talbot and Alan Dinehart, who often joined her for various benefits and fund raising events.

Prior to her relationship with Dr. Ross, several eligible bachelors were rumored to have "popped the question," but Glenda was too careful and *smart* to rush headlong into anything, especially something as serious as marriage. She focused on her family and friends, her homes (in Los Angeles and New York) and her work.

The text examines Glenda's entire career, with important projects and roles receiving a thorough treatment, while "lesser" material is mentioned in more brevity. A complete filmography, the most thorough listing of her television appearances (including several titles not included in earlier print and electronic sources), list of Broadway performances and biographical sketches of her best Warner Bros. friends and colleagues are included.

I extend my thanks to Barton H. Aikens, Cliff Aliperti, the American Film Institute, Hardwicke Benthow, the late Julie Harris, Michael A. Hoey, Todd M. Jacobsen, the Media History Digital Library, Harold N. Nollen, Shirley A. Nollen, Jay F. Tiarks, Turner Classic Movies and the University of Wisconsin–Madison.

But most of all, I thank Glenda, who deserves to kick this volume off herself:

Heads up ... A lady's comin' in!

Scott Allen Nollen
Harlan, Iowa
January 2014

Notes:

[1]*Hollywood*, April 1938, p. 58.

Chapter 1
Beautiful Aspirant

Glenda Farrell of 2320 Broadway, San Diego, California
—on *Motion Picture* magazine's "Honor Roll of Beautiful Aspirants" (1919)

In Enid, Oklahoma, on June 30, 1901,[1] a squalling baby daughter, Glenda, was born to Wilhelmina ("Minnie") and Charles Farrell, of Alsatian (French-German) and Irish-Cherokee descent, respectively. The growing family, which also included two sons, Eugene and Richard (born July 10, 1910), moved to Wichita, Kansas, when Glenda was about nine. Charles was a trader in animals, mostly horses and dogs, and little Glenda soon developed a love for pets that would last a lifetime.

Having longed to become an entertainer, a dream that unfortunately would remain unfulfilled, Minnie wholeheartedly supported her daughter's burgeoning interest in the dramatic arts. At age seven, Glenda was cast as Evangeline "Little Eva" St. Clare in an Elks Club amateur production of Harriet Beecher Stowe's *Uncle Tom's Cabin.*

Minnie and Charles raised Glenda with the tenets of Catholicism, a faith she would retain throughout her life. Part of her formal education included attending the Mount Carmel Catholic Academy, a girls' boarding school.

Following a move to Oregon, the family relocated to sunny San Diego. Twelve-year-old Glenda was eager to join the Virginia Brissac Players, a local stock company, in which she played children's parts in many old standbys, including Kate Douglas Wiggin and Charlotte Thompson's *Rebecca of Sunnybrook Farm.*

Studio portrait of Virginia Brissac in *Captain from Castile* (1947)

The Brissac Players were a very well-known professional company, providing a solid training ground for aspiring performers. On the stage with various West Coast companies since 1902, Virginia Brissac (1883-1979) had starred in William Gillette's *Secret Service* (1905), Paul Kester's *Sweet Nell of Old Drury* (1906), Oscar Wilde's *Lady Windermere's Fan* (1907) and Winchell Smith and Byron Ongley's *Brewster's Millions* (1912), among many other classics.

Since 1914, Brissac (who later would enjoy a successful film career) had focused on local theater, mainly in the San Francisco Bay area. The professionalism of her company certainly registered strongly with Glenda. The Brissac Players usually changed the bill every week, so rehearsals were very intensive, and the directors suffered no nonsense from their young actors.

Accompanied by her mother, Glenda toured with the stock company for several years, often playing one-night stands, quickly moving on from one town to another. While maintaining a hectic professional schedule, she somehow managed to attend school in San Diego.

Glenda's winning entry in *Motion Picture* magazine's "Fame and Fortune Contest" (January 1919). Of the thousands of young women who entered, only seven were chosen to be named to the "Honor Roll of Beautiful Aspirants."

In January 1919, Glenda entered the "Fame and Fortune Contest" sponsored by the popular *Motion Picture* and *Motion Picture Classic* magazines. Each contestant was required to submit a current photograph of herself for the chance to be named to the "Honor Roll of Beautiful Aspirants." Of the seven young ladies chosen from thousands of candidates, one was "Glenda Farrell of 2320 Broadway, San Diego, California."

Motion Picture reported, "Miss Glenda Farrell was born in Oklahoma, and has had some experience in the chorus, vaudeville and camp entertainments. She has light-brown hair, dark-gray eyes and is five feet three inches in height."[2]

Later in 1919, while performing a dance at San Diego's Navy Benefit Hall, 18-year-old Glenda became enamored with English-born Thomas Albert "Dick" Richards, a decorated, 20-year-old World War I veteran. "It was violent love at first sight," recalled Glenda.[3]

Minnie, disapproving of Richards' status as an unemployed sailor, repeatedly turned him from the Farrell door, leading to a blossoming of the romance at a local sweet shop. Carried away by youthful enthusiasm, Glenda accepted a train ticket from a Hollywood scout, and married Richards on the trip to Tinsel Town, where she planned to appear in a screen test. However, motion pictures would need *sound* before they were ready for Glenda.

Back in San Diego, the happy newlyweds, intent on taking a show on the road, tirelessly worked up a vaudeville act while living at the Farrell home. After a brief time playing small-time theaters in the area, Glenda became pregnant but kept acting and dancing as long as possible. When forced to put a hold on performing, she worked extra hours as a salesperson during the days and at an artificial flower factory in the evenings.

On October 7, 1921, Thomas Farrell Richards was born at his grandparents' home, while his parents continued attempting to eke out an existence. Though Thomas, Sr. eventually would work as a film editor on several bona fide classics (primarily at Warner Bros.), he often had difficulty finding jobs, and his increasing reliance on alcohol made things even worse. Glenda often had to improvise, using flour sacks to diaper their infant. She struggled to hold the marriage together, while her depressed husband disappeared for long stretches of time.

In 1925, Glenda accepted a part in the play *The Best People*, starring Charlotte Treadway, at the Morosco Theatre in Los Angeles. The Morosco stock company performed the same play, often a second-run title that had been a Broadway hit, for eight to 12 weeks.

Glenda with baby Tommy, sitting on the front porch of her parents' home (early 1922).

In February 1926, Glenda appeared in Winchell Smith and Tom Cushing's comedy *Thank-U* at the Majestic Theatre in Los Angeles. Among the other cast members was Gavin Gordon (who would share the screen with her seven years later in *Mystery of the Wax Museum*). Augustine Glassmire directed the play.

Back at the Morosco, again under the able direction of Glassmire and sharing the stage with Charlotte Treadway, Glenda landed a sizable role in *The Back Slapper*, a comedy by Paul Dicky and Mann Page. The play opened on February 28, 1926, with a cast including Richard La Salle, Ann McKay and Harry Hoyt.

Lucky Boy (**Tiffany-Stahl Productions, 1928; directed by Norman Taurog**). **Glenda had an uncredited bit part in this George Jessel silent with sound sequences, also known as** *The Ghetto.*

Glenda later spoke of having survived this period while "living in a trunk." She toted it from L.A. to San Francisco, spending 16 weeks in Frank Craven's *New Brooms*, and in a production of Lowell Brentano's *The Spider*.

In an uncredited bit part, Glenda made her first film appearance in *Lucky Boy*, a silent with sound sequences, for Tiffany-Stahl Productions in June 1928. The feature-film directorial debut of Norman Taurog, who previously had helmed dozens of comedy shorts, the project originally was titled "The Schlemiel" and "The Ghetto."

Now considered a "lost" film, *Lucky Boy* starred George Jessel as a Jewish jeweler's son from the Bronx who dreams of making it big in show business. Actor Charles C. Wilson, who played a bit part, also served as assistant director. The film was released on January 2, 1929. Glenda never considered it her actual screen debut, and believed that she lost out on potential film work because her face didn't photograph well.

In late 1928, Glenda was cast in the New York play *The Street Wolf*. With little Tommy left in the capable hands of her mother, she left for the Big Apple. Having scraped together just enough money for the transcontinental train trip, she survived the three long days and nights on several sandwiches packed by Minnie.

Eventually Glenda replaced actress Erin O'Brien-Moore in *Skidding* at the Nora Bayes Theatre, which was located on the roof of the 44th Street Theatre on Broadway. In February 1929, she suffered an attack of appendicitis and, with Adele Renson taking over her *Skidding* role, was admitted to Mount Morris Park Sanitarium, where she underwent an operation performed by Dr. M.J. Siegelstein.

From late September through early November, she played Vina Chase in 40 performances of Winnie Baldwin's murder mystery *Divided Honors*, directed by William B. Friedlander at the Forrest Theatre. Another of Glenda's 1929 accomplishments was of a more personal nature: She finally received a divorce from the wandering Thomas.

Glenda Farrell Operated On.

Glenda Farrell, leading woman of "Skidding," is at the Mount Morris Park Sanitarium, where she is recovering from an operation for appendicitis performed Tuesday night by Dr. M. J. Siegelstein. Adele Renson, who will play Miss Farrell's part in the Chicago company of the comedy, is acting it temporarily at the Bayes. Miss Farrell's condition was said to be satisfactory yesterday.

Feb. 8, 1929, the *New York Times* reported on Glenda's appendicitis.

On January 29, 1930, she opened in Preston Sturges' *Recapture* at the Eltinge 42nd Street Theatre. Running for 24 performances, the play, directed by Don Mullally, also featured Melvyn Douglas, Celia Loftus and Hugh Sinclair. The *New York Times* reported that Glenda was "funny, abrupt, slangy, blonde and very cute."[4]

Notes:

[1] Although most sources list her birthdate as 1904, the correct year of 1901 was confirmed by the 1910 and 1920 censuses, and the Social Security Administration (Glenda's SS number was 573-03-9877).
[2] *Motion Picture*, February 1919.
[3] Dan Van Neste, "Glenda Farrell: Diamond in the Rough," *Classic Images*, Vol. 275, May 1998.
[4] *New York Times*, 19 January 1930.

NDAY. SEPTEMBER 29. 1929.

FORREST Thea. W. 49th St. OPENING **TOMORROW NIGHT at 8:50**
K. A. I. presents a new play by WINNIE BALDWIN

DIVIDED HONORS

Directed by WILLIAM R. FRIEDLANDER—Settings by WILLY POGANY.

Ad for Farrell's Broadway plays from the *New York Times*

Chapter 2
Little Caesar

"Where—where would we go? Where would we run to? There's no place he wouldn't find us. There's only one thing for us to do: *Flaherty*.

"Well, I can do it. That gang must go. Rico must go. I want my happiness. Joe, I want you—and we'll never have any peace until Rico's gone. And I'm going to do it!"

—Olga Stassof, *Little Caesar* (1931)

Love, Honor and Betray (**Broadway, Eltinge Theatre, 1930; directed by Don Mullally). Alice Brady, George Brent and Glenda.**

Originally titled "The Fatal Woman," Fanny and Frederic Hatton's drama *Love, Honor and Betray* was given a tryout in Atlantic City before opening at New York's Eltinge Theatre on March 12, 1930. After rubbing shoulders with the likes of Melvyn Douglas in her previous Eltinge assignment, Glenda, again working with director Don Mullally, now had the pleasure of costarring with Alice Brady, George Brent and Clark Gable.

Following *The Widow from Chicago* (1930), starring Edward G. Robinson, and *Doorway to Hell* (1930), starring Lew Ayres with James Cagney in a supporting role, Warner Bros. planned a first-rate screen adaptation of W.R. Burnett's popular 1929 novel *Little Caesar*, featuring characters based on Chicago mobster Salvatore "Sam" Cardinella (Cesare Enrico Bandello) and then-dancer George Raft (Joe Massara), who had been involved with Harlem Cotton Club owner and racketeer Owney Madden.

Other characters are fictionalized versions of Chicago underworld characters Giacomo "Big Jim" Colosimo ("Diamond Pete" Montana), who reportedly was assassinated by Al Capone; William "Big Bill" Thompson ("The Big Boy"), the city mayor; Charles Dion O'Bannion, florist and bootlegger; and Samuel J. "Nails" Morton, a local gangster.

When casting the film, Hal Wallis initially told Robinson that he was being considered for the supporting role of Otero (which eventually went to George E. Stone), Rico's loyal henchman. Director Mervyn LeRoy was lobbying for Robinson, whom he had seen in the 1928 play *The Racket*, for the lead, and doing his best to dissuade Jack Warner from miscasting an inexperienced Clark Gable as Massara. (Gable's enormous ears ultimately cost him the role, which went to Douglas Fairbanks, Jr.) Warner later claimed that casting Robinson was his idea, but Eddie G. actually earned the Rico role by storming into the mogul's office, furiously chomping on his cigar and landing a screen test in a cloud of smoke.

When *Love, Honor and Betray* completed its run in April, Glenda accepted the female lead, Olga Stassoff, a dancer in love with Joe Massara, in *Little Caesar*. Lila Lee had been Warner Bros.' first choice for the role, but she had to drop out of the project after becoming ill. (A former child star on the stage, she suffered from alcoholism, though official publicity usually referred to her malady as tuberculosis.) Having seen her on Broadway, Mervyn LeRoy requested Glenda, and it was the start of a beautiful friendship. Uncertain about the new direction her career might take, Glenda wisely decided to maintain her apartment in New York.

Prior to leaving for Los Angeles to begin work on *Little Caesar*, Glenda appeared in a Warner Bros.' *Vitaphone Varieties* comedy short, "The Lucky Break," shot at the company's Eastern studio in Flatbush. Directed by short subjects department head Arthur Hurley from a script by Homer Mason and Stanley Rauh, this two-reeler depicted the considerable mayhem ensuing from the disastrous demonstration of an "unbreakable mirror" and the inventor's efforts to redeem himself with a group of businessmen. As support to star Harry Fox, Glenda joined Walter Regan, Leonard Jerome, Charles Hopkins, Edward Butler and Arthur Shaw. (Glenda's future colleagues Pat O'Brien and Allen Jenkins also gained film experience by playing small roles in Hurley's *Vitaphone Varieties*.)

Mervyn LeRoy shot *Little Caesar* over 31 days in July and August 1930, during which a "spy" planted by Al Capone observed the production. This fact made all the actors a bit nervous, with Robinson's uneasiness multiplied by the fact that, in 1930, live machine-gun rounds were still being used in screen shootouts. Even after being fitted with steel plates, Eddie, who was easily distracted by gunfire, accidentally moved off his mark. Fortunately, technician George Daly compensated, thus preventing the actor's serious injury or death.

Robinson later wrote,

> Those of us in *Little Caesar* who had come from the stage—
> Sidney Blackmer, Glenda Farrell, William Collier, Jr., and
> George E. Stone (for whom I felt a special affection because
> he was playing Otero, the role originally intended for me)—

Little Caesar (Warner Bros., 1931; directed by Mervyn LeRoy). Olga Stassof (Glenda) and Joe Massara in a tense moment.

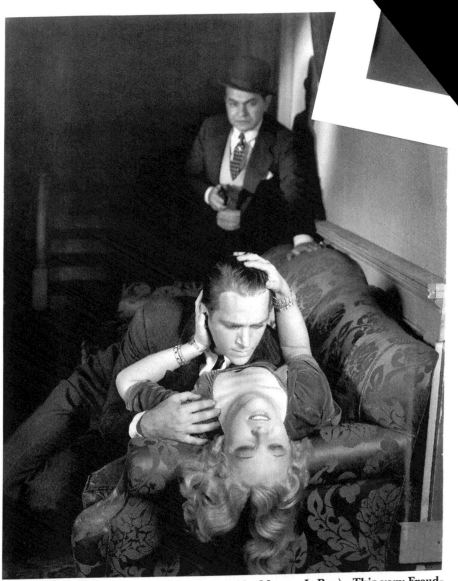

Little Caesar (Warner Bros., 1931; directed by Mervyn LeRoy). **This very Freudian, pre-Code publicity pose, featuring Edward G. Robinson, Douglas Fairbanks, Jr., and Glenda, bears no resemblance to any scene in the film.**

banded together. We were, I think, insufferable. Our conversation was a constant put-down of Hollywood, and our plans for our return to Mother Earth—Broadway. We were, I must admit, quite sickening.[1]

Though LeRoy was pleased with her work, Glenda made no bones about thinking her performance was "terrible." She later said, "Imagine a charac-

Little Caesar (Warner Bros., 1931; directed by Mervyn LeRoy). Joe Massara (Douglas Fairbanks, Jr.) and Olga Stassof (Glenda, in her feature film debut).

ter woman like me skipping around in organdie and a wide-eyed expression. Lord!"[2]

The film opens with a gas station robbery; then Rico and Massara are seen in a roadside diner, discussing their future as criminals. When Joe speaks of his love for dancing and dames, Rico replies that his pal is "soft." Little Caesar's oft-repeated mantra, "You can dish it out, but you're getting so you can't take it no more," ultimately becomes his own epitaph after Joe, egged on by his doll, Olga, survives, while Rico (having selfishly shunned romantic attachments) lies dead in the gutter behind a billboard promoting the loving couple.

A prototype for many later genre films, *Little Caesar* romanticizes the criminal antihero, but its conclusion supports law and order brought about by a former gangster and his assertive girl, who turns stool pigeon to save her man. At one point, Rico confronts Joe, accusing Olga of turning him into a "sissy" and threatening, "It's suicide for both of you."

Later, when Rico arrives at the couple's apartment to kill them, he is unable to pull the trigger. In an archetypal role, Robinson (often using only facial expressions and other nonverbal techniques) creates depth rarely seen on the screen during the early sound period, alternating Rico's confident animalism with an equally effective boyish innocence.

Rico's avoidance of women, and his close relationships with Joe and Otero, suggests possible closet homosexuality, an element mentioned by W.R.

Warner Bros. publicity portrait (1930): one of Glenda's first studio photos, taken during her trip to Hollywood to shoot *Little Caesar.*

Burnett after seeing the film. This overtone is present (Otero crawls onto Rico's bed while hanging out at his apartment), but anything further remains pure speculation. Rico and Joe genuinely care for each other, and when the mobster is unable to whack his pal, Otero tries to shoot him, claiming that his boss has "gone soft." Rico's inability to be completely ruthless is his tragic flaw, a sentimental action leading directly to his downfall in a hail of Thompson bullets. (His final line, "Mother of God, is this the end of Rico?" was censored to "Mother of *Mercy*, is this the end of Rico?")

tone of *Little Caesar* is hard-edged, dark and violent, but sporadic ts of subtle humor provide some respite. (The fact that the Chicago ization boss is called "The Big Boy" [Sidney Blackmer], is indicative of e absurdity of Mafia monikers.) Robinson's innate magnetism dominates the film, and its major success led to his signing a new two-year, six-film contract with the studio.

In her first major role, Glenda convincingly plays a sympathetic, standup dame, a contrast to the tough, fast-talking, sarcastic gold diggers she often would play in subsequent Warner Bros. pictures. At the beginning of the film, when Olga first kisses Joe, she feels the bulging pistol in his jacket pocket and immediately tries to talk him into quitting the mob. To save Joe from Rico's intended hit, she phones Sergeant Flaherty (Thomas E. Jackson), who then riddles him with submachine gun rounds under the billboard. The final image of the film shows, not Robinson, but artwork of the faces of Glenda and Douglas Fairbanks, Jr.

Little Caesar premiered in New York at Warner Bros.' Strand Theatre on January 9, 1931. Both Robinson and Fairbanks attended, helping to break the all-time attendance record for an initial run (11 screenings) at the venue, raking in a box-office gross of $50,000. *New York Times* critic Mordaunt Hall wrote, "Glenda Farrell is excellently authentic as Massara's 'moll'."[3]

After completing *Little Caesar*, a one-shot role with no offer of a contract, Glenda returned to New York, anxious to begin work on her next stage role. She signed to play Marie Pouliski, the female lead in Edgar Wallace's gangland play *On the Spot*, which ran for 167 performances, from

---

THE PLAY
By J. BROOKS ATKINSON.

Presenting Edgar Wallace.

ON THE SPOT, a play in a prologue and three acts, by Edgar Wallace. Settings by Rollo Wayne; staged by Lee Ephraim and Carol Reed; produced by Lee and J. J. Shubert, in association with Mr. Wallace and Mr. Ephraim. At Edgar Wallace's Forrest Theatre.

A Priest	John Wheeler
Interne	John Adair
Shaun O'Donnell	Mike Sullivan
Officer Ryan	George Spelvin
Captain Harrigan	Stanley Wood
A Nurse	Jeanne Winters
Tony Perrelli	Crane Wilbur
Minn Lee	Anna May Wong
Keriki	Suezo Tckero
Angelo	John Gallaudet
Con O'Hara	George Drury Hart
Marie Pouliski	Glenda Farrell
Jimmy McGarth	Alan Ward
Detective Commissioner John Kelly	John M. Kline
Mike Feeney	Arthur R. Vinton

"On the Spot" is sufficiently well acted by Crane Wilbur as a bogus wop gang leader, Anna May Wong as his inscrutably loyal Chinese jade, Arthur R. Vinton as a capitally hoarse rival gang leader, Glenda Farrell as a two-timing strumpet, John M. Kline as an upright detective—and several other good actors. As one of the neighbors remarked, it is a spotty play. But it is refreshingly amusing in the simple vein of footpad make-believe.

24

October 29, 1930 through March 1931 at the Forrest Theatre. John Adair, John Gallaudet, Crane Wilbur and Anna May Wong were also in the cast.

Glenda's performances were so sincere and convincing that her *On the Spot* role was expanded, and she received excellent notices in the New York press. After taking her last curtain call of the evening, she often thought of a comment her mother had made on numerous occasions: "I'll never rest until your name is up in lights."[4]

Glenda later recalled two milestones that occurred simultaneously during the run of the play:

> I was doing *On the Spot* for the Shuberts ... A man associated with producer Arthur Hopkins came to me and offered me more money and my name in lights if I'd step over and do a lead in *So This Is New York* ... The Shuberts wouldn't let me go ... But they bargained with me, "If what you want is your name in lights, we'll do that for you." Of course, I wired my mother the grand news immediately. The lights flashed my name, and the first night they did, I went into my dressing room and found a telegram ... Mother had died early that evening from the effects of an operation she had undergone. At the very moment undoubtedly that the lights were twinkling through the New York dusk, and the name Glenda Farrell appeared for the first time on any marquee, mother passed on, her life's work done.[5]

On January 29, 1931, Glenda and Charles Ruggles were the guests of honor at an AMPA luncheon held at the Dixie Hotel, located between 42nd and 43rd Streets in Manhattan. Though she believed that her looks weren't suitable for movie stardom, she was encouraged when *Photoplay* selected her as one of the "New Faces" for May 1931.

Back in Hollywood, Glenda accepted the small supporting role of Stella in a Universal newspaper expose adapted by Ralph Graves from the Emile Gauvreau novel *Hot News* and filmed under the working titles *Ambition* and *Scandal Market*. Directed by Russell Mack, and starring Charles Bickford, Pat O'Brien, Rose Hobart and J. Farrell MacDonald, the film was retitled *Scandal for Sale* (1932) prior to release.

The production, shot by ace cinematographer Karl Freund (who soon would direct Boris Karloff in Universal's *The Mummy* [1932]), was an attempt to cash in on the popular yellow-journalism subgenre including *The Front Page* (1931), costarring Adolphe Menjou and Pat O'Brien, and *Five Star Final* (1931), starring Edward G. Robinson in one of his best early roles. Charles Bickford plays Jerry Strong, a single-minded city editor whose con-

Scandal for Sale **(Universal, 1931; directed by Russell Mack). Newspaper editor Jerry Strong (Charles Bickford) questions Stella (Glenda).**

stant crusading for sensationalistic news takes its toll on his family life. After his star reporter, Waddell (Pat O'Brien), who has a fondness for booze, dies in a plane crash while on the job, Strong reevaluates his career.

Film Daily reported that *Scandal for Sale* "is the fastest moving yarn of its kind to come along, and in the person of Charles Bickford it presents about the toughest managing editor yet seen on the screen."[6]

Notes:

[1]Edward G. Robinson, with Leonard Spigelglass, *All My Yesterdays: An Autobiography* (New York: Hawthorn Books, Inc., 1973), p. 119.
[2]*Motion Picture*, March 1933, p. 93.
[3]*New York Times*, 30 January 1931.
[4]*Photoplay*, January 1937, p. 94.
[5]Dan Van Neste, "Glenda Farrell: Diamond in the Rough," *Classic Images*, Vol. 275, May 1998.
[6]*Film Daily*, 10 April 1932, p. 10.

Chapter 3
Life Begins

I didn't ask you for your opinion. Keep your trap shut!
I don't want to hear anything about 'em.
—Florette Darian, *Life Begins* (1932)

On March 28, 1932 Glenda opened at the Selwyn Theatre in Joseph Santley's production of Mary Macdougal Axelson's *Life Begins*, a powerful, realistic drama set in a hospital maternity ward. As

> **THEATRICAL NOTES.**
>
> Two plays will open in the Broadway theatres tonight. "Life Begins" will be presented at the Selwyn by a cast including Joanna Roos, Glenda Farrell and Alan Bunce, and "Intimate Relations," a comedy starring Blanche Ring, will have its first performance at the Ambassador.

New York Times, **March 28, 1932**

Florette Darian, she received enthusiastic notices for her portrayal of a former "worldly" chorus girl who eventually discovers the true miracle of motherhood. Unfortunately the play ran for only eight performances, closing in April.

But that didn't dissuade Warner Bros. from making a film version. Impressed with the production and Glenda's characterization, Jack Warner and Darryl F. Zanuck cast her in Earl Baldwin's adaptation, starring Loretta Young in the role performed on the stage by Joanna Roos. Director James Flood assembled an excellent supporting cast, including Aline MacMahon, Glenda (billed fourth), Preston Foster, Vivienne Osborne, Gilbert Roland, Paul Fix, Bobs Watson (in his film debut) and Frank McHugh (in the first of his many films with Glenda).

Although its stage origins are well on display, the performances keep the film consistently engrossing. With the possible exception of Eric Linden (who frequently seemed to be on the brink of a nervous breakdown), the actors are top notch. Young, MacMahon and McHugh are particularly believable, and Glenda, as a feather-clad showgirl reading *True Confessions* and swigging bootleg booze from her hot water bottle as she waits to deliver twins, positively steals the show.

"What are you grinning about?" Florette asks her doctor. "You going to tell me a dirty story?" Told about the legal process of adoption, and observing another woman's newborn child, she quips, "What can you do with it, now that they've passed a law that you can't sell 'em?" Later she stammers an improvised, off-key version of "Frankie and Johnny" as she drunkenly shuffles about the "waiting woman's" ward.

Though Florette tries her best to wisecrack away any interest in the impending bundles of joy, her motherly affection blossoms after they are

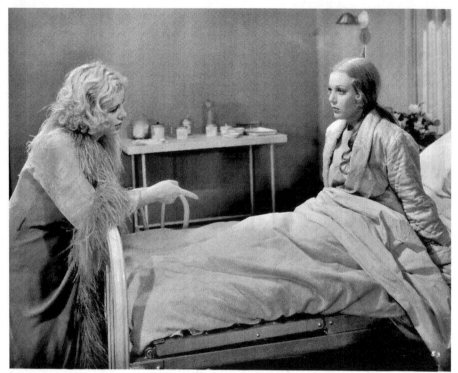

Life Begins (Warner Bros., 1932; directed by James Flood and Elliott Nugent). Maternity patients Florette Darian (Glenda) and Grace Sutton (Loretta Young).

delivered, and she overhears a prospective adoptive mother saying she will take the boy but not the girl, who isn't thriving. Having provided much-needed humor to balance the grim and dramatic story, Glenda then creates one of the most genuinely moving scenes of her film career.

Picture Play magazine enthused:

> Glenda Farrell is vividly successful as the rebellious tough girl, as fine in her hardboiled wisecracks as she is in her emotional scene and its aftermath of tenderness.[1]

Her redemptive moment occurs just before Grace Sutton (Loretta Young) dies following a Caesarean procedure. The film ends as "life begins" for the baby girl, in the arms of her stunned, suddenly widowed father (Eric Linden).

Hollywood Filmograph reported:

> *Life Begins* is really a grand picture ... Give Miss Young more of these parts ... Frank McHugh, as the expectant father, was a riot ... Glenda Farrell, Aline MacMahon, Preston Foster, Clara Blandick and Vivienne Osborne are the remainder of

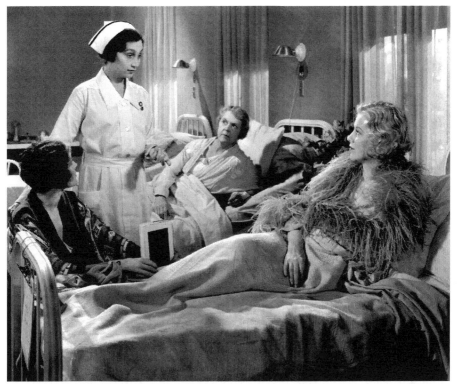

Life Begins (Warner Bros., 1932; directed by James Flood and Elliott Nugent). Miss Bowers (Aline MacMahon) attends to patient Florette Darian (Glenda). Dorothy Peterson (in bed on left) and Vivienne Osborne (seated) also appear in this scene.

> a perfect cast. Each one's performance was individual and outstanding ...
>
> *Life Begins* was made for adult minds ... so don't bring the kiddies if you want them to keep their illusions.[2]

Jack Warner, impressed with Glenda's work, signed her to a five-year studio contract. Unlike top Warner Bros. stars like James Cagney and Bette Davis, who consistently complained about their assigned roles, going so far as to go on suspension or simply walk out rather than appear in a particular film, Glenda calmly accepted every part, eventually appearing in an average of 10 films per year during the run of her contract.

While waiting for her next quality role to come along, Glenda *worked*. Initially many of the parts were small, with little room for character development, but they were all in top Warner Bros. projects.

Originally titled *Woman's Day*, *Three on a Match* (1932) is an uncompromising depiction of Great Depression tragedy with documentary-like sequenes. By the time Mervyn LeRoy directed the exciting trio of Joan Blondell,

Three on a Match (Warner Bros., 1932; directed by Mervyn LeRoy). **Glenda has a small part in this hard-hitting Great Depression drama starring three of Warner Bros.' top female stars: Joan Blondell, Ann Dvorak and Bette Davis.**

Bette Davis and Ann Dvorak, the Warner Bros. talkie technique had become more refined, and the measured pacing of *Little Caesar* had given way to a fast-moving, economical style. *Three on a Match* runs only 63 minutes, but it covers an impressive span of material.

The film opens in 1919, with images of Prohibition and the women's suffrage movement prefacing scenes depicting the trio as childhood friends. Following their high school graduation, Vivian Revere (Ann Dvorak) attends Miss Jason's School for Young Ladies, Ruth Westcott (Bette Davis) studies at Metropolitan Business College and Mary Keaton (Joan Blondell) winds up in reform school, where Glenda has a small part as Mrs. Black, a wisecracking inmate who warns her not to get "mixed up with a man—*any man*." Though limited to one brief scene dominated by a top-billed star, Glenda still manages to make a lasting impression.

Sinking into desperate alcoholism, Vivian is held captive by a trio of gangsters (Humphrey Bogart, Allen Jenkins and Jack La Rue), while her young son (Buster Phelps) is kidnapped by conman Michael Loftus (Lyle Talbot). These thugs mean business, and the humor that soon would creep into Warner Bros.' mob depictions is nowhere to be seen in this unrelenting film.

Following 10 days locked in a filthy sty, the gangsters assign the job of whacking the kid to Loftus, who refuses. In a scene that rivals the ending of Cagney's *Public Enemy* as the most spine-chilling in the entire Warner Bros. classic catalog, Vivian writes a note on her nightgown in lipstick; then, as the goons enter the room, she takes a glass-shattering dive through the window, falling several stories to her death on the sidewalk below. (These scenes, in the wake of the Lindbergh incident, greatly concerned censors across the nation, who persuaded the Hollywood moguls to refrain from producing films involving the kidnapping of small children.)

Notes:

[1]*Picture Play*, November 1932, p. 64.
[2]*Hollywood Filmograph*, 8 June 1932.

Chapter 4
I Am a Fugitive from a Chain Gang

When a fellow wants to ditch a girl, he'll do most anything—providing it doesn't land him back on the *chain gang*—where he probably belongs.
—Marie Woods, *I Am a Fugitive from a Chain Gang* (1932)

In February 1922, Robert Elliott Burns, a World War I veteran from Brooklyn, unemployed and penniless, was arrested in Atlanta, Georgia for unwittingly assisting two small-time crooks in robbing a small neighborhood grocery store. Though he had been scammed into the job, Burns was convicted and awarded a sentence of six to 10 years in the Georgia chain gang system. The entire haul from the caper: a whopping $5.80.

Four months later, Burns, with bloodhounds on his trail, escaped from one of the horrific camps, making his way to Atlanta and then to Chicago, where, for the next seven years, he worked as a laborer, real-estate manager and magazine publisher. A divorced landlady named Emily fell in love with him, and instigated his move up the ladder by using her family's connections to set up the couple as proprietors of an apartment house. Though he didn't share her feelings, Burns married Emily, who eventually discovered his true identity by reading a letter from his brother Vincent, a New Jersey clergyman. When Burns fell in love with another woman, the highly emotional and conniving Emily turned him over to the local authorities.

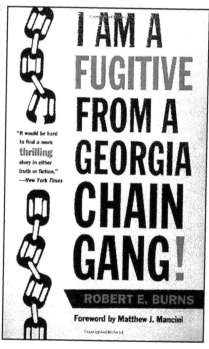

"It would be hard to find a more **thrilling** story in either truth or fiction." —*New York Times*

Burns' harrowing story soon made national headlines. Chicago businessmen, community leaders and the Chief of Police supported him, and they actually proposed a getaway plan. Incredibly, Burns voluntarily chose to return to Georgia, assured that he would not be reassigned to a chain gang. Instead he would be given a clerical job for 90 days, while the prison commission arranged for a parole.

However, all the bad press did not amuse the authorities and politicians in the South. Duped by corrupt authorities

Book written by Robert E. Burns on his real-life experience on a Georgia chain gang.

and shyster attorneys alike, Burns eventually was transferred from a trusty position back to swinging a pick and suffering the abominable "rack" and "sweatbox" on a chain gang. Though he paid an Atlanta lawyer to represent him, customary bribes for the prison commissioners were sought, and Burns continued to endure brutal conditions while Northern supporters vainly attempted to influence a parole decision.

Aided by a local farmer, Burns brilliantly managed a second escape. On September 4, 1930 he took it on the lam once more, cunningly slipping past authorities from Georgia to New Jersey, where he produced a memoir (ghost-written by his brother) based on an earlier article published in *True Detective Mysteries* magazine.

I Am a Fugitive from a Georgia Chain Gang! hit the streets in January 1932. Though it would later be evaluated as an "unsteady compound of hearsay, myth and stereotype," the embellished memoir "struck a resonant chord with the men and women of [Burns'] generation, especially after the start of the Great Depression."[1]

An instant bestseller, the book soon attracted the attention of Darryl F. Zanuck, who arranged for Burns (using the alias "Mr. Crane") to travel to the Warner Bros. studio in Burbank. He arrived on April 13, 1932 and soon became the official advisor for the film adaptation *I Am a Fugitive from a Chain Gang*. He was paid $12,500 for the screen rights. While working on the film, he kept in written contact with his brother. Zanuck dropped *Georgia* from the title because he didn't want to add extra fuel to the fire already raging among state authorities, considered that now California as well as New Jersey was harboring a dangerous felon.

The first of many Depression *social problem* films that would set the studio apart from the other Hollywood "majors," where escapist fare was usually the main order of the day, *I Am a Fugitive from a Chain Gang* merged the popular prison genre (MGM's *The Big House*, Fox's *Up the River*, Columbia's *The Criminal Code*) with Warner Bros.' own gritty gangster genre, begun with *Little Caesar* and *The Public Enemy*.

The *I Am a Fugitive* screenplay was assigned to young writers Brown Holmes and Sheridan Gibney, who set out to adapt the Burns account into a coherent narrative, while avoiding the more specifically controversial elements. Cast as James Allen (aka "Allen James"), Hollywood heavyweight Paul Muni (who had caused a sensation as the Al Capone-like Tony Camonte in Howard Hawks' gangster epic *Scarface* [1932]) began a series of research sessions with his real-life counterpart, who was enthusiastic about seeing a version of himself portrayed by such a lauded actor.

Meanwhile, RKO studios was gearing up for its own chain gang film, *Hell's Highway*, directed by Rowland Brown and starring Richard Dix, Tom Brown and Rochelle Hudson, hoping to hit theater screens before Warner Bros.

I Am a Fugitive from a Chain Gang (**Warner Bros., 1932; directed by Mervyn LeRoy**). **This publicity photo depicts the emotional stranglehold Marie (Glenda) exerts over James Allen (Paul Muni) in Mervyn LeRoy's "social problem" masterpiece.**

was able to release *I Am a Fugitive*. Fifteen weeks of work were required to complete the *I Am a Fugitive* screenplay, allowing RKO to sneak their film into theaters while the former was still in production.

Holmes wrote the original 86-page treatment, dated April 25, 1932, which was expanded into a screenplay by Gibney. The two then collaborated on a temporary script, handed over to Zanuck, who brought in Howard J. Green

to integrate the producer's own changes and suggestions into a final shooting script, completed on July 23.

Holmes and Gibney's "explicit critique of capitalism" was toned down, while transitional sequences and character introductions were added to smooth the flow of the narrative, which had been somewhat confusing.[2] One of Holmes and Gibney's most powerful scenes, the ending showing the pathetic, nerve-wracked Allen still on the run, was retained.

Zanuck beefed up the suspense and sexual elements, including the scene with a prostitute, Linda (Noel Francis), at a hotel run by a former chain gang inmate, Barney Sykes (Allen Jenkins) and the very nature of Marie Woods, the attractive, attention-seeking 26-year-old landlady whom James Allen reluctantly marries. Glenda was cast as Marie, which left behind the "fortyish and stout" description of Burns' actual wife.[3]

Director Roy Del Ruth, considering the material too uncommercial, had passed on the temporary script, and the 143-page final draft was assigned to Mervyn LeRoy, who (supervised by Zanuck) began shooting on July 28, 1932. The chain gang camp set was built at the Warner Ranch in Calabasas, California and a major scene involving the inmates swinging sledgehammers on a rock pile was shot in a working quarry at Chatsworth. Much of the project was filmed on five studio soundstages, with additional exteriors shot on the backlot.

The publicity portraits, opposite page and above, of Glenda and Paul Muni from *I Am a Fugitive from a Chain Gang* **gives no indication of the adversarial relationship that develops between their characters in the film.**

Production was wrapped on September 7, exactly on schedule. Ultimately, LeRoy's work, including a large amount of "coverage," was turned over to Zanuck, who (as he would throughout his career at Warner Bros. and 20th Century-Fox) oversaw the editing of the finished film, including the addition of dramatic touches, such as sound effects, to heighten the suspense and tighten the pace.

More than eight decades after its release, *I Am a Fugitive from a Chain Gang* remains a cinematic tour de force and a monument to man's inhumanity to man. A film that helped lead to actual social awareness and legal change, it depicts a litany of deadly sins: lying, chicanery, negligence, greed, blackmail, corruption, brutality, sadism, racism and manslaughter. The human appetite for destruction has rarely been cinematically symbolized as well as in the scene where James Allen, highly accomplished engineer and builder of bridges, must detonate one with TNT to escape from a carload of officers blasting away with rifles.

Mervyn LeRoy's direction is brisk, with Sol Polito's mobile camera, William Holmes' editing and the effective use of sound (the clang of the blacksmith's hammer on the leg shackles; the rhythmic singing of the African American prisoners as they swing their sledgehammers; Allen's footsteps trailing away into the darkness during the final, haunting shot) all adding up to a transcendent work. Of course, all their contributions were overseen and polished by Zanuck.

The acting, too, is uniformly impressive, with Muni's performance arguably his most naturalistic screen effort to date. Though the supporting characters have been faulted for being underdeveloped and two-dimensional, they admirably do not derail the narrative focus from the powerful central figure of the fugitive.

Glenda is viscerally sexy in her introductory scene, and she builds Marie's selfish, vindictive nature like a musical crescendo (which is particularly impressive, since her screen time is limited). She captures exactly the description of the scene in the original screenplay:

> INT. BOARDINGHOUSE ROOM
> It is a rather nice room. Marie and Allen have just come in.
> She is twenty-six, dark and sexy looking. She is the kind of
> a girl that must have her man. Allen is inspecting the room as
> she talks. He is paying but little attention to her, but she is
> eyeing him critically, and she likes him.

The subtle nonverbal touches Glenda integrated into her performance, as in the way Marie slowly withdraws Reverend Allen's (Hale Hamilton) "chain gang" letter from between her breasts before she hands it to James, are striking. *Picture Play*'s Norbert Lusk wrote:

> Mr. Muni handles his meaty role with the reserve of a master
> craftsman ... Miss Farrell is so attractive one wonders why
> Allen ever took a room at her house, unless he really wanted
> to get entangled.[4]

Motion Picture magazine ran a full-page photo of Glenda, claiming:

> It all depends on your frame of mind whether you can resist
> the charm of Glenda Farrell, a newcomer out Hollywood way.
> Doubtless she'll conquer you when you see her in *Life Begins*.
> The girl doesn't miss. She left Broadway because *Little Caesar* called—and found herself on the spot. Naturally, she was
> rewarded. Just now she has placed herself in a frame of mind
> to keep Paul Muni from running away with the acting honors
> in *I Am a Fugitive*.[5]

Marie (Glenda) scoffs at her husband, James Allen's (Paul Muni), concern over her reckless spending and carousing.

Glenda was grateful to share scenes with Muni under LeRoy's direction. Having both come from the theater, she and Paul prepared and rehearsed their roles in a similar fashion. Glenda became so immersed in her character that she didn't realize the truly evil nature of Marie until she finally saw the film on television more than two decades later.

Warner Bros. had quite a challenge in promoting such bleak, relentless subject matter. The trade press expressed concern over the film's commercial possibilities, but Zanuck and his crew forged ahead with a sweeping publicity campaign, taking extra care to pitch its "romance" angle to women. One of the merchandising suggestions made to department stores was the displaying of a "Glenda Farrell Gown" based on the alluring attire she wears on screen.

Even the most optimistic Warner Bros. employees were a bit surprised when the film was a box-office smash, opening to long lines of patrons in 210 U.S. cities, including New York, where attendance records were broken and throngs of people had to be turned away from repeat showings. Zanuck had been proved right in his dedication to the socially relevant material, and he had the moxie to know just how to craft a screen story (especially during the post-production phase) to capture the attention of a mass audience. The film has been called "a high point in Zanuck's regime and the coming of age of Warners' Depression-era style."[6]

I Am a Fugitive from a Chain Gang was nominated for three Academy Awards: Best Sound Recording, Best Actor and Best Picture. Though its makers left the Oscars empty-handed, the National Board of Review named it Best Film of 1932. Muni eventually would receive a total of five Best Actor Oscar nominations (plus a strong write-in campaign for *Black Fury* [1935]), but he won only once, for his (more theatrical) performance in the Warner Bros. prestige biopic *The Story of Louis Pasteur* (1936), directed by William Dieterle.

Robert E. Burns took a risk becoming involved in such a major media event, and 13 more years would pass before Georgia authorities gave up trying to extradite him from New Jersey. In 1942, Vincent Burns, revealing that he indeed had ghostwritten his brother's famous book, published a sequel, *Out of These Chains*, in which he gives a detailed but carefully bowdlerized account of his family's continuing struggle for Robert's freedom.

Vincent deplored the film's sanctimonious depiction of "Reverend Allen" (especially the performance of Hale Hamilton) so much that he sued Warner Bros. for $250,000. (However, the characterization actually mirrors Vincent's own high-handed and self-righteous writing style.) In *Out of These Chains*, he actually claims that he should have played himself in the film. Like its predecessor, the sequel ends with a big question mark. Would Georgia authorities ever catch Robert if he should travel outside the borders of New Jersey?

In the end, the fugitive was not so much freed as he was *let go*. The hardliners against Burns never really gave up. However, in 1945, Georgia Governor Ellis Arnall personally won a commutation of his sentence from the Pardon and Parole Board, whose members apparently considered the $5.80 (from 1922) finally to have been repaid.

The amassing of huge sums of cash was the topic at Warner Bros. when, on August 29, 1932, Howard Bretherton began directing *The Match King*, Houston Branch and Sidney Sutherland's adaptation of the novel by Einar Thorvaldson, who based his material on Swedish industrialist Ivar Kreuger (1880-1932), creator of a worldwide safety match empire. An engineer, entrepreneur and financier, Kreuger, through business acquisitions, innovative (sometimes extralegal) investment schemes and lending operations, eventually developed match monopolies with several European and Latin American governments. At his peak, Kreuger controlled 200 companies and nearly three-fourths of global safety match production. He also became deeply involved in speculation and the creation of dummy companies to provide fronts for his illegal activities.

The Great Depression hit Kreuger hard, and he lost millions while gambling with securities and making deals without having any idea how and from where he was going to raise the necessary funds. In March 1932, with struggling Swedish banks no longer able to lend him any money, he was discovered dead from a gunshot wound in the bed of his Paris apartment. After a brief in-

The Match King (Warner Bros., 1932; directed by Howard Bretherton). **Paul Kroll (Warren William) and his hapless girlfriend, "Babe" (Glenda), about to part ways.**

vestigation, a physician and the French police concluded that he had committed suicide. A 9-mm semiautomatic handgun and a sealed envelope containing three separate sealed notes were found near the body.

For *The Match King*, Warren William was cast as "Paul Kroll," the man who rises from shifty Chicago street cleaner to debauched megalomaniacal capitalist, while the female lead, "Marta Molnar," was assigned to French actress Lily Damita after Darryl Zanuck was unable to borrow Greta Garbo from MGM. (Interestingly, it was widely reported that Garbo had lost a sizable sum she had invested in actual Kreuger stock.)

After *I Am a Fugitive*, Glenda dutifully moved on to play less venomous versions of her tough-cookie dame character. In *The Match King*, a sprawling epic packed into 78 minutes, she receives third billing as "Babe," Kroll's Chicago girlfriend, from whom he steals enough money to jumpstart his business affairs. Her two brief scenes occur at the beginning of the film, and she has just enough time to enact her somewhat dazed floozy routine.

Bretherton wrapped *The Match King* in early October 1932 for a final cost of $165,000. Many of the trade advertisements pitched the film as another chapter in the studio's sensational crusade against social evils:

39

WARNER BROS. again is first on the screen with the facts of the most sensational news of a decade! As revealing as a search of the Match King's Park Avenue penthouse! The picture his 10,000,000 victims have been waiting for! It shows … why women cried for his kisses … why men cried for his blood! YOU were on his sucker list! You — and the gorgeous women he used and misused — will hail this picture as your revenge!

One review referred to Kreuger as an "international reprobate," the film as a "thoroughly deodorized life story," and Glenda's characterization as its "redeeming influence."[7] Much of the film is devoted to Kroll's many romantic affairs, with Damita's character being based on Kreuger's longtime lover, Ingeborg Hassler Eberth (1889-1977). To make Kroll's suicide more dramatic, he dies, not in bed like the real Kreuger, but falling off his balcony and into the street after he shoots himself. The ending fades out on the surrounding rubbish being swept up by street cleaners, much like the street cleaner he had been back in Chicago before all the scamming begun.

During production of *The Match King*, *Film Daily* reported that Warners had cast Glenda, a "screen luminary," in the lavish musical *42nd Street* (1933).[8] Director Lloyd Bacon and choreographer Busby Berkeley began shooting the film, starring Warner Baxter and Bebe Daniels, on October 5, but Glenda had been dropped from the supporting cast, which includes Allen Jenkins. (Joan Blondell and Frank McHugh also had been announced for roles but do not appear in the film.)

On November 22, the *New York Times* featured Glenda in the column "Who's Who in Pictures," referring to her as "a citizen of the theatre" whose family has possessed "an abundance of theatrical and musical talent for several generations."[9]

Notes:

[1]Matthew J. Mancini, in Robert E. Burns, *I Am a Fugitive from a Georgia Chain Gang!* (Athens: University of Georgia Press, 1997), ps. vi, ix.

[2]John E. O'Connor, in Tino Balio, ed., *I Am a Fugitive from a Chain Gang* (Madison: University of Wisconsin Press, 1981), p. 21.

[3]O'Connor, p. 23.

[4]*Picture Play*, January 1933, p. 47.

[5]*Motion Picture*, November 1932, p. 32.

[6]Thomas Schatz, *The Genius of the System: Hollywood Filmmaking in the Studio Era* (New York: Pantheon Books, 1988), p. 142.

[7]*The New Movie Magazine*, December 1932, p. 107.

[8]*Film Daily*, 1 September 1932, p. 6.

[9]*New York Times*, 22 November 1932.

Warner Bros. publicity portrait (1932).

Glenda personally signed this 1932 publicity portrait, "For Mrs. Benthall, with my sincerest wishes, Glenda Farrell."

Warner Bros. publicity portrait (1932) used to promote Glenda's upcoming appearance in *The Mystery of the Wax Museum*.

Chapter 5
Mystery of the Wax Museum

All right, all right. You raise the kids, I'll raise the roof. I'd rather die from an apoplectic heart from shaking cocktails and bankers than expire in a pan of dirty dishwater.
—Florence, *Mystery of the Wax Museum* (1933)

Shortly after completing *The Match King*, Glenda moved on to a major supporting role in Warner Bros.' horror film *Mystery of the Wax Museum*, Michael Curtiz' follow-up to *Doctor X* (1932), starring Lionel Atwill and Fay Wray. Shifting from mad doctor to the mad sculptor "Mr. Ivan Igor," Atwill again appears in two-strip Technicolor. (Cinematographer Ray Rennahan's work on this film marked the final time this color process was used for a theatrical feature film.)

Shooting these Expressionistic thrillers in color was Warner Bros.' attempt to attract filmgoers who were enjoying the current wave of black-and-white horror films spurred by Universal, whose *Dracula* (1931), *Frankenstein* (1931) and *The Mummy* (1932) had cleaned up at the box office. The bluish two-strip process had its limitations but (for better or worse) did offer audiences something new. (Following the release of the Warner Bros. color duo, the horror genre would return primarily to moody monochrome for the foreseeable future).

An unpublished story, "Wax Works," by Warner Bros. dialogue writer Charles Spencer Belden became the source material for *Mystery of the Wax Museum*. Don Mullaly, with whom Glenda had worked with on the stage, and Carl Erickson, wrote the screenplay. The studio saved time and money by retaining much of the same cast and crew from *Doctor X*, going so far as to reuse composer Bernhard Kahn's opening theme music to begin the new film.

While preparing for her role in *Wax Museum*, Glenda said:

Really, I don't think much of my picture roles. They're too standardized. There's no art in repeating the same characterization. On the stage I did a variety of parts. I'm no ingénue and I don't mind playing bad girls. But smart-remarking women were never my line in the theater, and here I am ripping off bright repartee whenever I'm not menacing ...

I'm glad to be wanted in pictures, of course. But life here isn't as much fun as it was in New York. I've had my pick of parts on Broadway for the past five years. I always earned a good salary, as much as I'm getting now. There was always a job in the East, so I'm no better off financially ...

IN A WAXWORKS

"THE MYSTERY OF THE WAX MUSEUM," with Lionel Atwill as the man of mystery and Glenda Farrell sharing the feminine hysteria with Fay Wray, will bring its cargo of violence into the Strand on Wednesday night. The film, which has been photographed in Technicolor, was suggested by the burning of Mme. Tussaud's celebrated waxworks in London more than a decade ago.

A number of interesting production problems rose to plague the technicians during the making of the film, but one which might have caused considerable delay and expense had been foreseen and was solved in advance. This had to do with the susceptibility of ordinary wax dummies to heat. In filming a Technicolor picture about five times the amount of light needed for ordinary motion-picture photography is required. After ten or twelve hours of exposure to the extreme heat of a sound stage under such conditions the wax comes to the melting point. This was provided against by building the dummies of a specially durable composition material which stood the wear and tear exceedingly well.

The human players in "The Mystery of the Wax Museum" move among a variegated array of figures that to all appearance are human also, lacking only the breath of life. Some of these figures reproduce the physical appearance of living characters in the story; thus plaster casts were made of the head and shoulders of Fay Wray and of Edwin Maxwell, while Monica Bannister was encased in plaster for half an hour.

Column in the *New York Times*, Feb. 12, 1933

In Hollywood I work practically every day—twice as many hours as a play requires. I miss my friends in the East, and I haven't had time to make but a few here.[1]

Curtiz encountered a major problem during the *Wax Museum* production, as the high temperatures created by the Technicolor lighting setup caused many of the wax sculptures to melt. He solved the problem by casting extras as the figures (thus imitating Mr. Igor's use of corpses in the film). As he proved time and again, the director was a master of light and shadow in both black-and-white and color.

Tommy Farrell, then 12 years old, recalled visiting his mother on the set:

Lionel Atwill ... had this terrible mask on. One day I was coming in the door to the stage as Mr. Atwill was coming out. I looked up, and I saw that face and let out a holler that you could hear in Cleveland.

Mother came running. She said, "I know that voice. That's Tommy. Now what happened?"

Atwill, of course, was laughing so hard, and he said, "It's Lionel Atwill."

And I said, "What happened to you?"

And he said, "This is for the picture."

I said, "Oh, my god!" He scared the living hell out of me![2]

The film opens in "London, 1921," when Igor's impressive wax exhibits are burned by Joe Worth (Edwin Maxwell), an impatient investor wishing to collect on a fire insurance policy. His dirty deed done, Worth locks Igor in the blazing building. Flashing ahead to 1933 New York, the miraculously still-breathing Igor (wearing a wax mask) watches a New Year's celebration before (sans mask) stealing a body from the local morgue.

The morbid subject matter of *Wax Museum* is balanced by a judicious use of pre-Code comedy, expertly served up by Glenda (as Florence, a "girl" newspaper reporter) and Frank McHugh (as her editor and divorced boyfriend, Jim). When he attempts to pull his tough newspaperman act, she responds, "Is 'Mama's Little Dumpling' getting tough?"

Sashaying into police headquarters, she slaps an officer (Wade Boteler) on the back before asking Sergeant Joe (Robert Emmett O'Connor), "Hello, sweetheart. How's your sex life?" He replies by asking a colleague to "call out the riot squad."

Glenda (who never looked better on screen) consistently brings a delightful energy to this well-paced, at times genuinely frightening, film. She provides the perfect counter to Atwill's splendidly measured madman. Fay Wray

Mystery of the Wax Museum (**Warner Bros., 1933, directed by Michael Curtiz**). **Intrepid reporter Florence (Farrell) tours the Wax Museum with love-struck George Winton (Gavin Gordon).**

adds further sex appeal (as Florence's roommate, Charlotte Duncan), showing plenty of leg in a pair of *short* shorts.

Florence's skills as a reporter extend to the investigative variety, and she eventually discovers that Igor is using real corpses as armatures for his sculptures. Following her initial visit to the museum, she tells him, "So long, Pop. See you in jail."

"There's something *cockeyed* about that joint," she informs Joe, "and I'm going to find out what it is!" Known for her verbal gifts, Glenda also displays a considerable talent for physical comedy, and she easily dominates all her scenes. On two occasions, she unleashes earsplitting screams. (Wray, however—in a warm-up for *King Kong* [1933]—adeptly handles most of the shrieking.)

As the preface for a marriage proposal, George Winton (Gavin Gordon) admits to Florence, "I never dreamed there were women like you in the world."

Dropping a gold-digger barb, she asks, "How much money have you got?"

Though Wray dominates the climactic terror scene (in which she is strapped down, "nude" under a sheet, to Igor's wax-embalming table), Glenda gets the final fade-out, locked in the classic Hollywood "let's get married" embrace with McHugh.

Mystery of the Wax Museum advertises Fay Wray and Lionel Atwill as its stars. But it is Glenda Farrell who steals the show, managing to hold her own with the flamboyant Atwill. Farrell would make her mark as a tough-talking blonde in the Jean Harlow mold. Before appearing in *Wax Museum* she had appeared in *I Am a Fugitive from a Chain Gang* and *Little Caesar*. The wise-cracking blonde would come into her own with the Torchy Blane series in 1938.

Farrell portrays mouthy reporter Florence Dempsey, roommate of the dull Charlotte Duncan (Wray). As Florence makes fun of Charlotte's boyfriend, she is chided for her frivolous ways. Florence embraces life while Charlotte hides behind it.

Charlotte: "I don't think you could have a real affair. I don't think you could care for anyone."

Florence: "I've been in love so many times my heart's callused. But I never hit one with dough. I'd rather die with an apoplectic heart from shaking cocktails and bankers than expire in a pan of dirty dishwater."

Lionel Atwill, as the demented Ivan Igor, has been masterminding the theft of bodies and using them to restock his wax museum. When Charlotte visits her artist boyfriend at the studio, Florence discovers an amazing resemblance between Joan of Arc and a missing body. She rushes to her newspaper office where she engages in snappy patter with despised editor, Jim (Frank McHugh).

Florence: "Hello, light of my life."

Jim: "Well, well, Prussic Acid."

Florence, visiting the exhibit with Charlotte, sneaks over to the Joan of Arc and scrapes a bit of wax from her foot then follows a henchman of Igor's to a deserted basement. She's accompanied by a rich young man, Winton (Gavin Gordon), she met the night before in the slammer. He is a little hesitant to get involved, having had enough interaction with the police. "OK, brother, then you can go to some nice warm place and I don't mean California." Florence climbs in a basement window and explores the area, scaring herself as she bumps into things. Unfortunately, Florence is not only adventurous, she tends to jump to conclusions, notably when she calls the cops convinced a body is in an oblong box she has discovered. The police burst into the room and approach the box with trepidation; however, it's not a murderer who inhabits the house, but bootleggers. Florence grabs a couple bottles as they leave.

In the car Winton professes his love for the daring Florence.

Winton: "I've only known you for 24 hours, but I'm in love with you."

Florence: "It doesn't usually take that long."

Florence heads back to the newspaper office where she tackles her considerably unhappy editor.

Florence: "Mitt me kid, I got a classic."

Jim: "...an evil spirit to mar my happiness."

Florence heads back to the museum where she is just in time to save the wretched Charlotte from a wax bath. Actually, she sensibly runs screaming for the police—a nice touch—rather than stay and put her pretty neck in jeopardy; she actually uses her head for something other than a hat rack.

Florence returns to the newsroom in glory, jovially accepting congratulations from her colleagues.

Florence: "Well, how about it Poison Ivy?"

Jim: "Rotten. You had a million dollars worth of luck with you."

Florence: "Could I possibly do anything that would meet with your approval?"

Jim: "Yeah. Cut out this crazy business, act like a lady, marry me."

Florence: "I'm gonna get even with you, you dirty stiff. I'll do it."

Will they live happily ever after? Maybe; however, we all know she'll be back in the newsroom before the honeymoon's over. And we're glad.

Farrell spiels forth her newswoman patter with the zeal of an early Rosalind Russell and is a welcome change from your comparable '30s scream queens.

—Susan Svehla, *Bitches, Bimbos and Virgins, Women in the Horror Film*, MMP 1996

Glenda stole *Mystery of the Wax Museum* from under the feet of Fay Wray (top left) and Lionel Atwill (top right). Roommates Charlotte (Fay Wray) and Florence (Glenda)

Theaters promoted *Mystery of the Wax Museum* with posters and prop displays.

"Don't take the kiddies," warned *Photoplay*, noting, "Glenda Farrell, Frank McHugh, Holmes Herbert and Allen Vincent [are] excellent in support."[3]

Never reissued after its initial 1933 release, *Mystery of the Wax Museum* was long considered a "lost" film. When the Technicolor Corporation upgraded to the three-strip process in 1936, the studios, requiring storage space for new films, disposed of many obsolete two-strip titles. Without a support system for the old prints, Warner Bros. retained only its color cartoons.

However, Warners' London film exchange had retained a 35mm color print of *Wax Museum* and a well-preserved nitrate print; a similar print of *Doctor X* was later discovered in Jack Warner's personal vault on the Burbank lot. Various copies were made over the years, from inferior dupes used for television distribution to a color-corrected preservation negative from which new theatrical prints were struck. (In 1953, Warner Bros. remade the film, in Technicolor and 3D, as *House of Wax*, starring Vincent Price.)

After signing a new long-term contract with the studio, Glenda continued to work for Warner Bros.' top directors, playing the unimaginatively named "Blondie" in William Dieterle's *Grand Slam* (1933), adapted by Erwin Gelsey and David Boehm from the novel *Grand Slam: The Rise and Fall of a Bridge Wizard* by Benjamin Russell Herts. Though Alfred E. Green had been an-

Grand Slam (Warner Bros., 1933; directed by William Dieterle). Party girl "Blondie" (Glenda) is restrained by boyfriend Philip "Speed" McCann (Frank McHugh) during some drunken nightclub mischief.

nounced as director, Dieterle replaced him, and shot the film over three weeks for a total cost of $164,000.

Paul Lukas stars as Russian waiter turned bogus bridge wizard Peter Stanislavsky, and Loretta Young is Marcia, his beautiful young wife, who urges him on. Frank McHugh plays Blondie's boyfriend Philip, aka "Speed," a ghostwriter who creates the book explaining the revolutionary "Stanislavsky System." Without doubt, Glenda's dizzy, drunken (and very funny) dame *is* the one true dumb blonde of her film career.

A high point of *Grand Slam* is its opening titles sequence, in which each actor appears on a separate playing card. The film's big playoff game between Stanislavsky and Van Dorn (Ferdinand Gottschalk) is a satirical version of "The Bridge Battle of the Century," a real challenge match played by the Romanian-born Ely Culbertson, "the man who made contract bridge," and Sidney S. Lenz, held at two New York hotels during December 1931 and January 1932. Like Culbertson, who was famous for often partnering with his wife Josephine, Stanislavsky widely publicizes his partnership with Marcia (whose temporary split from him provides much of the film's drama).

Glenda received top billing in her next Warner Bros. assignment, *The Blue Moon Murder Case*, directed by Robert Florey. Heavyweights Walter Huston

51

Warner Bros. publicity candid (1933) taken on the set of *Girl Missing*.

and William Powell were considered for the male lead, but the role eventually
went to Ben Lyon. Florey managed to shoot this quickie, retitled *Girl Missing*
(1933), in just 13 days on a budget of $107,000.

Glenda did justice to her billing. Energetic, wise, determined and tough
Kay Curtis is arguably the quintessential Glenda Farrell film performance.
Cast with her best friend Mary Brian, the dialogue flows effortlessly and hu-
morously throughout the film. Viewers may get lost amidst the convoluted plot

Girl Missing (Warner Bros., 1933; directed by Robert Florey). "Burn my clothes!" announces Kay Curtis as her partner in crime-solving, June Dale (Mary Brian), waits for the roll of the dice. "Hot-cha!"

involving a shakedown predicated on a bogus kidnapping, but the excellent acting and crackling script more than compensate.

Pre-Code elements abound. Kenneth Van Dusen (Guy Kibbee) tells June Dale (Brian), "I want to make love to you in the very worst way." Kay (an electric Glenda) slaps Van Dusen on the cheek while calling him "a sweet old potato." Kay and June are labeled "The G.D. Sisters": Does it stand for "Gold Diggers" or "another word?"

Glenda's antics at a casino crap table are a highlight. "Burn my clothes!" Kay exclaims as she tosses the dice. "*Hot-cha!*"

Eventually her attempt to solve the crime nearly lands the "sisters" in the slammer. "One more thought out of you and we'll be electrocuted," June tells her.

In the end, Kay pulls a rod on all concerned (including the police inspector [Edward Ellis]) and forces the truth from the culprits (Lyle Talbot and Peggy Shannon), who tried to fleece millionaire Henry Gibson (Lyon). She even threatens, "To turn [the woman] into a sieve."

"You'd make a good copper," the inspector tells Kay. Although the .38 she held on the assemblage wasn't loaded, the wily wisecracker then brandishes her own heater (presumably loaded). The G.D. Sisters triumph and collect a

53

Warner Bros. publicity portrait (1933) used to promote Glenda's appearance in
The Keyhole.

$25,000 reward from Gibson. Though the plot may contain a few too many twists, *Girl Missing* is essential viewing.

Though Glenda had been announced as the female lead in Warner Bros.' *The Mayor of Hell* (1933), directed by Archie Mayo and starring James Cagney, the part eventually went to Madge Evans. Instead, she played another major supporting role for Michael Curtiz, in *The Keyhole* (1933), a shipboard romance starring Kay Francis and George Brent (who replaced William Powell),

The Keyhole (**Warner Bros., 1933; directed by Michael Curtiz). Two gold-diggers at work aboard a cruise ship: Hank (Allen Jenkins) and Dot (Glenda). Both are in for a rude awakening.**

in which she is pursued by none other than the studio's most prolific sidekick, Allen Jenkins. Based on an original story, *The Adventuress*, by Alice D.G. Miller, the film was shot over 25 days for $169,000.

The film literally begins and ends with the camera turning the viewer into a true *voyeur*. Tracking through a keyhole, the opening scene irises-in on Maurice LeBrun (Monroe Owsley), a shady man who has refused to give his wife, Anne Vallee (Kay Francis), a divorce and is now blackmailing her. Tracking out through a keyhole, the closing scene irises-out as Neil Davis (George Brent) embraces Anne, now free of LeBrun (who accidentally killed himself).

During the entire voyage from New York to Havana, Neil has been paid by Anne's "current" husband, millionaire Schuyler Brooks (Henry Kolker), who knows nothing about her previous marriage, to spy on her, hoping to catch her in an act of infidelity. Meanwhile, Neil's sidekick, Hank Wales (Allen Jenkins), posing as his valet, becomes involved in a mutual gold-digging entanglement with Dot (Glenda).

Dot is one of Glenda's most blatant professional gold-diggers. During and after the voyage, she is in cahoots with several confederates, including a bartender and a jeweler, who give her a cut of the cash fleeced from Hank (actually expense money supplied by Old Man Brooks). While Hank believes

Central Airport (**Warner Bros., 1933; directed by William A. Wellman**). **Though Glenda's scenes were cut from the final print, her name still appeared prominently on the posters used to promote the film. This title lobby card bills her just below the three stars of this excellent aviation drama.**

Dot is a tobacco heiress, she thinks he is living off his "retired" father's dough. When she finds out he is a detective, she takes a powder, leaving behind a lipstick Dear John letter on the mirror in his hotel room.

Glenda and Jenkins provide many comic moments, including a drunk scene that begins with Dot declaring the expensive champagne "atrocious." Later, after she pulls a "diamond ring" scam on Hank, Dot tells him, "Let's go to some nice quiet place where I can *really* thank you."

The March 1933 issue of *Movie Classic*, noting that Glenda "plays hardboiled wenches on the screen and is shy and timid in real life," also linked her romantically with none other than—Allen Jenkins![4]

Glenda had a brief role in Warner Bros.' *Central Airport* (1933), starring Richard Barthelmess, Sally Eilers and Tom Brown, but it was left on the cutting room floor. One of many aviation adventures directed by William A. Wellman, who shot the film as *Grand Central Airport* over 30 days on a $365,000 budget, this very adult drama (even for the pre-Code era) benefits from the stunning aerial photography of Elmer Dyer and special effects of Fred Jackman.

A major scene involving a plane crash was filmed, but after the aviation board of the Los Angeles Chamber of Commerce screened the original cut, the footage was removed. Glenda had played a crash victim in the sequence.

However, her name still appeared prominently on the posters and title lobby cards, which Warner Bros. already had printed. Her name also was included in *The Hollywood Reporter*'s March 21, 1933 negative review of the film.

After directing her in three major films, Mervyn LeRoy had grown very fond of Glenda's unique talent. In the June 1933 issue of *The New Movie Magazine*, he related his appreciation—and a shocking story (bearing a real-life similarity to the ending of *Three on a Match*):

> Glenda Farrell just telephoned ... to say she hadn't slept a wink all night. A woman who lives on the seventh floor of her apartment house jumped out of the window about 10 o'clock last evening. Glenda lives on the sixth floor. She saw her go by ...
>
> That Farrell girl's a great actress ... Watch her! ... I take some credit for Miss Farrell, and for Aline MacMahon, too ... because I brought them out here to play in my pictures.[5]

Glenda's working relationship with LeRoy would continue over the following decade. Their close friendship would last even longer. She considered him her favorite director, and one of the very finest in the film industry, for the patience and respect he showed every actor with whom he worked. In an article devoted to LeRoy's practice of giving aspiring film actors a break, *Movie Classic* reported:

> The man with the kindliest eyes and biggest heart in Hollywood is director Mervyn LeRoy. An unassuming man, he is averse to talking about the fact he has discovered some of the greatest stars in Hollywood ...
>
> Encouragement and intelligent understanding are inspiring things to those with talent who are struggling. Stars like Loretta Young, Boris Karloff, Aline MacMahon and Glenda Farrell can testify to that—thinking of the encouragement and understanding that Mervyn LeRoy gave to them, when others scorned and doubted their possibilities.[6]

Warner Bros. loaned Glenda to Paramount for *Gambling Ship* (1933), based on four short stories by Paul Cain published in *Black Mask* magazine the previous year. Top-billed Cary Grant was paired with Benita Hume, in a role originally announced for Carole Lombard. Glenda received fourth billing, behind heavy supreme Jack La Rue.

Director Louis Gasnier hired a technical advisor, known only as "Mr. 100," to coach the actors in the art of gambling, which was legal in floating

Gambling Ship (**Paramount, 1933; directed by Louis Gasnier and Max Marcin**). **Pete Manning (Jack La Rue) is taught some manners by Ace Corbin (Cary Grant), as Jeanne Sands (Glenda) is grateful for his protection.**

casinos anchored outside a three-mile radius from the California shoreline. San Pedro provided the locations used by cinematographer Charles Lang and his assistants, Robert Pittack and Cliff Shirpser.

Gambling Ship falls squarely into the "retired bootlegger" subgenre that emerged during 1933, most famously in the lively Warner Bros. spoof *Little Giant* starring Edward G. Robinson and Mary Astor. Spurred by the Hays Office, the "golden age" of the gangster film, which had lasted only two years, began to give way to parody and satire. A former beer baron, laid low by the end of Prohibition, leaves the rackets behind in favor of new conquests, namely gambling and *dames*. Whereas Eddie G. pursues Ms. Astor in the Warner Bros. opus, here Grant's Ace Corbin goes after the desirable Ms. Hume's Eleanor La Velle. Glenda appears in a supporting role as Jeanne Sands.

Glenda recalled the busy, hectic days at Warner Bros, where she appeared in seven films, plus another three on loan-out, in 1933:

> It all went so *fast*. I used to ask myself, "What set am I on today? What script am I supposed to be doing—this one or this one? Up at 5 every morning, start work at a quarter of 6, work till 7 or 8 at night. By the time you got home, it was 9. Then you had to study your lines, have your dinner and bath

and go to bed. You worked till midnight on Saturday. All I ever really wanted was a day off. Our contracts gave us six weeks' vacation each year, but they got around that by loaning us out to other studios. I could have gone on suspension, but I had responsibilities—my father to support, my son in military school, all that.[7]

Glenda was among the Warner Bros. stars riding the cross-country train "42nd Street Special" used to promote *42nd Street*. Christened by California Governor James Rolph and Senator William Gibbs McAdoo, the train, scheduled to arrive in the nation's capital for the March 4, 1933 inauguration of President Roosevelt, left Hollywood on February 21. Among the passengers were James Cagney, Bette Davis, Bebe Daniels, Joe E. Brown, Helen Vinson, Preston Foster, Lyle Talbot, Alice White, Laura LaPlante, Dolores del Rio, Mary Astor, Fay Wray, Eleanor Holm, Leo Carrillo, Claire Dodd, Tom Mix, Jack Dempsey and Glenda, who was called back to the studio when the party reached Philadelphia. Jack, Harry and Albert Warner also attended the inaugural festivities.

Warner Bros. cast Glenda in a short film, "Position and Back Swing," the second installment in the *How to Break 90* series starring golf champion Bobby Jones. George Marshall directed the episode, which also features Guy Kibbee as "Himself, a Bad Golfer!" The previous installment, "The Grip," guest stars Joe E. Brown, while four subsequent efforts, all directed by Marshall in 1933, include W.C. Fields, William B. Davidson, Warner Oland, Richard Arlen, Regis Toomey, Sheila Terry, Ruth Donnelly and J. Farrell MacDonald.

Glenda initially had been cast as "Blondie," but now was handed the even more uninspired name "Glenda," in *Mary Stevens, M.D.* (1933). Adapted by Rian James and Robert Lord from a story by Virginia Kellogg, and directed by Lloyd Bacon, the film is a well-acted pre-Code soap opera with some of Warner Bros.' progressive and "social problem" elements (a "woman doctor," drinking on the job, political corruption, pregnancy, divorce) tossed in for good measure.

MARY STEVENS, M.D.
KAY FRANCIS
LYLE TALBOT · GLENDA FARRELL
THELMA TODD · UNA O'CONNOR
DIRECTED BY LLOYD BACON
A WARNER BROS. & VITAPHONE PICTURE

Mary Stevens, M.D. **(Warner Bros., 1933; directed by Lloyd Bacon). Nurse Glenda (Glenda) and Dr. Mary Stevens (Kay Francis) admire the latter's baby boy.**

Glenda's role is a substantial one, with her serving as Dr. Stevens' (Kay Francis) Woman Friday throughout the picture. She often provides commentary on the state of things, particularly Mary's affair with the married Dr. Donald Andrews (Lyle Talbot). Among her pithy one-liners is a reference to the good doctor's being with child, "without benefit of clergy": "I'm glad what ails you isn't catching." (In 1936, when Warner Bros., intending to reissue the film, applied for a certificate from the Production Code Administration, Joseph Breen denied the request.)

Mary Stevens becomes quite a tearjerker when the doctor's baby boy, born abroad to avoid a possible scandal, fatally contracts infantile paralysis while at sea. The fine supporting cast also includes Thelma Todd, Charles C. Wilson and Una O'Connor (who was borrowed from Fox).

Notes:

[1]*Picture Play*, January 1933, p. 43
[2]Dan Van Neste, "Glenda Farrell: Diamond in the Rough," *Classic Images*, Vol. 275, May 1998.
[3]*Photoplay*, March 1933, p. 61.
[4]*Movie Classic*, March 1933.
[5]*The New Movie Magazine*, June 1933, p. 33.
[6]*Movie Classic*, March 1936, ps. 51, 68.
[7]*New York Times*, 9 February 1969.

Lady for a Day (Columbia, 1933; directed by Frank Capra). Glenda looms large in the artwork on this one-sheet poster, also featuring Warren William, May Robson, Guy Kibbee, Jean Parker and Barry Norton.

Chapter 6
Entirely on Merit

You wouldn't want me to start a scandal around here, would
you? Or have you jugged for non-support? It might not be so
good for your job, you're such an important guy around here.
Come on, Butch—be nice.
—Belle Saunders, *Bureau of Missing Persons* (1933)

On loan to Columbia, Glenda was cast in a top-supporting role, nightclub
owner Missouri Martin, in Frank Capra's *Beggar's Holiday*, starring Warren
William, May Robson and Guy Kibbee. In production from May 9 to June
6, 1933, the film, retitled *Lady for a Day*, also features Ned Sparks, Walter
Connolly, Jean Parker, Nat Pendleton and Halliwell Hobbes. Adapted from
Damon Runyon's 1929 short story "Madame La Gimp" by Capra's frequent
collaborator, Robert Riskin, the project involved the director's failed attempt
to borrow other Warner Bros. players, including William Powell, James Cagney and Allen Jenkins, but he did manage to land William and Kibbee, as well
as MGM stars Robson, Connelly and Parker.

Glenda's loanout also resulted in her catching the eye of Riskin, who
squired her about some of Hollywood's top nightspots. They began seeing
each other on a regular basis, including weekend outings with 12-year-old
Tommy, and at one point the relationship became quite serious. The popular movie magazines naturally began tossing around words such as "fiancée,"
"honeymoon" and "shopping for furniture."

Originally published in *Cosmopolitan*, "Madame La Gimp" was transformed by Riskin into a screenplay of greater depth, tying the "Apple Annie"
character, played by the 75-year-old Robson, to other unfortunate though colorful characters affected by the Great Depression, which naturally resonated
with filmgoers throughout the nation. Unlike many authors who are inevitably
disappointed by the film adaptations of their work, Damon Runyon considered
Riskin and Capra's efforts a great improvement on his story.

After casting a group of Columbia contract players to the supporting roles,
Capra combed through downtown Los Angeles, looking for real street people
to give the film the touch of realism he was seeking. This, coupled with the fact
that the Australian-born Robson, primarily a stage actress, was unfamiliar to
many Americans, made audiences feel as if they were seeing a true depiction
of real Depression down-and-outers.

Lady for a Day premiered at New York's Radio City Music Hall during the
week of September 7, 1933. As a publicity stunt, Columbia recreated events
from the film by locating Ellen McCarthy, a 73-year-old Shubert Alley apple

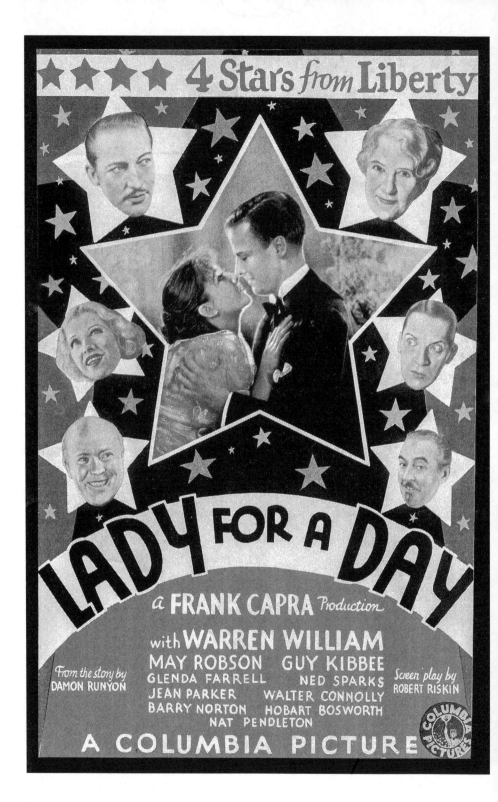

Lady for a Day (Columbia, 1933; directed by Frank Capra). [Front] Apple Annie (May Robson) and Judge Blake (Guy Kibbee); [rear] Louise (Jean Parker), Dave the Dude (Warren William) and Missouri Martin (Glenda).

seller, purchasing a lavish wardrobe and booking a room in an expensive hotel before parading her to the premiere. This overblown ballyhoo was repeated in several major cities across the nation, but Columbia executives ultimately regretted their acquisitive decision. The following year, McCarthy and her husband, subsisting on home relief in a tiny apartment, were found dead from natural gas suffocation.

This populist fantasy may be labeled "Capracorn" more than eight decades after its release (it was called "improbable" during its own day), but it is a thoroughly entertaining, witty, Runyon-fueled ride driven by a stellar cast. It is exactly the sort of relevant yet escapist film Depression audiences ate up, like Dave the Dude (Warren William) and the fruit he buys from "Apple Annie" (May Robson) on the screen. Shortly after it went into general release on September 13, *Lady for a Day* grossed $600,000, twice its budget.

When Dave the Dude's increasingly elaborate scheme to make a Spanish count (Walter Connelly) believe that his prospective daughter-in-law (Jean Parker) hails from an American society lineage begins to unravel, he asks the incensed police commissioner (Wallis Clark), "You believe in *fairy tales*, don't you?"

Arguably the funniest line in the film is delivered just a short time later, by "Happy" McGuire (the inimitable Ned Sparks, deadpanning his signature plant on a family basis. All department heads sit in on the Thursday night conferences, all executives ~~have lunch at one large table each~~ day and discuss production, and almost any employe can tell what the box office reports for Columbia's product were at Dubuque, Seattle or Miami. Mr. Cohn pounds the desk and shouts and his employes pound and shout back. Blunt things are said on both sides, but every problem is settled in no uncertain terms and every one is happy. Nepotism is forbidden and executives, no matter how important, are prohibited from giving out even $3 a day extra jobs to friends. Many of Hollywood's maddest stories have been traced to incidents at Columbia. But through all the serious business of making pictures is a strain of humor and rough camaraderie.

Mr. Cohn will go to London shortly with Lewis Milestone to establish an English company and see if his system of production will work in a more sedate atmosphere. May Robson and Robert Montgomery have been borrowed from MGM. Richard Cromwell has been loaned to Cecil De Mille in exchange for Carole Lombard. Warren William, Guy Kibbee and Glenda Farrell have been borrowed from the Warners. Leslie Howard has been engaged. Columbia is recognized in Hollywood as in the big league.

May 7, 1933 *New York Times* lists studio loan-outs to Columbia for *Lady for a Day*.

monotone), who asks a gubernatorial assemblage of balding authority figures the same question, and then follows it up with an aside to the Dude: "Look at their *skulls*."

Glenda's witty nightclub owner with a heart-of-gold matched Sparks' sarcasm, and she combines indelible charm with just the right humorous edge. Missouri Martin is one of her most likeable film characters. "Look at 'em. Look at 'em," she says when a fleet of "artists" gathers to give Apple Annie a makeover. "Their tongues are hanging out!"

Glenda's first scene is one of her most sensual on film. Missouri appears on stage at her club, shimmying and shaking her breasts as she sings, "I'm so hot, I'm smoking. I want a *man*!" And that man is Dave the Dude, who rebuffs her advances until the very end, when she tells him she loves him for what he's done for his "good luck charm," Apple Annie.

May Robson is simply superb in a role that demands a full spectrum of emotions. And she is given fine support by the rest of the cast, especially the ever-reliable Guy Kibbee, who appeared in many films with Glenda over the next several years.

Lady for a Day (Columbia, 1933; directed by Frank Capra). **The crew assembled to transform Apple Annie into a "lady for a day" is observed by [far left] Dave the Dude (Warren William), Shakespeare (Nat Pendleton) and Happy (Ned Sparks); and [far right] Pierre (Leo White), Missouri Martin (Glenda) and Apple Annie (May Robson).**

Film Daily selected *Lady for a Day* as one of the 10 Best Films of 1933, and four Academy Award nominations were announced for Best Picture, Best Director, Best Screenplay and Best Actress for Robson, who later teamed with Jean Parker in an audio version for *Lux Radio Theater* on May 1, 1939. The film remained one of Glenda's favorites.

In early May 1933, Glenda joined two of her best Warner Bros. pals, Mervyn LeRoy and Allen Jenkins, at the Club Ballyhoo on the Sunset Strip in West Hollywood to see a new show featuring comedian Jerry Lester, singer Maxine Lewis, female impersonator Leon Le Verde and the Earl Burtnett Orchestra. *Hollywood Filmograph* reported:

> One of the most representative audiences that has so far visited the café actually stood on their feet and applauded, demanding encores and many bows from the artists in the show.[1]

During the spring, Loretta Young formed a bicycling and skating club for Warner Bros. contract players. By June 1, the club boasted 47 members, including Glenda, Joan Blondell, Mary Brian, Dick Powell, Patricia Ellis and

Claire Dodd. On jaunts to local resorts, they carried their picnic essentials on "butcher boy" bicycles fitted with large baskets.

In July 1933, *Movie Classic* magazine ran an article, "Legs! Do They Have to Show Them?" offering this hook for the reader:

When they're stars, actresses can cover their legs. But when they're newcomers, they have to reveal them—to attract attention. It's one of the Hollywood rules. Joan Crawford and Clara Bow and Marlene Dietrich—yes, and all the others—obeyed it when they started. But Glenda Farrell is a rebel. She's going to fight to win attention by acting alone. Can she do it?[2]

July 1933 *Movie Classic* **featuring an interview with Glenda.**

Referring to Glenda as an exception to the rule and a "phenomenon," the article continues:

"We expect great things of Glenda Farrell," [Warner Bros.] said. "She has established a place for herself on the stage. She will go even further on the screen."

The public seemed to agree. Her fan mail has grown by leaps and bounds. Her performances have won high praise and the press, always alert for new film faces, has called for interviews and photographs ... There have been plenty of pictures depicting Glenda's every mood, from smiles to tears. But wonder of wonders—not a single bit of leg art.[3]

Such a heretical departure from the status quo bewildered members of the Hollywood publicity and press communities. What—Glenda Farrell was against depicting innocuous cheesecake on the screen? Farrell explained to the magazine:

I hope I am neither a prude nor a Puritan. It is just that I can't see the slightest excuse for posing in undies of any sort. This is entirely a personal opinion and judging by the numbers who differ with me, decidedly a wee voice in the minority.

If what success I am able to attain on the screen should make me an important figure in the film industry, my pictures will be published entirely on merit ... We had all this out at the studio months and months ago. The ink on my contract was hardly dry when I was called into the photographic gallery for a portrait sitting. The first thing I was handed was a cute little bunny suit ...

I lost no time announcing that they had picked on the wrong rabbit ... I fear I was abrupt in my positive refusal. I wasn't sure but what my contractual status might suffer. Still, I felt I was right. Since then I have done many things in the name of publicity, even to going to a zoo to be photographed aboard an elephant in an effort to be a good fellow.

The public will never have my insufficiently clad person thrust upon them without cause. Advancing a screen characterization is one thing. Posing in a bunny suit is quite another.[4]

During late July 1933, Glenda and Robert Riskin attended the Terry Dantzler Orchestra's opening engagement at the Patio Roof of the Roosevelt Hotel. Dantzler was the brother of Mary Brian, who had quite a retinue at her table. Joining Glenda and Bob were George E. Stone, Guinn "Big Boy" Williams, Ken Murray, William Wyler and many other Hollywood luminaries.

Based on the book *Missing Men* by Captain John H. Ayers and Carol Bird, *Bureau of Missing Persons* offered Glenda a one-trick role in a fast-moving,

Bureau of Missing Persons **(Warner Bros., 1933; directed by Roy Del Ruth). Belle Saunders (Glenda) digs for gold from her husband, "Butchy Wutchy" (Pat O'Brien).**

69

social-problem crime drama directed by Roy Del Ruth and featuring the ubiquitous Allen Jenkins and Hugh Herbert. Released on September 16, 1933, *Bureau of Missing Persons* stars Bette Davis as Norma Williams, an innocent woman accused of murder, Lewis Stone as Captain Webb and Pat O'Brien as Butch Saunders, one of his detectives who continually attempts to escape the gold-digging interruptions of his nagging wife, Belle (Glenda), who ultimately proves to be a bigamist!

A pre-Code extravaganza, *Missing Persons* includes flagrant and sometimes lurid references to drugs, sex, adultery, rape and dismembered murder victims. The film ends in rather misogynistic fashion with Butch actually *beating up* Belle. The final shot shows a disheveled Glenda, bending over toppled office furniture, with a pocketbook perched on her rear end. Repeating Belle's oft-repeated clarion call, she cries, "Butchy Wutchy!"

Glenda accepted the role of singer Fay La Rue, the "other woman" who briefly entices Bill (Spencer Tracy) away from Trina (Loretta Young) in Columbia's *Man's Castle*, which director Frank Borzage began shooting on July 28, 1933. Ralph Bellamy and Anita Louise had been considered for the leads, and Spencer Tracy had requested Fay Wray for the Trina role, but her recent success in *King Kong* had kept her working at Columbia, Fox, RKO and Paramount throughout the year. While costarring with Tracy, Glenda enjoyed going to work every day.

After the film was completed, Borzage sent a telegram to Columbia, expressing his satisfaction with the project:

> I enjoyed directing *Man's Castle* more than any picture I have ever made, and judging by first cut, which I have just seen, [the] result is most gratifying. *Man's Castle* represents just about the best job of casting in talking pictures so far. Swerling's script is great, Joe August's photography superb, Gooson sets could not be improved. I owe sincere thanks to Spencer Tracy, Loretta Young, Glenda Farrell, Walter Connolly, Arthur Hohl and Marjorie Rambeau for magnificent performances.
> Frank Borzage[5]

Borzage had every right to be satisfied with this very unusual dramatic, romantic film. "When people got nothing, they act like human beings," says Bill early in the film. Though he purposely projects a tough, apathetic, irresponsible demeanor, always threatening to hop a freight train for 1,000 miles from anywhere, he eventually is won over by the all-encompassing love of Trina, who has become pregnant with his child. After bungling a burglary intended to net some cash for the expected kid, Bill hops a freight but takes Trina with

Man's Castle (Columbia, 1933; directed by Frank Borzage). This one-sheet poster gives more prominence to Fay La Rue, the "other woman" (Glenda) of Bill (Spencer Tracy), than to his wife, Trina (Loretta Young).

Man's Castle (Columbia, 1933; directed by Frank Borzage). Bill (Spencer Tracy) waits to serve a writ to Fay La Rue (Glenda), as soon as she finishes her "sexy" number.

him. The final shot, showing the couple embracing in a boxcar filled with hay, is unforgettable.

Borzage makes the most of this pre-Code project, which includes scenes of skinny-dipping, two-timing (courtesy of Glenda, who resembles a slim Mae West), drunkenness, sexual harassment (courtesy of Arthur Hohl's slimy Bragg, who squeals on Bill and then tries to conquer Trina) and murder (Marjorie Rambeau's Flossie kills Bragg to end his reign of sleaze). Jo Swerling's screenplay is inventive, and the acting, particularly by the leads, is outstanding.

Billed fourth, Glenda appears in only three brief scenes, but the fact that she *sings* in two of them makes this an atypical entry in her film catalog. Decked out in a shimmering, silvery, floor-length dress and backed by an equally iridescent band, Fay La Rue—and Her Jazbos—entices her audience of balding, middle-aged men, just before receiving a summons (delivered by Bill) to appear in court to answer an "alienation of affection" suit.

Later, while lounging on Fay's sofa, Bill tells her, "You don't need a bodyguard. You look like you can take care of yourself."

"I always have," she replies.

Hollywood magazine reported:

> With typical finesse, Glenda [Farrell] makes sin doubly attractive in her expert delineation of the siren in *Man's Castle*.

Funny things, movies. Glenda in real life, devoted to her son, is not at all like her screen self.[6]

Motion Picture Daily predicted great success for the film:

Another artistic achievement for Frank Borzage, who direct-ed this romance of derelict squatters with an attentive eye on the box-office. Rich in human appeal and handled with tender charm, this picture will without doubt meet unanimous ap-proval of entertainment seekers. Spencer Tracy is excellent and elicits swell support from Loretta Young, who chalks up one of her best performances to date. Glenda Farrell, Walter Connelly, Marjorie Rambeau, Arthur Hohl and Dickie Moore, in different difficult assignments, contribute "ace" showings.[7]

The New Movie Magazine concurred:

Just about a satisfactory job of acting as you're likely to see ... makes this story of life in shacks of the unemployed squatters a moving and worthwhile picture. Thanks to the skill of all concerned, *Man's Castle* is sentimental without being syrupy and heart stirring without becoming hokum ... [The film] has flavor and a soft, moonshiny luster because of Miss Young's beautiful portrayal of the world-hounded girl and Mr. Tracy's characterization of the roughneck who hides his love under mock brutality. Some of the scenes between these two are as lovely as any a screen ever has reflected.[8]

Unfortunately the film did not do as well as expected at the box office. (When it was reissued in 1938, the Production Code Administration's insis-tence on nine minutes of cuts removed much of the film's gritty edge.) One of Glenda's benefits from appearing in the film was her friendship with screen-writer Jo Swerling and his wife.

Glenda now was living in a Spanish-style home she had purchased in North Hollywood. To help provide a family environment for Tommy, she bought a residence for her father in Laurel Canyon. Her brothers, Gene, who served as her manager, and Dick, who worked as a film editor, also were living in the Los Angeles area. Filmmaker Michael A. Hoey, who worked with Dick Farrell at MGM during the 1960s, remembered:

What a nice man he was—a very pleasant guy. He always had a great attitude, was very friendly and was a good editor. He was our editor on one of the Elvis pictures [*Speedway* (1968)] during that period when we [Hoey and director Norman Taurog] were at MGM. He did a great job on the picture.

Glenda was quite a sexy little lady in the early days—and a good actress.[9]

Tommy was away at military school during the week, but he came home to spend every weekend with Glenda. This arrangement worked very well, since she was constantly busy making one film after another. At his request, Tommy had his surname legally changed from Richards to Farrell the previous year, and the relationship with his mother was referred to as "one of the tenderest [sic] ... of all Hollywood" by at least one movie magazine.[10]

Joan Blondell described Glenda's Hollywood home:

It was substantially built and the grounds were lovely but the house wasn't one bit attractive. Glenda walked through it, talking as she went.

"I'll knock out that wall and build on a bedroom which will open out onto the patio. I'll take that closet out and put in bookshelves. The fireplace is clumsy. It will have to be rebuilt. It's rather dark in the living room. French windows at the end would fix that. There's plenty of room over the garage for a play room, etc."

She did all that and you should see the place now! The minute you step into her home you realize that it is the home of a woman. It is all done in delicate shades of rose, green, blue, gold and white, yet it isn't fussy and frilly.[11]

Though she had been dating screenwriter Robert Riskin, whom she did consider marrying at one point, Glenda remained single. Other beaus with whom she had serious relationships, including comedian Jack Durant (whom she had met in San Francisco), saw their relationship crumble. She told a reporter:

I don't believe in forgetting old friends, but my career is, after all, the big thing. You see, I've Tommy, my child. No! Hollywood will never make me deny him. I'm divorced, but Tommy is really the one that counts with me."[12]

In the August 1934 issue of *Hollywood* magazine, Richard English reported:

Studio portrait from *Man's Castle*

Glenda's romance with Robert Riskin is one of Hollywood's happier idylls. During the filming of *Lady for a Day* they were introduced; Glenda was a member of the cast and Bob, the writer of the screen story. From their first dinner date they plunged into a romance that has become one of the cinema city's most widely discussed topics.[13]

Glenda spoke about being married amongst the temptation of Hollywood:

> This isn't a bad town, by any means, but the straying from the straight and narrow is just a little easier here than any place else. Too much money, too much leisure, too much beauty! I know what it means to be in love, marry and to lose that love. Marriage would be hard enough to keep, as it should be, in any town so why risk it here where the odds are so high against marrying and staying married?[14]

Glenda also elaborated on the difference between her on-screen persona and her actual personality:

> Really, I'm not the least bit like the roles I play ... In movies I'm usually cast as a wisecracking, gold-digging dame, you know. But actually I never wisecrack ... And as for gold digging, I've never been able to wangle a thing. Everything I've ever had, I've worked for and paid myself ... I don't wish to give Tommy everything he wants, but I do want to give him understanding and good times. I want him to feel that he is a person of importance in the Farrell household.[15]

Glenda's talent for acting hardboiled was so convincing that she often disappointed fans when meeting them in public. She said:

> I don't consider myself sophisticated, either. Though I'm old enough to be. I've been advised to live up to my screen illusion. It would be better business, but I've been an actress since I was seven, and when I'm acting I love to act. And when I'm through with a job I'm through.[16]

Glenda disliked Hollywood parties and fancy nightclubs (which the studios encouraged their stars to frequent). She drank very little and was a non-smoker. She much preferred taking a drive to the beach or attending a late movie.

She enjoyed entertaining in her home, and especially liked having children over for parties and various activities with Tommy. She also loved to cook, and had a great penchant for Siamese cats. Her felines eventually included a Siamese pair, "Frankie" and "Johnny," but when Johnny ran away, Frankie was given to Glenda's father, who had bought a replacement, "Taki," of which the older cat disapproved. Glenda also owned a white Persian named "Annie," plus a mixed-breed dog, "Heinzie," who fared splendidly with the cats.

Glenda poses with one of her beloved cats.

Frequently coming home from the studio exhausted, she didn't have much time for reading. However, the books on her nightstand included works by Joseph Conrad and Ernest Hemingway, and she was quite fond of the prolific C.B. Kelland, whose stories often were adapted for the screen.

One of Glenda's favorite domestic additions was her outspoken Hungarian housekeeper, Teresa, who could be somewhat intimidating to guests. On one occasion, when Glenda's pal Hugh Herbert came calling, lugging a basket of fruit and wearing old, worn clothing, Teresa, thinking him a peddler, gave him the bum's rush. Rescued from the dreaded "Magyar distaste" by Glenda, the befuddled Herbert attempted to explain and was laughingly welcomed into the kitchen.[17]

Another incident involved Teresa, who had despised cats prior to her employment with Glenda, and Taki. Glenda explained:

> One night I was entertaining a few friends and had a buffet supper spread in the snack bar. When I took my guests into the bar, every shrimp and anchovy hors d'oeuvre had been plucked clean. Obviously, Taki was the offender. But did Teresa scold him? Not by a single word. Instead, she hastily substituted fresh hors d'oeuvres from the kitchen.[18]

Joan Blondell added, "Glenda is forever doing things for others and she seems instinctively to know just what to do and when to do it."[19]

Notes:

[1]*Hollywood Filmograph*, 6 May 1933, p. 6.
[2]*Movie Classic*, July 1933, p. 26.
[3]*Movie Classic*, July 1933, p. 72.
[4]*Movie Classic*, July 1933, pp. 72-73.
[5]Frank Borzage, Western Union telegram to Columbia Pictures, 21 September 1933.
[6]*Hollywood*, January 1934, p. 18.
[7]*Motion Picture Daily*, 30 December 1933, p. 4.
[8]*The New Movie Magazine*, April 1934, p. 51.
[9]Michael A. Hoey, conversation with Scott Allen Nollen, 6 November 2013.
[10]*Picture Play*, August 1933, p. 26.
[11]Joan Blondell, "My Pal, Glenda," *Hollywood*, January 1936.
[12]*The New Movie Magazine*, June 1933, p. 83.
[13]*Hollywood*, August 1934, p. 14.
[14]*Hollywood*, August 1934, p. 15.
[15]Dan Van Neste, "Glenda Farrell: Diamond in the Rough," *Classic Images*, Vol. 275, May 1998.
[16]*Picture Play*, August 1933, p. 72.
[17]*New York Times*, 3 April 1938.
[18]*Hollywood*, July 1936, p. 72.
[19]Joan Blondell, "My Pal, Glenda."

Warner Bros. publicity candid (1933): Cat fancier Glenda enjoys hanging out with a member of the studio's feral feline menagerie.

During a night out, Glenda chats with Lois Wilson and Winslow B. Felix (December 1933).

Chapter 7
Gimme Girls

We came all the way over here so we could grab up a millionaire and get out of show business. Now, you don't want to
spoil our only chance, do you?
We've got our fall guy all hooked. Now all we've got to do is
land him. Oh, he's a cinch to go for plenty of dough.
—Sadie Appleby, *Havana Widows* (1933)

Glenda's teaming with fellow hardboiled dame Joan Blondell was not exactly planned. For Warner Bros.' *Havana Widows* (1933), director Ray Enright had cast the equally wisecracking Aline MacMahon as Sadie Appleby,
but when she became unavailable, the role went to Glenda, who was putting
her finishing touches on *Man's Castle* at Columbia. She recalled:

We were a very close group—Cagney, Kibbee, Hugh Herbert,
Aline MacMahon, Dick Powell and Joan Blondell ... They
used to call Joan and me "the gimme girls." We were always
out to get a man with money. But those movies were risqué ...
sophisticated and *fun*.[1]

Havana Widows is not only the first of the "Blondell-Farrell" pictures,
but also the sexiest (being released pre-Code) and funniest. Like all great
comedies, the film builds a crescendo of craziness from start to finish, when
total chaos ensues. Joan and Glenda's comic timing is crackling (their mutual double-takes are priceless), and Allen Jenkins (tossing off one-liners with
aplomb) and Frank McHugh (whose never-sobering souse is one of the best
comic drunks on film) support them splendidly. By tossing in Guy Kibbee,
Ruth Donnelly and Lyle Talbot (who comprise a family), Warner Bros. created
one gem of a comedy, cleverly and crisply written by Earl Baldwin.

The film begins with Joan and Glenda as showgirls Mae Knight and Sadie Appleby supporting Broadway's current Russian phenomenon, "Iwanna
Shakitoff." Joan's skimpy, jaw-dropping costume is only the first of many
she wears throughout the fast-moving 62-minutes. In order to get to Cuba
"to land a millionaire," Mae borrows $1,500 from her "boyfriend," Herman
(Allen Jenkins), who is advanced the dough by his "boss," gambler Butch
O'Neill. Herman loses it at roulette and then forges his name to a rubber check
in connection with an insurance policy he purchases from Mr. Otis (Hobart Cavanaugh). As straying married man Deacon Jones, Guy Kibbee makes his first
appearance in bed, passed out in the girls' Havana hotel room, having ended

Havana Widows (Warner Bros., 1933; directed by Ray Enright). **Sadie Appleby (Glenda) and Mae Knight (Joan Blondell) learn how to "land a millionaire" from Gladys Gable (Noel Francis, center).**

the previous night's party by stripping down on their balcony. (Blondell holding up Kibbee's boxer shorts is unforgettable.) He makes his final appearance in court, after being set up for a shakedown, accosted by two thugs who yank off his clothes and send him running across the rooftops in his underwear.

"I'll try anything once," Mae tells Deacon's son Bob (Lyle Talbot) at one point. "That's my undoing." Trying anything and everything to wring some dough out of the Deacon (with the help of drunken attorney Duffy [Frank McHugh]), the girls also get "slapped in the cooler." Given "24 hours to get out of Cuba," they hurry onto a ship, where they are married: Mae to Bob, and Sadie to Herman. (Glenda always liked working with Allen Jenkins, and a great friendship did result from their frequent collaborations.)

A gala opening of *Havana Widows* at New York's Strand on November 22, 1933 included a dozen "Vitaphone Chorus Girls" handing out small boxes of candy to the audience members. The special filling inside the confections: Bacardi rum straight from Havana! Three days later, *Film Daily* reported:

> Hilarious comedy about gold diggers prospecting in Havana.
> Plenty of action and laughs. Considered strictly on its mer-

Havana Widows (**Warner Bros., 1933; directed by Ray Enright**). **World-class gold-digger Sadie Appleby (Glenda) toasts to a successful scam with attorney and perpetual drunkard Mr. Duffy (Frank McHugh).**

its as entertainment, this production is calculated to provide plenty of glee for any audience ... A lot of gag comedy, sousing and other action keeps the affair going at a lively pace throughout.[2]

The 1934 New Year brought Glenda and some of her colleagues a fine compliment from *The New Movie Magazine*, whose editor selected various readers' letters for the article "The People's Academy." Lucille Hanson of Milwaukee, Wisconsin, wrote:

Why is it we all like Marie Dressler, Guy Kibbee, Glenda Farrell and Aline MacMahon? Because they act natural, not affected, as most stars do. They are like people you know in real life, and that is the way they are in reel life.

All the world abhors artificiality in any form, so why make movies where the actors and actresses do not act like human beings? I am sure that much of the Depression in the Hollywood studios could be traced to this one fault—artificiality.[3]

Charles **FARRELL** Bette **DAVIS** in **THE BIG SHAKEDOWN**

A FIRST NATIONAL & VITAPHONE PICTURE

The Big Shakedown (**Warner Bros., 1934; directed by John Francis Dillon**). **Spurned girlfriend "Lil" Duran (Glenda) squeals to the coppers about the racketeering activities of former beau "Dutch" Barnes (Ricardo Cortez).**

Glenda again supported Bette Davis in Warners' *The Big Shakedown* (1934), directed by John Francis Dillon from the story "Cut Rate" by Sam Engels and Niven Busch. However, the two women never appear together on screen.

Young druggist Jimmy Morrell (Charles Farrell) becomes involved with former bootlegger "Dutch" Barnes (Ricardo Cortez) when the latter creates a new racket involving the production of counterfeit toothpaste. Soon, Morrell, a talented chemist who can not only reproduce a product but improve upon it, is in over his head, and he must continue to work for Barnes after the life of his fiancée, Norma (Bette Davis), is threatened.

Glenda plays Barnes' spurned girlfriend, "Lil" Duran, who gladly informs on the racket to the D.A., fully expecting to testify in court. Her slang-ridden affidavit, featuring Glenda at her fast-talking, streetwise best, is a highlight of the film. Lil doesn't remain a state's witness for long, however, and is gunned down in front of her apartment while under "police protection."

Several comic moments lighten the mood of this Warners "social problem" film, including a scene of Barnes' gang (Allen Jenkins plays "Lefty") brushing their teeth together. But the most amusing sequence involves Lil giving a swift

The Big Shakedown (Warner Bros., 1934; directed by John Francis Dillon). "Lil" Duran (Glenda) gets the big gun down from the "Dutch" Barnes mob.

kick in the tush to Dutch's new girlfriend, who then proceeds to start a wild, hair-pulling catfight that goes on for some time.

Working steadily at Warner Bros., Glenda was reunited with Paul Muni and Mervyn LeRoy for the newspaper drama, *Hi, Nellie* (1934). As in *I Am a Fugitive from a Chain Gang*, she was promoted to second billing, behind Muni, and given the female lead. Although she already had played a newspaperwoman in *Mystery of the Wax Museum*, her new character, Gerry Krale, is a former ace reporter now suffering through duty as "Nellie Nelson," the pen name for the lonely hearts editor.

Muni is Samuel N. Bradshaw, the managing editor and Gerry's former beau who was involved in "breaking" her from her former position. Now Bradshaw is demoted for soft-soaping a story that all the other New York papers have played up big. He is handed the "Nellie" job, while Gerry is moved up to the city staff.

After Bradshaw trashes his office and tears off on a drunk, Gerry tells him he's "short on guts," inspiring him to solve the mystery of prominent attorney Frank J. Canfield, whom the other papers had accused of embezzling a huge sum of money and then disappearing. Bradshaw proves that the crime was actually pulled off by Canfield's rival, Thompson, in league with Beau Brownell (Robert Barrat), a notorious gangster, who had the innocent man whacked and

Hi, Nellie (Warner Bros., 1934; directed by Mervyn LeRoy). **Reporter Gerry Krale (Glenda) and demoted former managing editor Samuel N. Bradshaw (Paul Muni) discuss his occupational options.**

framed. The film concludes with Bradshaw back in his old job, with Gerry secure in her new position.

Gerry Krale is not merely a repeat of Glenda's Florence in *Wax Museum*. She is not a wisecracking dame this time, but a standup female who longs to get back into a "man's" job. Required to smoke in the film, Glenda was given specially made cigarettes containing only a small amount of tobacco. Though she consistently has one burning throughout the first half of the film, she takes only a single drag in one of her scenes with Muni.

LeRoy admired Glenda's abilities enough to make sure she again was cast alongside the studio's biggest dramatic star in a role that was grittier and more down to Earth than the others he had been given by the studio since his success in *I Am a Fugitive*. She rose to the occasion, and LeRoy would not forget her work.

Glenda was excited when she was reteamed with Edward G. Robinson for Warners' *Dark Hazard* (1934). Tommy Farrell later remembered Eddie G. as "a sweetheart ... the nicest man in the world."[4]

Adapted from W.R. Burnett's bestselling, Book-of-the-Month Club novel, *Dark Hazard* chronicles the exploits of Jim "Buck" Turner, a compulsive gambler, who, in the opening scene, accompanied by Valerie Wilson (Glenda),

Hi, Nellie (Warner Bros., 1934; directed by Mervyn LeRoy). You're "short on guts," Gerry Krale (Glenda) informs the binging Samuel N. Bradshaw (Paul Muni), who has temporarily forsaken his typewriter for the bottle.

wins 20 grand at a horse race and then blows the entire roll at an after-hours casino. At a local boarding house, he rents a room-with-breakfast for $9.00 weekly, and then lands a job as cashier at the Bel Port racetrack.

Seeking "respectability," Turner marries Marge Mayhew (Genevieve Tobin), the "proper" daughter of the old boarding house woman (Emma Dunn), and then attempts to go straight by working as a hotel clerk. His job ends quickly, however, when he tosses a key at John Bright (Sidney Toler), a lodger who has continually taunted him. Later, Bright, admitting that he'd "been riding" Buck, places him in charge of a dog racing track in California.

Now Turner has no way to break his addiction, particularly after he falls in love with a black greyhound named Dark Hazard. To make matters worse, Valerie (who continually appears from coast to coast) makes casino sobriety impossible. "Don't tell me you turned decent on me?" she asks him.

Marge tells Buck that she's "going to have a baby," and then, upset by his continued wagering, selfishly orders, "Go away! I never want to see you again!" Out on the town with Val, he gambles until 6 a.m., winning another 20 grand before going home with her.

Buck can't cheat on his wife, however, and Val picks up the phone to request "a wheelchair." Listening to the reply, she adds, "I didn't do anything to him—or vice versa."

Dark Hazard (**Warner Bros., 1934; directed by Alfred E. Green**). **"Val" Wilson (Glenda) enjoys seeing her pal "Buck" Turner lose all his dough at the gaming tables.**

"This is the first time I disappointed you," Buck says as he leaves. Back at his own digs, while in a deep sleep, he finally loses Marge when she splits with all his dough, leaving only $500 behind.

For the next two years, Buck rides the rails, trying to scrape up enough bread to get back to his wife and the tiny son he has never seen. Marge claims she will avoid a divorce if Buck reforms, and he accepts a cashier job from Pres Barrow (George Meeker), his wife's "friend."

At the Bel Port track, Buck runs into Tex Willis (Robert Barrat), the owner of Dark Hazard, now "practically a three-legged dog." When the leg bone snaps during a race, Buck saves his beloved pooch from the gas chamber for $25. Back at home, he complains about the family while getting loaded with Marge's brother George (Hobart Cavanaugh), punches out Barrow and then leaves with Dark Hazard. Bumming rides, he eventually gets the dog back into racing trim and then, after winning a fistful of lettuce, happily walks into the final fadeout with Val on his arm.

Unable to experience true affection from his wife, Turner receives his only real moments of pleasure from either Valerie or Dark Hazard (both of them castoff characters). Val, described by Marge as a "frowsy, over-painted creature," is one of Glenda's finest characterizations. No other actress of the period

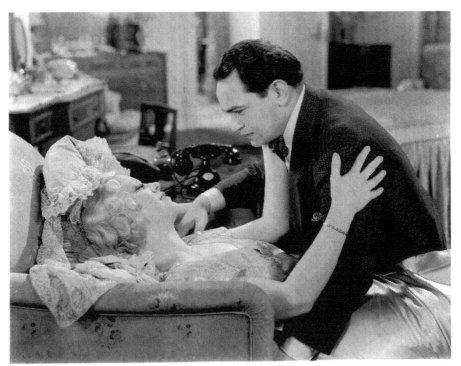

Dark Hazard (Warner Bros., 1934; directed by Alfred E. Green). "Val" Wilson (Glenda) does her best to seduce the married "Buck" Turner (Edward G. Robinson).

could better deliver lines like, "Heads up, you dimwits. A lady's comin' in," and (as Val and Buck stroll into the fade) "C'mon, let's go home. I have an idea."

"This time, I *won't* disappoint you," Buck replies.

In its advertising campaign, Warner Bros. played up the *Little Caesar* connection by mentioning W.R. Burnett. In a special trailer, Burnett actually appeared on screen with Robinson, who also was joined by other famous actors (who aren't in *Dark Hazard*) hired specifically for the publicity project. Following a November 1933 preview of the film, *Motion Picture Daily* reported:

> [The film] omits none of the more popular games of chance, with Edward G. Robinson portraying the gambler deluxe ... The production as a whole carries exciting moments intermingled with humorous incidents, heart interest and human touches contributed by an able supporting cast including Glenda Farrell ...[5]

In the May 1934 issue of *Photoplay*, advice columnist "Sylvia" wrote:

Dear Glenda: I've certainly got to hand it to you. You're one of Hollywood's prize "picture stealers." When you're on the screen, nobody looks at anything but you—and there's a reason.

Hundreds of girls can learn a big lesson from you. When you step in front of the camera you seem to be entirely unconscious of your attraction. That's the lesson. I want every girl and woman in the world to make herself as beautiful as she can be—but when that is accomplished, she shouldn't be preening herself all the time and giving off the attitude, "Look at me, see how beau-ti-ful *I* am?"

Believe me, Glenda, you and I have seen plenty of that in Hollywood ... That's why I hand it to you, Glenda. You're not that sort. And you're smart in another way. You know you haven't regular features, but I'll stake my reputation on the fact that 10 years from now you'll still be going strong on the screen. That's because you're intelligent and make the most of what you have ...

I saw you recently in *Dark Hazard*. It was a racing picture, with you supplying most of the raciness. It's wonderful to see that vitality just oozing from the screen. And vigor is what I'm most enthusiastic about ... A picture career is a tough racket. Life is a tough racket, too, and unless you're loaded to the eyebrows with vitality you'll never get by successfully in either.[6]

(Sylvia then continued with her advice, giving beauty and exercise tips [including nude dancing] to Glenda.)

Ray Enright began shooting *I've Got Your Number* in early November 1933, just prior to the release of *Havana Widows*. Although both actresses are in it, *I've Got Your Number* is not a "Blondell-Farrell" project, but a film in which both appear. Joan is the star, Glenda has a small supporting role and they share no scenes together.

Originally titled *Hell's Bells*, the film features Pat O'Brien as sarcastic telephone repairman Terry Reilly and reliable Allen Jenkins as his "boyfriend," John. Glenda plays Bonnie, aka "Madame Francis," a phony fortuneteller, while Joan appears as switchboard operator Marie Lawson. During production, Joan was rushed to the hospital for an emergency appendectomy, but Enright kept the cameras rolling, including a bedroom scene shot at Blondell's house while the star was recuperating.

When Marie becomes the innocent victim in a bond theft from her employer, Terry rushes to her rescue, gets pinched by a mob and is freed by his pals from the telephone company. Marie marries Terry, but the gang again shows up to repair the telephone on their wedding night. Glenda appears in one "séance" at the beginning (in which Louise Beavers and Allen Jenkins share a humorous palm-reading moment) and again at midpoint, when Bonnie and John, both drunk, attempt to join Marie and Terry for a double date.

I've Got Your Number (**Warner Bros., 1934; directed by Ray Enright). During work hours, telephone repairman Terry Reilly (Pat O'Brien) takes a break in the lap of phony fortune teller "Madame Francis" (Glenda).**

Warren Duff and Sidney Sutherland's screenplay is peppered with double entendre. In an attempt to distract Terry from tearing out her phone, Bonnie says, "I'd like to show you my crystal."

Trying to put the make on Marie, Terry explains, "I guess I'd better go over your apparatus. Maybe you're not hooked up right." (Later, Joan displays quite a bit of her "apparatus," just before climbing into the wedding bed.)

The overall hijinks in the film are perhaps best described by a comment made by telephone company president Joe Flood (Eugene Pallette) to John: "If you ever had a mind, I'd swear you lost it."

Notes:

[1]*New York Times*, 9 February 1969.
[2]*Film Daily*, 25 November 1933, p. 3.
[3]*The New Movie Magazine*, January 1934, p. 69.
[4]Tommy Farrell, in Dan Van Neste, "Glenda Farrell: Diamond in the Rough," *Classic Images*, Vol. 275, May 1998.
[5]*Motion Picture Daily*, 20 November 1933, p. 6.
[6]*Photoplay*, May 1934, p. 54.

**Warner Bros. publicity portrait (1934): Glenda relaxing on the patio of her
North Hollywood home.**

Warner Bros. publicity candid (1934): In her spare time, Glenda enjoyed play-ing games, particularly croquet.

Chapter 8
A Woman's Job

You know, I don't feel it a bit myself. (Holding up a glass of
Coke.) I think it's a fake, this rumor about putting aspirin in
this stuff—completely a fake.

Fortunately I can discard any fakes I may find and go on
to something better. Frank, bring me a bottle of beer.

—Mrs. "Feathers" Tifton, *Heat Lightning* (1934)

With Mervyn LeRoy again at the helm, Warner Bros. cast four of their
finest contract actresses, Aline MacMahon, Ann Dvorak, Glenda and Ruth
Donnelly, in *Heat Lightning*, also featuring Preston Foster, Lyle Talbot and
Glenda's frequent costar, Frank McHugh. Based on the play by Leon Abrams
and George Abbott, the film was shot on location at a hotel and diner located
in Vacamville, California, from November 20 to December 7, 1933.

Released on March 3, 1934, four months prior to enforcement of the Production Code, the film was banned by the Catholic Legion of Decency, particularly for its sexual innuendoes and the scene in which Glenda takes a bath *al
fresco*. The film opens in the hot, dusty desert as travelers struggle toward the
rural diner (an establishing scene that would be varied slightly by Archie Mayo
for Warner Bros.' *The Petrified Forest* two years later).

Dvorak and MacMahon appear first, as Myra and Olga, two sisters who
operate the establishment, which also includes a service station and auto camp,
without "any men." Told that a man is needed to remove a radiator cap, Olga
proves to a tourist couple (Edgar Kennedy, Jane Darwell) that it's really a
woman's job. While Myra yearns to leave the dust of the desert behind, to "go
someplace," Olga is content to wear her bib overalls and red bandana while
laboring as a mechanic in a greasy pit beneath the automobiles.

Two lamming bankrobbers/killers, Jerry and Jeff (Preston Foster, Lyle
Talbot), soon roll in for sandwiches and beer. "An old baboon and a couple
tomatoes" follow, much to Jerry's delight. Unfortunately the dames leave with
"the old thigh pincher" on "the way of all flesh." Olga then recognizes Jerry
(credited as "George") from their days "back in Oklahoma."

Mrs. Tifton and Mrs. Ashton-Ashley (Glenda, Ruth Donnelly), two
wealthy divorcees who've just returned from Reno, arrive, chauffeured by
Frank (Frank McHugh). After they exit to book some rooms, Jerry asks Jeff,
"Did you see the rocks on those babies?"

"Frank will have to stay on guard all night to protect us," says the
beer-drinking "Feathers" Tifton, while "Tinkle" Ashton-Ashley mentions how

Heat Lightning (Warner Bros., 1934; directed by Mervyn LeRoy). Mrs. "Feathers" Tifton (Glenda) and Mrs. "Tinkle" Ashton-Ashley (Ruth Donnelly) drop in at the desert diner for a visit they'll never forget.

her friend ably protected herself against her "last husband." Frank is summoned to help Feathers with her bath, which must be taken in a metal tub "out back of the shed."

"After all, that's where it all started, isn't it?" comments Tinkle, as Feathers disrobes (LeRoy and cinematographer Sid Hickox tastefully show Glenda's silhouette on the screen door's canvas shade). A piercing scream rends the evening just as Feathers, clad only in a towel, flies around the shed toward her room.

"I ain't used to seeing dames taking a bath out in the middle of the desert!" says Jeff, claiming that he's ogled "better" specimens. (Glenda makes the most of the insulting moment.)

When Jerry, packing a rod, orders Jeff to rob the diner's safe, Olga guns him down. "You're a good kid, Olga," he mutters while dying on the floor.

"I found a big rat running around in the lunchroom," Olga tells the rest of the gang.

Although *Heat Lightning* runs only 64 minutes, the witty script by Brown Holmes and Warren Duff features some depth due to its depiction of four distinct "types" of women, all played superbly by the dynamite Warner Bros. ensemble cast. Contemporary reviews praised the film both for the women's

Merry Wives of Reno **(Warner Bros., 1934; directed by H. Bruce Humberstone).**
Bunny (Glenda) and her "sheep-fancying" husband, Colonel J. Kingsley Fitch
(Hugh Herbert).

performances and the realistic setting provided by the desert location shoot
and fine cinematography of Hickox. Eight decades after its release, the fe-
male-dominated film holds up very well as an excellent example of pre-Code
boldness.

Released two months after *Heat Lightning*, Warners' *Merry Wives of Reno*
(1934) makes very good use of the "stock company," but does them a disser-
vice with a substandard script by Robert Lord and Joe Traub. Glenda receives
second billing behind Guy Kibbee, and Donald Woods, Margaret Lindsay,
Hugh Herbert, Ruth Donnelly and Frank McHugh offer support.

This absurd "divorce comedy" involving several New York couples features many repetitive situations, but the comic talents of Kibbee, Herbert and
McHugh often rise above the stale material. Kibbee, who performs an un-
canny drunk routine, nearly steals the show but is topped by Herbert (in a
fairly restrained performance), who is hilarious as Colonel J. Kingsley Fitch, a
"sheep fancier" (as described by his wife, Bunny [Glenda]) who buys a ranch
near Reno. The Fitch character also provides the punchline of the divorce-rid-
den story: He and his pet sheep "Eloise" enjoy the only stable relationship in
the film! (Woody Allen would cinematically take the idea much further four
decades later.)

The Personality Kid (**Warner Bros., 1934; directed by Alan Crosland). Washed-up boxer "Ritzy" McCarty (Pat O'Brien) and his "with child" wife, "Babes" (Glenda, in one of her most touching performances).**

From February 12 to March 5, 1934, Glenda costarred with Pat O' Brien in Warner Bros.' *One Man Woman*, directed by Alan Crosland and released as *The Personality Kid* on July 7, just one week before the Production Code took effect. O'Brien's previous experience as a boxer at Marquette University, coupled with training from former welterweight champion Jackie Fields, added some realism to the fight scenes, including bouts with former welterweight champ Mushy Callahan and USS *Arizona* champ Myron Schlecter. Though the fights feature more dancing than punching, some rapid montage techniques (courtesy of editor Terry Morse) energize one of the scenes.

O'Brien is "Ritzy" McCarty, "the sensational flash and dancing master," and Glenda his wife and manager, Joan, aka "Babes." While Ritzy is often an arrogant, two-timing heel, Babes is sincere and on the level. "You don't have to wear pants and talk out of the side of your mouth to be a fight manager," she tells some chauvinistic promoters.

After Ritzy handily "wins" some bouts, he learns that they've all been fixed. "You want to wait until your head looks like a vegetable and there's nothing between your ears but a vacant lot?" Babes forcefully asks him.

The knowledge that his wife knew about the fight fixing, combined with his interest in attractive magazine artist Patricia Merrill (Claire Dodd), leads to

Glenda and beau Robert Riskin attend the 6th Academy Awards ceremony at the Ambassador Hotel (March 16, 1934). Riskin had been nominated for Best Writing, Adaptation, for *Lady for a Day*.

a separation. Ritzy is washed up, sleeping in a train station and eating pretzels and onions in a cheap beer joint. Soon he is working for a sideshow snake-oil racket.

Glenda is genuinely moving, particularly in the scenes when Babes is mistreated by Ritzy. However, when he learns that she "is going to have a baby," he bucks up and signs on for another fight. He risks his life by refusing to take a dive, demonstrates that he has a real punch and receives an offer to become a legitimate fighter. With his wife and new baby boy, he plans to fight just long enough to raise money for a family farm.

On May 9, 1934, William Keighley began directing Warners' next Blondell-Farrell film, *The Kansas City Princess*, which was held from release for three months to allow for the birth of Joan's son, Norman. The studio didn't want to risk keeping Blondell off the screen for too long.

"*Kansas City Princess* is a knockout," raved "Lindy" of the *Hollywood Filmograph*:

> Joan Blondell and Glenda Farrell make one of the greatest girl
> mirth provoking teams in pictures, getting into some remark-

Glenda and intermittent beau Addison Randall (May 1934).

ably tight spaces, then extricating themselves by using the old
noodle ... Hugh Herbert, the perfect nut, cleans up plenty of
giggles ... Should pack them in with this grand cast and clean
wholesome fun.[1]

This time, Joan and Glenda are Rosie Sturgis and Marie Callahan, roommates and manicurists in Kansas City. Dynamite Carson (Robert Armstrong),
called "a super colossal mug" by Marie, is Rosie's boyfriend, who gives her
a stolen diamond ring, which is then pinched from her. Most of the film's 64
minutes are devoted to the mayhem that ensues while Dynamite chases and
the ladies run away, going so far as to "join" the Outdoor Girls of America as
a way to get to New York.

Accidentally remaining aboard a ship bound for Paris, Rosie and Marie
become involved with millionaire Junior Ashcraft (Hugh Herbert, playing his
comedy pretty straight) and his marital troubles. The chaos finally ends with
Rosie back with Dynamite, and Marie receiving a marriage proposal from Junior, though he first must get a divorce! Warner Bros. was continuing to con-
clude Glenda's films by marrying off her character to the obligatory comic
fool.

Kansas City Princess (**Warner Bros., 1934; directed by William Keighley**). **Manicurists Rosie Sturgis (Joan Blondell) and Marie Callahan (Glenda) are under the surveillance of the intrepid Quincy (Vince Barnett), henchman of Rosie's gangster boyfriend.**

Delightfully, the Blondell-Farrell team of *Havana Widows* is back in *Kansas City Princess*. Manuel Seff and Sy Bartlett's screenplay is not without its zingers, even though the film was released after enforcement of the Production Code. The booze flows freely, infidelity abounds and there is even a reference to narcotics. Dynamite, questioning the reliability of his right hand man Quincy (the ever obtuse Vince Barnett), asks, "You been sniffin' that nose candy again?"

The film's most memorable line is delivered by Glenda when Marie explains to Rosie the true gold-digger's mantra: "A girl's got to have three things these days—*money*, *jack* and *dough*."

During the early summer of 1934, Glenda maintained a long-distance relationship with Robert Riskin, who had traveled to Europe while she remained behind in Hollywood, with plenty of film work to keep her busy. Riskin called nearly every day and brought back a gift that delighted her: a new Persian cat for her menagerie.

On July 23, 1934, Glenda underwent another operation following an appendicitis attack. In the care of surgeon Dr. Herbert C. Chase, she spent 10 days at the Polyclinic Hospital in Harrisburg, Pennsylvania. This time she had the organ removed. The *Regina Leader-Post* reported,

The Secret Bride (Warner Bros., 1934; directed by William Dieterle). Hazel Normandie (Glenda), on trial for her life, is questioned by Lieutenant Forrest (Charles C. Wilson).

After nearly two years of "pinch-hitting" for the Warner Bros. studio, it looks as though Glenda Farrell really is going to get a break.

She has just been handed the leading role in *Women are Bum Newspapermen*, a story of a sob sister and a breezy reporter in love with each other but working on competing papers ...

For the last two years Glenda has been shoved around pretty badly, being put in anything or everything that came along. And she has taken it like a lady — not even getting much rest until she was forced to go to a hospital for an appendicitis operation recently.[2]

(*Women are Bum Newspapermen* was announced several times in the press but was never made. The later "Torchy Blane" films feature similar plot elements.)

During September 1934, Glenda played the top supporting role opposite costars Barbara Stanwyck and Warren William in *The Secret Bride*, directed by William Dieterle and loosely based on the play *Concealment* by Leonard Ide.

101

This tale of political conspiracy and murder involves Robert Sheldon (Warren William), a state attorney general, and Governor Vincent (Arthur Byron), who fall victim to the machinations of financier Jim Lansdale (Henry O'Neil) and his stooge, Dave Breeden (Douglas Dumbrille), who has been planted in Sheldon's office.

Glenda plays Sheldon's secretary, Hazel Normandie, who is unintentionally framed for the murder of Breeden. Having witnessed the killing, Ruth Vincent (Barbara Stanwyck), the governor's daughter and Sheldon's "secret bride," cannot come forth without causing further political and personal scandal for her father and husband.

"A wildcat, that one is," claims a female jailer when referring to Hazel, who retains her tough demeanor even when faced with a potential walk to the electric chair! Though she is saved by Ruth just as the jury is about to render its guilty verdict, Hazel is an underdeveloped character. She is last seen in the witness box, and the lack of a scene showing her relief at being freed suggests that some footage may have been cut from the finished film, which runs a scant 62 minutes.

Painted by artist Marland Stone, Glenda was featured on the cover of the September 1934 issue of *Motion Picture*. In October, *Photoplay* ran a story on her "personality and beauty secrets." She talked extensively about humor and her ability to take, as well as make, a good joke. She emphasized modesty, as reporter Carolyn Van Wyck explained:

Glenda warns you above all of the girl with the self-importance complex. The Sarah Bernhardt slant, she calls it. We all dramatize ourselves at times, but indulge in this little pastime for yourself only. Don't inflict it on others if you want your

Gold Diggers of 1935 (**Warner Bros., 1935; directed by Busby Berkeley**). **Publicity portrait of Glenda used to promote the film.**

telephone to ring frequently. Glenda tells me that because of having several brothers, her own sense of self-importance was shot to pieces at an early age, and nothing better could happen to any girl, she believes.[3]

Glenda got the New Year of 1935 off to a good start by indulging in one of her favorite pastimes: going to see a new film featuring *other* actors, namely W.C. Fields, Lionel Barrymore, Maureen O'Sullivan, Basil Rathbone and

Freddie Bartholomew, in MGM's *David Copperfield*, which had its West Coast premiere at Grauman's Chinese Theatre. At the gala event, she was photographed with her friend Minna Gombell, Minna's husband Joseph Sifton and *Movie Classic* magazine executive head Captain Roscoe Fawcett.

By January 1935, Glenda's once serious relationship with Robert Riskin had cooled off to the point where she was referring to their status as "just friends." Though they loved each other, both had bad experiences in previous marriages and thought that they were "temperamentally unsuited to the wedded state."[4]

On January 14, Glenda completed her first Dick Powell musical at Warner Bros. Directed by Busby Berkeley, who spent four months on the project, the spectacular *Gold Diggers of 1935* costars Powell with Adolphe Menjou, Gloria Stuart and Alice Brady, and features Glenda with "usual suspects" Hugh Herbert and Frank McHugh. Harry Warren and Al Dubin wrote three new songs for the film, "The Words are in My Heart," "I'm Going Shopping with You," and "Lullaby of Broadway," which won the Academy Award for Best Song that year.

The film is beautifully directed and choreographed, its narrative scenes seamlessly incorporated with the elaborate, mind-boggling production numbers. The numbers are really "films within the film." The stunning "Lullaby of Broadway," featuring Winifred Shaw, tells the story of a beautiful New York lass who sleeps all day and parties all night and ends in macabre fashion when she suddenly is pushed to her death from a high-rise balcony.

In the incomparable "Words are in My Heart," 56 white grand pianos, moved by carefully hidden stagehands dressed entirely in black, were used. The sumptuous costumes, sets and choreography were all captured strikingly by cinematographer George Barnes (who was married to Joan Blondell at the time). Unfortunately, tragedy struck when 26-year-old dancer Jack Grieves died during production, reportedly from "acute indigestion."[5]

While vacationing at a summer resort with her daughter Ann (Gloria Stuart) and son Humboldt (Frank McHugh), Mrs. Mathilda Prentiss (Alice Brady) is talked into putting up the money to produce a lavish charity show. One humorous scene features Betty (Glenda) attempting to extort a piece of the action from Nicoleff (Adolphe Menjou), the director, and Schultz (Joseph Cawthorn), the set designer. Her attempts at extortion continue with her suit against "snuffbox historian" T. Mosley Thorpe (Hugh Herbert), who is accused by Mrs. Prentiss of "lollygagging around with a stenographer."

As stenographer Betty Hawes, Glenda dexterously takes gold digging to its apex. While typing the dictation of Thorpe, Betty transforms "song lyrics" into a marriage proposal, has him sign it and then sues him for breach of promise! At one point, she sings, "*I'm* in the money ..." Though her character could

Gold Diggers of 1935 (**Warner Bros., 1935; directed by Busby Berkeley**). **While typing the dictation of T. Mosley Thorpe (Hugh Herbert), Betty Hawes (Glenda) transforms "song lyrics" into a marriage proposal, and then sues him for breach of promise!**

easily have become lost amidst all the spectacular showmanship, Glenda's performance makes it memorable.

In his somewhat negative *Picture Play* review of *Gold Diggers of 1935*, Norbert Lusk praised elements wrought by the Production Code:

> There are those who say this edition of Warners' annual [sic] is not as riotous as its ... predecessors, but it has superior qualities that none of them possessed. A ... virtue is that raucous humor and double meanings are absent from the story and depravity isn't even hinted at. True, everybody's a chiseler, more or less, but it's all in the nature of good-humored fun far removed from the barroom. In fact, believe it or not, this chapter is refined and is capitally acted ... The outstanding song — and there is only one — is "The Lullaby of Broadway," imaginatively staged by Busby Berkeley and gorgeously sung by Winifred Shaw. But there is a number employing countless girls at revolving, white pianos which is startling and tasteful.[6]

Traveling Saleslady (**Warner Bros., 1935; directed by Ray Enright**). **Drugstore mogul Claudette Ruggles (Glenda) provides irresistible bait for peddling toothpaste to amorous conventioneers.**

Traveling Saleslady (1935), directed by Ray Enright from an original story by Frank Howard Clark, could be considered the "feminist" entry in Warner Bros. "social problem" films of the 1930s. Blondell and Farrell are back once again, although they don't work as a team in the film. George Barnes shot the film using a new camera developed by Warner Bros. that created greater depth of field, resulting in higher definition of the actors against the background.

Focusing on the toothpaste industry, *Traveling Saleslady* first depicts Angela Twitchell (Blondell) and Claudette Ruggles (Glenda) as acquaintances, then as rivals and finally as friends. Angela is an ambitious, intelligent young lady who wants to work for her father's toothpaste company, but he is a thorough chauvinist. "Isn't the Secretary of Labor of the United States a woman?" she asks him. "What's the matter with women?" (Frances C. Perkins served as Franklin Roosevelt's Secretary of Labor for his entire presidency [1933-1945].)

They are "unstable and unreliable," her father (Grant Mitchell) responds.

Claudette obviously is an exception to the old man's rule, as she already owns a chain of drugstores. However, even Angela is surprised to see her sitting behind the boss' desk at her company.

Angela takes a new toothpaste idea to Schmidt (Al Shean), her father's competitor, who signs a contract with her. On the road, using an assumed name, she becomes interested in Twitchell salesman Pat O'Connor (William Gargan), who doesn't know her true identity. Eventually they become fearsome sales rivals, and Claudette joins forces with Pat. Everything is resolved following a convention in Chicago, and the two companies arrange a merger.

Hugh Herbert gives another brilliant comic performance, as former bootlegger and "nutty" inventor Elmer Niles, who develops the new line of "Cocktail Toothpaste" (available in bourbon, martini, scotch, rum and many other "intoxicating" flavors) that causes all the uproar. At one point, he tells Angela, "I wish your old man had half the brains that you've got."

Schmidt offers a similar remark about her abilities: "So it's a businesswoman you are, and not just a pretty girl."

Although *Traveling Saleslady* doesn't reach the same level of comic chaos offered by *Havana Widows* and *Kansas City Princess*, the film offers an interesting look at two very strong women's roles in an era that usually depicted Joan, Glenda and *many* others as gold-diggers. Much like Glenda's own life and career, there is no need for such scheming in the lives of Angela and Claudette, two working "girls" who can take care of themselves.

Under contract to Warner Bros., it was inevitable that Glenda would cross paths with one of the true phenomena of American popular culture. Billed third in the cast, she supports "The World's Greatest Entertainer," Al Jolson, and his wife, Ruby Keeler, in *Go Into Your Dance* (1935), a dramatic musical directed as *Casino de Paris* by Archie Mayo (assisted by the uncredited Michael Curtiz and Robert Florey).

Harry Warren and Al Dubin contributed seven songs, including some Jolson standards: "Latin from Manhattan," "This Evening About a Quarter to Nine," "Go Into Your Dance," "The Little Things You Used to Do" (sung by Helen Morgan), "Mammy, I'll Sing About You," "Casino de Paree" and "An Old Fashioned Cocktail with an Old Fashioned Girl" (performed by Keeler). Two of Warner Bros.' top cinematographers, Tony Gaudio and Sol Polito, worked on the production, adapted from the Bradford Ropes novel by Earl Baldwin. Bobby Connolly created and staged the dance numbers, and Bernhard Kahn contributed the incidental music.

Go Into Your Dance marked the only time Jolson and Keeler were paired on screen. Thereafter, "Jolie" refused to make any more films with his wife, whom he eventually divorced in December 1940. Ward Bond appears on screen for a few seconds, as an enraged husband who punches out Al Howard (Al Jolson) for showing interest in his wife.

As Al's sister Molly, Glenda plays the important role of the only person who attempts to revive the "washed-up" singer's career. When he suddenly ducks out on a Broadway engagement to take a "vacation" in Mexico, she doggedly tracks him down. Talking Dorothy Wayne (Ruby Keeler) into teaming up with him, she helps land them a job in a Chicago revue. Soon the pair is an

Go Into Your Dance (**Warner Bros., 1935; directed by Archie Mayo**). **Struggling Broadway belter Al Howard (Al Jolson) revives his career with the help of his sister, Molly (Glenda).**

enormous hit, but the big New York producers are still unimpressed. Dorothy falls in love with Al and wants to quit, but Molly persuades her to stay.

Bankrolled by "The Duke" (Barton MacLane), a Detroit gangster, Al plans to open his own lavish nightclub on Broadway. Duke's motivation is his wife, Luana Wells (Helen Morgan), a fading torch singer in search of a gig. Feeling threatened by Luana's attention to Al, Dorothy sparks a confrontation in her dressing room.

Just when Al is about to open his joint, Molly is arrested on suspicion of murdering Tom McGee (William Davidson), a tough guy she had met in Chicago. Bailed out by Al, who used the money Duke put up for an Equity bond, Molly "disappears," attempting to find a girl who was with her when McGee was shot by some goons who had burst in on them with rods blazing. Upon hearing the news, an unimpressed Duke sends some hit men (Mark Lawrence, Huey White) to whack Al.

In the nick of time, Molly returns and is cleared of the murder charge. But the "mugs" are still on their way to the club. Duke calls off the hit, but Luana does not deliver the message. Just before Jolson's obligatory blackface number (Fred "Snowflake" Toones appears as his valet), shots are fired and Dorothy is hit. As she lies wounded backstage, Al declares his love for her. "To think I had to get shot to hear you say that," she replies.

Al goes on stage and sings "Go Into Your Dance." The doctor (Henry Kolker) pronounces Dorothy "fine," and Al kisses her before performing an encore of "About a Quarter to Nine." "You ain't heard nothing yet!" he declares to Dorothy.

Glenda does not reappear after the jail sequence. Throughout the film, she dons her usual quota of current fashions, including a stunning off-the-shoulder dress designed by Orry-Kelly (providing quite a contrast to her jailhouse duds). Though she plays Jolson's sister, she does share a kiss with the renowned entertainer.

Lloyd Bacon had begun production on Warner Bros.' *In Caliente* (1935), partially filmed in Agua Caliente, Mexico shortly after the 1934 Christmas holiday. With numbers created and directed by Busby Berkeley, this lavish musical features a score by Harry Warren and Al Dubin ("Muchacha") and Mort Dixon and Allie Wrubel ("The Lady in Red," "In Caliente," "To Call You My Own"), plus an all-star cast including Dolores del Rio, Pat O'Brien, Leo Carrillo, Edward Everett Horton, Phil Regan and Winifred Shaw.

Glenda began working on the film in January 1935 but, by February 5, she was laid low by a flu bug that currently was decimating the Hollywood ranks. Her recent fatigue and appendectomy may have contributed to continued poor health. She did recover, however, and completed her work on *In Caliente* in March.

Although she has the top supporting role as Clara Thorne, "a calculating, gold-digging blonde," Glenda has very little to do until the final scenes, when she takes her act on the road from New York to Agua Caliente, where her prospective husband, magazine editor Larry MacArthur (Pat O'Brien), has been unwittingly kidnapped into protective custody by his assistant, Harold Brandon (Edward Everett Horton). The threadbare plot involving Larry's pursuit of dancer Rita Gomez (Dolores del Rio), whom he previously criticized in his magazine, exists to tie together Berkeley's elaborate production numbers. Del Rio's scantily clad dancing and swimming scenes are also visual highlights.

Throughout the 1930s, Pat O'Brien's Warner Bros. performances often fell into two categories: serious dramatic roles (such as the priest in *Angels with Dirty Faces* [1938] and the title role in *Knute Rockne: All American* [1940]) that he played superbly; and brash, bossy types (such as in *Devil Dogs of the Air* [1935], *Ceiling Zero* [1936] and *Boy Meets Girl* [1938]) who yell their way through most of the picture. Larry MacArthur falls into the latter category, though O'Brien eventually tones things down after arriving in Mexico.

Edward Everett Horton turns in his usual solid performance, and the scene in which Harold and Clara steal a car, in pursuit of Larry and Rita, and then end up facing "practically capital punishment" or "eloping," is the comic high point. The formula of having Glenda married off to the "geek" was, by this point, tried and true: Clara gets hitched to Harold. Of course, O'Brien and del Rio end up married as well. The film concludes with a shot of Glenda pursuing Horton into the Agua Caliente Hotel to start their honeymoon.

In early 1935, Glenda made her final payment on the house in the San Fernando Valley. To celebrate the occasion, she consigned to the flames her "original home": the wardrobe trunk that she had used during her days as an itinerant actress.

By this point in her career, Warner Bros.' typecasting of Glenda began to concern many of her fans who longed to see her in a variety of roles. In particular, they called for characterizations, not involving smart remarks and gold digging, but ones that more closely mirrored her own persona. In a letter to *Photoplay*, J.B. Dean of Kansas City, Missouri, wrote:

> I'm demanding a pardon for one of my favorites. She's been sentenced too long to one type of role. I mean Glenda Farrell and her gold-digging parts. She's a fine woman, and in her real life is an intelligent person with generous impulses, warmth and understanding.
>
> I would like to see her cast as a young mother, for example. Anyhow in some role that would permit her own personality to shine through.[7]

In the March 1935 issue of *Picture Play* magazine, Whitney Williams described the process by which Glenda memorized her film scripts:

> Glenda Farrell always reads her lines aloud, in this way impressing upon her hearing the sound of the words as well as to give them the proper shading. She rehearses the night before the scenes are to be shot, until she knows she can do no better. Then she completely forgets the next day's work, and just before going under the lights, runs over the lines again.[8]

The April 1935 issue of *Movie Classic* magazine posed the bold question, "Which Stars Will Survive Color?" Optimistically claiming that "Technicolor will bring another boom to pictures," Sonia Lee predicted:

> Here are the new stars of tomorrow: Frances Dee, Glenda Farrell, Lilian Bond, Ginger Rogers—a star today, but not nearly as great as she will be in color; also a girl playing unimportant roles today—Betty Furness. All these girls share a vitality which Technicolor will not underkey.[9]

Fourteen-year-old Tommy Farrell holds one of Glenda's beloved Siamese cats, who's sporting a custom-made pair of feline spectacles (1935).

In May 1935, *Photoplay* published "My Mom," a charming essay by Tommy Farrell, in which he described an odd aspect of Glenda's loving attachment to Siamese cats, one of which had unusual special needs:

> [O]ne of them's cockeyed. Can't see worth a darn, either. She tried to tell me that was a sign of being rare or some such stuff. So finally I had to tell her that that was the bunk. I said, "Poor cat, going around the house bumping into chairs all the time," appealing to her sympathy, see? Well, we finally set-

Glenda talked with George Bilson and Hugh Herbert on the set of *We're in the Money* (1935).

tled that. Now Mom's had a pair of specs made for the cat. They're strapped on like goggles sorta, and they're all right. What's more the cat can see now, even though he makes you die laughing, just looking at him.[10]

Tommy also confirmed the public impression of the real Glenda:

[T]here's one thing I ought to have good and well understood about my Mom. She's a very sweet and big-hearted woman, not at all like the parts she plays on the screen. I have to laugh seeing her all decked out in diamonds on the screen. For a fact, I guess my Mom's one of the few women in the world who hasn't even got a diamond to her name. She just never spends her money on stuff like that.[11]

Tommy often felt self-conscious going out in public with Glenda, who of course elicited a lot of stares from passersby. However, when she accompanied him to a school party, many of the children didn't realize that she was a movie star.

"What's the girl's name you're with?" asked one of the boys.

"That's not a girl—that's my Mom," answered Tommy.

The boy replied, "Gosh, she's good looking, isn't she?"

Ray Enright directed the trio of Blondell, Farrell and Hugh Herbert again in *We're in the Money*, shot at Warner Bros. from May 8 to June 12, 1935. This time around, Harry Warren and Al Dubin contributed one of their most famous songs, which inspired the film's title. *We're in the Money* marked the first of two films Glenda made with Ross Alexander, an ill-fated young actor whose closeted gay lifestyle damaged his once-promising career at the studio, where he would appear in both *A Midsummer Night's Dream* and *Captain Blood* that year.

The dynamic Blondell-Farrell combination is again the highlight of the film, this time as Ginger Stewart and Dixie Tilton, respectively, two process servers out to make $1,000 for delivering

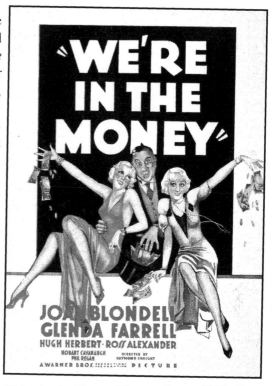

We're in the Money (**Warner Bros., 1935; directed by Ray Enright). The artwork on this window card poster features a very delighted Hugh Herbert sandwiched between Glenda and Joan Blondell.**

subpoenas in a breach of promise suit. Referring to their continual gold-digging lifestyle, Ginger admits to Dixie, "I'm sick of this racket of ours."

Dixie, however, says, "For $1,000, I'd make a sap out of any man!"

Later, after Dixie delivers a subpoena to C. Richard Courtney (Ross Alexander), Ginger's fiancé, due to a case of mistaken identity, Ginger explains, "You and your gold-digging ideas have dug me into a nice, deep hole."

F. Hugh Herbert (at Warner Bros. from 1933-1936, but no relation to Hugh Herbert) and Brown Holmes' screenplay isn't as sharp as those for *Havana Widows* and *Kansas City Princess*, but it does have its moments. Much of the humor is physical and visual, particularly an out-of-control boat scene in which lunatic lawyer Homer Bronson (Hugh Herbert) attempts to reach Courtney's yacht. After Ginger and Dixie jump into the craft from the pier, the former goes plunging into the sea (Blondell does her dunking routine three times). Homer is no better behind the wheel of an automobile, allowing Herbert to perform more of his trademark shtick. (By this point in his career, he was beginning to use his bizarre laugh a little too often.)

Joan Blondell and Glenda Farrell "arrest" musician Harry Busse in this studio publicity photo from the set of *We're in the Money*.

The film's comedy does not build into the chaotic crescendo of the earlier Blondell-Farrell team efforts, but Joan and Glenda, troupers that they were, provide plenty of charm and laughs. The scene in which they appropriate "No'th Car'lina" accents in order to serve a subpoena to wrestler Man Mountain Dean is a highlight.

Notes:

[1]*Hollywood Filmograph*, 11 November 1934, p. 5.
[2]*Regina Leader-Post*, 17 November 1934, p. 5.
[3]*Photoplay*, October 1934, p. 70, 82.
[4]*Motion Picture*, September 1934, p. 37.
[5]*Daily Variety*, 15 January 1935, p. 1.
[6]*Picture Play*, June 1935, p. 51.
[7]*Photoplay*, January 1935, p. 14.
[8]*Picture Play*, March 1935, p. 69.
[9]*Movie Classic*, April 1935, p. 73.
[10]*Photoplay*, May 1935, p. 114.
[11]*Photoplay*, May 1935, p. 114.

Warner Bros. publicity shot (1935): Glenda strikes an alluring pose.

Warner Bros. publicity still (1935): Glenda enjoys posing at the well.

Chapter 9
The Ultimate Professional

Well, you certainly picked a swell time to walk out on him.
The Greeks have a word for that.
—Verna Kennedy, *Here Comes Carter*

In 1935, Warner Bros. executives decided they needed their own version of Fox's box-office queen Shirley Temple, then seven years old, who recently had earned a special Juvenile Academy Award for her film work of the previous year. They believed they had discovered her in Sybil Jason, a seven-year-old South African girl who could do it all: act, sing, dance and do impressions of top Hollywood stars.

After seeing Jason in the British film *Barnacle Bill* (1935), Warner Bros.' London studio head Irving Asher arranged for a screen test, which landed her a contract. For her first vehicle, *Little Big Shot* (1935), Harrison Jacobs crafted a Runyon-style Broadway story loosely patterned on *Little Miss Marker* (1934), which had proved a huge hit for Temple on loan-out to Paramount.

Jerry Wald, Julius Epstein and Robert Andrews all worked on the screenplay, and Michael Curtiz was assigned to direct, with Frank McDonald assisting as dialogue director. Glenda received second billing, above Robert Armstrong and Edward Everett Horton, and Jack La Rue (as two-bit mobster Jack Doré) was assisted by a terrific group of mugs, including J. Carrol Naish, Joseph Sawyer, Ward Bond and Marc Lawrence.

This charming comedy features little Sybil performing songs and impressions of Greta Garbo and Mae West. But the film includes plenty of serious material, particularly the very unpleasant gangsters who murder the girl's father (Addison Richards), kill her puppy and then kidnap her. The two sidewalk con men, Steve (Robert Armstrong) and Mortimer (Edward Everett Horton), get in all kinds of hot water, but are aided by Jean (Glenda) all the way, even to the point of her bringing in the police to save Steve from the wise guys and then marrying him. The happy couple adopts the little girl and, together with Mortimer, opens a roadside diner.

Little Big Shot **(Warner Bros., 1935; directed by Michael Curtiz). Jean (Glenda) cares for homeless little Gloria (Sybil Jason).**

Jason creates an entertaining and at times genuinely moving version of Shirley Temple with a South African accent, and is well supported by a fine cast. If Sybil is a little over-emotive at times, she is well balanced by Glenda's solid, naturalistic performance.

Of Glenda, Sybil Jason later recalled:

> I just adored her on and off the set … First of all, she was the ultimate professional on camera, line perfect and always easy to work with. Off screen, we had a marvelous relationship. I often went to her home, and it was a must on the 4th of July when she had a very professional fireworks display in her backyard. She had the enthusiasm of a child and had a marvelous sense of humor. How often I would go into the house and hear Tommy and Jackie Cooper playing the drums. It was always a fun time with Glenda![1]

Unfortunately the Independence Day festivities got the best of Glenda when she contracted a serious case of food poisoning, missing a few days of work while under a doctor's care.

Remaining friends with Glenda and Tommy, Jason appeared in several Warner Bros. films before being hired by 20th Century-Fox as support to Shirley Temple in two films, *The Little Princess* (1939) and *The Blue Bird* (1940), after which she retired. Originally intended as a rival to Temple, Jason instead became her lifelong friend.

From August through October 1935, *Motion Picture* magazine ran a story, "The Mystery of Glenda Farrell's Missing Necklace," as part of a readers' contest. Following the third installment, entrants were to write, in 250 words, their choices for the party responsible for the theft, the motive and how the heist was accomplished. The suspects included James Gleason, Joan Blondell, Bradley Page, Pat O'Brien, Joel McCrea, Frances Dee, Mary Brian, Ralph Bellamy and John Mack Brown. The first-prize winner was to receive "an exact replica of Miss Farrell's lucky pendant."[2] Second through seventh prizes included various items of jewelry and crystal, all presented by the "suspects." The conclusion of "Missing Necklace" appeared in the December issue. All seven prize winners were women.

On September 9, 1935 Glenda, Joan Blondell and Hugh Herbert reteamed for *Miss Pacific Fleet*, directed by Ray Enright. The screenplay, by Peter Milne, Lucille Newmark and Patsy Flick, was based on a Frederick Hazlitt Brennan short story published in the June 23, 1934 issue of *Colliers*. On August 30, 1935 *Film Daily* reported:

Miss Pacific Fleet (**Warner Bros., 1935; directed by Ray Enright**). **Mae O'Brien (Glenda), Virginia "Vergie" Matthews (Marie Wilson) and Bernard "Kewpie" Wiggins (Allen Jenkins, in the ring).**

Miss Pacific Fleet **(Warner Bros., 1935; directed by Ray Enright). A battered Kewpie (Allen Jenkins) receives some much-needed inspiration from Mae O'Brien (Glenda) and Gloria Fay (Joan Blondell).**

> The briny deep is new battleground for Blondell-Herbert-Farrell laugh trust as Warners name 'Miss Pacific Fleet' for trio's next. Their *We're in the Money* is currently living up to its name in key runs.[3]

In *Miss Pacific Fleet*, former showgirls Gloria Fay (Blondell) and Mae O'Brien (Glenda) are working a ring toss game at an amusement park on the

San Pedro pier when the fleet, 83,000 sailors strong, sails into port. Thinking that Gloria is "his girl," Bernard "Kewpie" Wiggins (Allen Jenkins), "middleweight champ of the Pacific Fleet," plunges them into debt by skillfully winning all the prizes in their booth. Mae hatches a plan to raise some easy dough, and Gloria becomes the frontrunner in the Miss Pacific Fleet popularity contest.

As contest promoter J. August Freytag, Hugh Herbert is again in top form. At one point, during a nightclub scene, Mae mocks Freytag's laugh. (After appearing in a fleet of films with Herbert, Glenda had a chance to do her impression of him.) After Mrs. Freytag (Minna Gombell), imagining that her husband is interested in Gloria, arranges for her to be abducted, the kidnappers make a major mistake: They grab the jealous wife instead! A frantic boat chase and brawl precedes Gloria arriving at the contest to win in the nick of time.

The comic highlight is a boxing bout between the seriously undertrained Kewpie and brawny Butch Fitts, who repeatedly bashes him to the canvas. But when the bruised and battered Kewpie sees "his girl" in the arms of fellow marine Sergeant Tom Foster (Warren Hull), he quickly knocks out his superior opponent, but then gives the prize, 5,000 contest votes, to dizzy dame Vergie Matthews (Marie Wilson), who nearly tops Gloria as Miss Pacific Fleet. The film concludes with the triumphant girls taking a train back to their theatrical jobs in New York.

Glenda enjoyed working in all of the films with Joan Blondell, who remained a close friend for decades after the wrap of *Miss Pacific Fleet*. The Warner Bros. comic "stock company" that also included Allen Jenkins, Hugh Herbert, Guy Kibbee and Frank McHugh had been so successful that specific writers had been assigned to craft dialogue to each of their respective styles. Glenda received snappy one-liners because she could fire them off much faster and with more panache than anyone else. But by the time *Miss Pacific Fleet* was completed, Blondell was ready to move on to other things, especially more A-films with Dick Powell.

Glenda was surprised when Blondell filed for divorce from cinematographer George Barnes, whom she married in January 1933. *Photoplay* gossip columnist Cal York reported:

> Glenda ... had always considered their union romantically perfect, and was really all cut up and dumbfounded when it went to the divorce court. In fact, they say that it is making things tough for the several ardent gentlemen who would lead Glenda *altar*wards. One in particular, Addison Randall, who rumor insists has popped the question repeatedly.[4]

On the subject of love, Glenda told *Photoplay*:

It's the most important thing in the world ... Oh, I don't just mean the popular-song type of thing ... I mean the deep affection I have for my family, for my friends, even for the menagerie I keep. And they must love me in return ... Maybe I just have a warmhearted nature. But I *can't* hate anyone—and I can't bear it if somebody doesn't like me. Of course I fight like the dickens with my family, but we always make up six minutes later. I can't think of a person I dislike—there's always something lovable in everyone, you know. I say if you radiate love, others are bound to love you; overlook things in other people, be willing to give—of yourself and of your time and of your thoughts. If you don't enjoy doing that there's no happiness for you.[5]

"Should a Girl Marry Her Boss?" was the question offered by Harmony Haynes in the October 1935 issue of *Hollywood*. Glenda's answer:

I don't approve of the girl going on with her office work after she marries, for in that case, no matter how hard they tried to be husband and wife, they would continue to be just what they were in the first place—a girl and her boss.

The boss shouldn't bring his "bossing" home with him, either ... But he should bring his ambitions, his plans, his hopes and his dreams home to his former secretary ... Any girl who has worked side by side with a man, has absorbed some of his ambition to succeed. Then if she loves him enough to marry him, she will carry that feeling home with her and she'll be mighty lonely if she is robbed of her interest in his business.[6]

On November 20, Glenda and Ray Enright moved on to *Snowed Under* (1936), based on a Lawrence Saunders story and scripted by F. Hugh Herbert and Brown Holmes. Assigned third billing, Glenda was joined by George Brent, Genevieve Tobin, Patricia Ellis, Frank McHugh, John Eldredge, Porter Hall and Helen Lowell.

Brent plays Alan Tanner, once "the leading playwright in America," who currently cannot bring himself to complete the third act of his new opus. About to be married for the third time, to young Pat Quinn (Patricia Ellis), he is holed up in a rural cabin, where wife number one, Alice Merritt (Genevieve Tobin), arrives to help him finish the play.

Wife number two, Daisy Lowell (Glenda), "just a farmer's daughter from Nebraska," arrives with a deputy sheriff Orlando Rowe (Frank McHugh) and attorney McBride (John Eldredge) in tow, to have Tanner arrested for welching

Snowed Under (Warner Bros., 1936; directed by Ray Enright). **Insanity ensues when these characters are trapped under the same roof: Alice Merritt (Genevieve Tobin), McBride (John Eldredge), Orlando Rowe (Frank McHugh), Daisy Lowell (Glenda) and Pat Quinn (Patricia Ellis).**

on back alimony. Daisy blasts into the cabin like the blizzard raging outside (with Glenda performing double takes worthy of the great Stan Laurel), and soon everyone is snowed in for the evening.

Glenda and McHugh create a hilarious scene when Daisy, drunk on applejack, refuses to stay in the cabin with the rest of the "wives and women." Orlando, telling her it's time to turn in for the night, carries her up the stairs, kicking and screaming, and tosses her onto the bed. Glenda unleashes a piercing scream that rivals anything she emits in *Mystery of the Wax Museum*. Unable to get a moment's peace to work on the play, Tanner bolts into the storm, to hole up with his typewriter at the home of his neighbor, Mrs. Canterbury (Helen Lowell).

The following day, the sheriff (Olin Howland) arrives via dogsled with Tanner's agent, Arthur Leyton (Porter Hall), who desperately needs the completed play. When he hears Daisy still carrying on about having Tanner arrested, Leyton, chomping on a cigar, declares, "She's a hardboiled, lowdown, no good dame!" (This is the one time a description of Glenda's screen image is actually included in the dialogue of a film.)

Hollywood Reporter, claiming that the film would appeal to "unsophisticated audiences," added:

Glenda out with Dr. Herbert Gaillard at the President's Ball, Los Angeles Biltmore (January 1936).

> The box-office will be aided … by a quartette of names—
> George Brent, Genevieve Tobin, Glenda Farrell and Patricia
> Ellis—an all-youth cast that lends verve to this rather racy
> affair.[7]

For nearly four years, Glenda had worked constantly, always delivering her best performance and keeping her complaints, if any, to herself. Although her contract allowed for two six-week layoffs per year, Warner Bros. always trumped them by loaning her out to another studio. Unlike other contract stars like James Cagney and Bette Davis, who loved providing headaches for Jack Warner, Glenda didn't give him any problems. However, in late 1935, she offered the following New Year's resolution:

> In 1936 I'm going to learn to relax even if it kills me. I've been
> on a figurative rollercoaster for years—and I've promised my-
> self to take things easy, and not get excited about anything.[8]

By early 1936, Glenda's relationship with Addison Randall had waned. She was photographed in the company of Dr. Herbert Gaillard at the Presi-

The Law in Her Hands (Warner Bros., 1936; directed by William Clemens). Two "woman lawyers," struggling to get a case: Dorothy Davis (Glenda Farrell) and Mary Wentworth (Margaret Lindsay).

dent's Ball held at the Los Angeles Biltmore, an event covered by the popular movie magazines. She also dated architect Drew Eberson, but still had no intentions of tying the knot. On one evening, the very democratic Glenda threw a well-attended party at her home, at which Randall, Gaillard and Eberson all were there, along with Mary Brian, Cary Grant, Hugh Herbert and Barton MacLane.

William Clemens began shooting *Lawyer Woman*, based on an original story by George Bricker, at Warner Bros. in early February 1936. This time around, Glenda was paired with top-billed Margaret Lindsay, supported by Warren Hull, Lyle Talbot and Eddie Acuff. George E. Stone also was cast, but when he contracted pneumonia, character actor Al Shean replaced him. Scripted by Bricker and Luci Ward, the film was released as *The Law in Her Hands* on May 16.

Mary Wentworth (Margaret Lindsay) and Dorothy Davis (Glenda) have just passed the New York bar and are eager to establish a law practice together. As senior partner, Mary takes the few relatively unimportant cases that come their way. In the process, she becomes interested in Assistant District Attorney Robert Mitchell (Warren Hull), whose antiquated views include the maxim,

"The law is no profession for a woman." Agreeing to give her practice one year to prove him wrong, she eventually loses a case deliberately and marries him.

Many familiar Warner Bros. elements, including racketeering and shyster attorneys, populate *The Law in Her Hands*. But Bricker and Ward could only go so far with the "feminist" issues in 1936. Terms such as "girl mouthpiece" and "woman lawyer" are tossed around with impunity.

Glenda plays second fiddle to Lindsay, adapting her gold-digging persona to depict Dorothy's consistent prodding of her partner to accept lucrative cases, even if they involve notorious gangster Frank Gordon (Lyle Talbot), who is boss of multiple rackets in the city. When Mary learns that Gordon is responsible for the poisoning deaths of seven people, however, she turns the tables on him and is subsequently disbarred. Eddie Acuff lends some comic relief as a process server who is injured more severely as the film progresses.

Nobody's Fool (**Universal, 1936; directed by Arthur Greville Collins**). **On loan out to Universal, Glenda was teamed with frequent costar Edward Everett Horton.**

After Clemens wrapped *The Law in Her Hands*, Glenda was loaned out to Universal, where she played the female lead in *Nobody's Fool* (1936), also featuring Edward Everett Horton, Cesar Romero, Frank Conroy, Warren Hymer and Edward Gargan. Adapted by Ralph Block from a Frank Mitchell Dazey, Agnes Christine Johnston and Ben Markson story, the film, originally titled *Unconscious*, was directed by Arthur Greville Collins.

Horton plays Will Wright, a small-town waiter, who gets mixed up with racketeers in New York. Eventually, Wright persuades the gang, including Ruby Miller (Glenda), to go straight. The film ends with Ruby expressing her romantic interest in Will. The *New York Times* reported that:

> [The] "film works an unfair hardship on such talented comedians as Edward Everett Horton, Glenda Farrell and Warren Hymer—not to mention its audience.[9]

Remaining on loan-out, Glenda moved to 20th Century-Fox to play the female lead in Allan Dwan's *Trouble Makers*, which began shooting on April 27,

High Tension (20th Century-Fox, 1936; directed by Allan Dwan). **Remaining on loan-out, Glenda moved on to 20th Century-Fox, where she costarred with Brian Donlevy and Norman Foster.**

1936. Based on the J. Robert Bren and Norman Houston story "Here Comes Trouble," the project, retitled *High Tension* (1936), also features Brian Donlevy, Norman Foster, Helen Wood, Hattie McDaniel, Murray Alper and Ward Bond.

Glenda plays Edith McNeil, a writer of pulp fiction, who is in love with Steve Reardon (Brian Donlevy), a danger-loving cable layer whose specialty is working underwater in the Pacific. Impressing his boss, he lands a $1,000 bonus and a two-week vacation so he can marry "Mac." But before any marital bliss can occur, they argue and Steve accuses her of merely using him as inspiration for her stories. Following a series of fruitless efforts to rekindle their romance, resulting in endless troubles, Steve makes a heroic dive to save a trapped coworker (Norman Foster) and finally marries Mac, winning a five-year contract and permission for his new wife to travel with him so she may continue to receive material for her popular pulp stories.

The *New York Times* opined:

> *High Tension* is a loud and funny comedy written almost entirely in the vernacular, which is well suited to Miss Glenda Farrell's aptitude for robust comedy.[10]

Here Comes Carter (**Warner Bros., 1936; directed by William Clemens**). **Press agent turned radio commentator Kent Carter (Ross Alexander) and secretary Verna Kennedy (Glenda) make a deal.**

Back with Brian Foy's never-resting B-unit at Warner Bros. in mid-June 1936, Glenda worked opposite Ross Alexander in *Loudspeaker Lowdown*, directed by William Clemens from a screenplay by Roy Chanslor and original story by M. Jacoby. Released on October 24 as *Here Comes Carter* (after another working title, *The Tattler*, was jettisoned), the film benefits from a good supporting cast including Anne Nagel, Craig Reynolds, Hobart Cavanaugh, George E. Stone and John Sheehan.

"I'm a press agent, not a *suppress* agent," announces Kent Carter (Ross Alexander) of Premium Pictures. After being asked to cover up aspiring actor Rex Marchbanks' (Craig Reynolds) selfish refusal to support his wife and young son, Carter objects and loses his job. To get even with Marchbanks, he accepts a new job as a radio commentator to peddle potentially libelous information about the denizens of Hollywood. Carter's girlfriend, Linda Warren (Anne Nagel), objects to his mudslinging behavior, but reunites with him after he aids the police in nabbing Marchbanks and his brother, gangster Steve Moran (Norman Willis).

Billed below Glenda, Anne Nagel enjoys more screen time, including her performances of two songs, "You on My Mind" and "Through the Courtesy of Love," by M.K. Jerome and Jack Scholl. Glenda does deliver several zingers, however. When Carter arrives at the office of radio gossip commentator

Mel Winter (Hobart Cavanaugh), a chronic tippler, he asks the secretary Verna Kennedy (Glenda) about her boss' status.

"Drinking," she replies. "Maybe you can catch him before he passes out."

Later, when Carter asks Verna to refrain from passing on certain potentially dangerous information, she vows, "I'd rather cut my tongue out."

Glenda also is able to work in some good physical comedy, particularly a hilarious, very convincing faint for Verna when Moran and one of his ace henchmen, "Slugs" Dana (John Sheehan), arrive to whack the obstinate Carter. When she regains consciousness, Verna believes that Carter had struck her on the head.

Here Comes Carter proved the penultimate film in the career of Ross Alexander, who had attempted to cloak his homosexuality with two disastrous marriages: the first, to actress Aleta Friele, ended with her suicide; and the second, to Anne Nagel, whom he had met while filming Warner Bros.' *China Clipper* (1936), with his death by his own hand. At their ranch in Encino on January 2, 1937, an acutely depressed Alexander walked into the barn, placed a pistol to his head and pulled the trigger. His final film, Warner Bros.' musical *Ready, Willing and Able* (1937), costarring Ruby Keeler, Lee Dixon and Allen Jenkins, was released posthumously.

After the police and emergency crews, along with the drooling reporters, had finally left the scene of Alexander's suicide, the 21-year-old Nagel, alone and attempting to recover from the initial shock of the tragedy, heard a knock at her door. It was Glenda, with whom she had become friendly two years prior to shooting *Here Comes Carter*.

Glenda not only felt like consoling her friend: It was she who had introduced Anne to Ross Alexander. During the 14-week marriage, the couple had stayed out of the limelight, preferring to spend their evenings having quiet suppers together. Glenda hadn't seen Anne on a social basis since the wedding on September 16, 1936.

THRU THE COURTESY OF LOVE

Warner Bros Present

HERE COMES CARTER

With ROSS ALEXANDER · ANN NAGEL · GLENDA FARRELL

Directed by Wm CLEMENS

M. WITMARK & SONS
NEW YORK

JACK SCHOLL
M. K. JEROME

CUPID'S JOB COMPLETED

As shown here, Ross Alexander and Anne Nagel met on a studio set three months ago. Yesterday they eloped in a plane to Yuma and were married.

Film Pair Elopes to Yuma by Plane for Wedding

Ross Alexander and Anne Nagel, film players, yesterday departed Hollywood by plane and eloped to Yuma. They were married there by Judge E. A. Freeman, the marrying justice. Alexander gave his real name as Ross Alexander Smith and Miss Nagel signed her off-screen name, Anne E. Dolan.

Their romance began about three months ago when they worked opposite each other at Warner Brothers studio. She is 21 years of age.

Alexander's first wife, Aleta Friele, Broadway dancer, committed suicide last year.

Sadly, Anne Nagel would be a widow a mere 14 weeks after their marriage.

In the days that followed Alexander's death, Glenda spent a great deal of her off-work hours with Anne, providing, not sympathy, but an attitude of positive thinking. She also suggested that Anne get back to work on a film as soon as possible. The opportunity came when RKO requested a loan-out from Warner Bros., a move that helped Nagel focus on her acting career, which boomed with small parts at her home studio and female leads at Monogram. Over the next year, she appeared in over a dozen films. A short time later, when Glenda's beloved father passed away, Anne reciprocally offered strong support for her friend.

Glenda's career track improved with her appearance in Lloyd Bacon and Busby Berkeley's major production, *Gold Diggers of 1937*, which began shooting in mid-July 1936. Teaming Glenda with Dick Powell and Joan Blondell, the film, based on the Richard Maibaum, Michael Wallace and George Haight play *Sweet Mystery of Life*, includes a superb score featuring songs by Harry Warren and Al Dubin ("All's Fair in Love and War," "With Plenty of Money and You"), and Harold Arlen and E.Y. "Yip" Harburg ("Speaking of the Weather," "Let's Put Our Heads Together," "Hush Mah Mouth," "Life Insurance"). Though Arlen and Harburg had been hired to write all the songs for the film, Berkeley preferred Warren and Dubin, with whom he had worked before.

There are plenty of gold-digging dames in the film, and Glenda's Genevieve Larkin effortlessly leads the pack, first setting her sights on Morty Wetherad (Osgood Perkins) but eventually falling for 59-year-old J.J. Hobart (Victor Moore), whom she describes as having "two feet in the grave already."

Gold Diggers of 1937 (Warner Bros., 1936; directed by Lloyd Bacon and Busby Berkeley). Genevieve Larkin (Glenda) easily out-digs Norma Perry (Joan Blondell) in this musical-comedy extravaganza.

Unaware that his partners have squandered his fortune, Hobart learns that he cannot produce a big Broadway extravaganza because he is broke. After his cast engages in some fun-filled extortion efforts, however, the show goes on — to smashing success.

Having hooked up with the likes of Allen Jenkins, Frank McHugh and Hugh Herbert in earlier films, Glenda scored a comic hit by marrying the delightfully goofy Victor Moore this time around. Busby Berkeley also rose to the occasion, receiving an Oscar nomination for his direction of the "All's Fair in Love and War" dance number.

Berkeley needed an upturn in his life. During September 1936, shortly after the wrap of *Gold Diggers of 1937*, Glenda, Guy Kibbee and Pat O'Brien testified at the director's third "traffic murder" trial in Los Angeles Superior Court. After being involved in a serious auto accident on the Roosevelt Highway during a major film-colony soiree the previous autumn, Berkeley had been charged with second-degree murder for causing fatal injuries while intoxicated. Following two well-publicized trials that ended in hung juries, he was acquitted at the third, partially due to his three colleagues' testimony that he was sober at the time of the crash.

Gold Diggers of 1937 **(Warner Bros., 1936; directed by Lloyd Bacon and Busby Berkeley). Hugo (Charles D. Brown), Genevieve Larkin (Glenda) and Morty Wetherad (Osgood Perkins) plan their gold-digging scam.**

Joan Blondell, in her 1936 *Hollywood* article "My Pal, Glenda," wrote,

> Working with Glenda is splendid for me, but hardly fair to her … Glenda and I do the same type of role, which means that she must share her honors with me. With most girls such a state of affairs just wouldn't work, they would want their honors all to themselves. Not so with Glenda. In fact, she goes to the other extreme to build me up in my comedy.
>
> Glenda is at all times very natural. She isn't one bit camera-conscious … Her movements are always quick and her speech spontaneous. When she goes into a scene she never follows the script to the sacrifice of her naturalness. She acts just as she would if the same situation arose in her everyday life. In other words, she suits the part to her personality instead of trying to suit her personality to the script … Glenda will come out with some expression entirely her own which means that I have to ad lib back and do it pretty quickly or the scene will die on us.
>
> Glenda is like James Cagney in that respect … She is the fastest thinker I have ever known. She can have a dozen

Gold Diggers of 1937 (**Warner Bros., 1936; directed by Lloyd Bacon and Busby Berkeley**). **Genevieve Larkin (Glenda) and J. J. Hobart (Victor Moore).**

things on her mind at the same time and not get them bawled up. Her body keeps up with her mind. She moves swiftly and accurately and makes every move count.[11]

Notes:

[1]Sybil Jason, in Dan Van Neste, "Glenda Farrell: Diamond in the Rough," *Classic Images*, Vol. 275, May 1998.
[2]*Motion Picture*, August 1935, p. 56.
[3]*Film Daily*, 30 August 1935, p. 3.
[4]*Photoplay*, December 1935, p. 41.
[5]*Photoplay*, November 1935, p. 106.
[6]*Hollywood*, October 1935, pp. 68-69.
[7]*Hollywood Reporter*, 9 March 1936, p. 3.
[8]*Movie Classic*, February 1936, p. 88.
[9]*New York Times*, 4 June 1936.
[10]*New York Times*, 11 July 1936.
[11]Joan Blondell, "My Pal, Glenda," *Hollywood*, January 1936.

(Above) During a break in the Warner Bros. commissary, Glenda chats with good friend and colleague Hugh Herbert (1936).

(Below) Warner Bros, publicity "candid" (1936): Glenda cooks a roast in her home kitchen.

Warner Bros. publicity shot (1936): Glenda prepares to serve on her home tennis court.

Chapter 10
Glenda Runs for Mayor

These guys aren't hopheads, they're *businessmen*. A murder
has to get them something definite before they pull it.
—Teresa "Torchy" Blane, *Smart Blonde* (1937)

During the autumn of 1936, Glenda began working on a new film with
Bryan Foy's B-unit at Warner Bros. *No Hard Feelings*, based on a Frederick
Nebel short story, would cast her in a role with which she would be identified
thereafter: the bright, brassy, fast-talking, persistent newspaper reporter and
amateur detective Teresa "Torchy" Blane, a variation on her earlier character
in *Mystery of the Wax Museum*. Much of the fan mail Glenda had received
praised her characterization of the newspaperwoman in *Wax Museum* and *Hi,
Nellie!*

But Torchy Blane does not appear anywhere in Nebel's story. Screenwrit-
ers Kenneth Gamet and Don Ryan (with assistance from Harold Buckley and
Ben Grauman Kohn, who contributed to the treatment) transformed the author's male detective, "Kennedy," into the female equivalent, tailor made for
Glenda.

Receiving top billing, she was teamed with straight-shooting tough guy Barton MacLane, who had specialized in both crooks and cops at the studio for several
years, as Detective Lieutenant Steve McBride. Unlike their predecessors, Nick
and Nora Charles, in MGM's *Thin Man* series, Steve and Torchy are not a couple, but instead they are a coordinated unit setting out to solve crimes.

While Torchy does aid Steve in his investigations, she acts independently,
following him to murder scenes and doing her own sleuthing. Most important-
ly, she is the most intelligent character in the film, and it is she who ultimately
solves the crime. Glenda was one of the first actresses to play an amateur female detective (Joan Blondell had preceded her, in Warner Bros.' *Miss Pinker-
ton* [1932]) and, as future events would prove, with her own series, she helped
blaze a new trail for women in Hollywood.

Glenda took the role seriously, seeking to develop, not a caricature of a
newspaperwoman, but a believable *character*. She recalled:

> [B]efore I undertook to do the first Torchy, I determined to
> create a real human being—and not an exaggerated comedy
> type. I met those who visited Hollywood, and watched them
> work on visits to New York City. They were generally young,

Smart Blonde (**Warner Bros., 1937; directed by Frank MacDonald**). **Teresa "Torchy" Blane (Glenda) and Dolly Ireland (Winifred Shaw).**

> intelligent, refined and attractive. By making Torchy true to
> life, I tried to create a character practically unique in movies.[1]

Released on January 2, 1937 as *Smart Blonde* (a perfect title for an actress who rarely played a dumb one), the film, directed by Frank MacDonald, also features dimwit specialist Tom Kennedy as Gahagan, McBride's childlike, doggerel-spouting sidekick. The film opens with Torchy's byline and an article concerning Tiny Jorgensen (Joseph Crehan), a friend of Fitz Mularkey (Addison Richards), who buys his buddy's nightclub and sporting interests to free up Fitz to marry socialite Marcia Friel (Charlotte Winters).

Glenda is first seen in the back of a taxi as the cabbie races to catch up to a speeding locomotive. Climbing aboard the train, Torchy interviews Jorgensen about his plans to take over Mularkey's enterprises as a legitimate concern. (Glenda's earnest performance draws in the viewer, making Torchy an instantly likeable character.)

At Union Station, Torchy plans to share a cab with Jorgensen, who is gunned down in the street. Later, McBride's prime suspect, Chuck Cannon (Max Wagner), Fitz's right-hand man, is also murdered. Steve first suspects Fitz, and then nightclub singer Dolly Ireland (Winifred Shaw), but Torchy's investigation proves that Marcia Friel and her brother Louie (David Carlyle), career crooks from Boston, are after Fitz's wealth and guilty of the crimes.

When he had learned that Jorgensen recognized Marcia as an imposter, Louie shot him.

Glenda delivers some memorable dialogue, demonstrating Torchy's constant desire for food (Steve is usually too preoccupied to eat) and "advanced" female abilities. "But I'm a newspaper *man!*" she declares at one point. On another occasion, observing Steve, she claims, "That big palooka can't even think without me around." Her most amusing moment arrives when, at the Million Club, Torchy tells the hatcheck girl (a young Jane Wyman), "All he needs is a leopard skin."

"It's a lucky thing you've got Torchy," Fitz informs Steve in the closing scene.

"You ought to be a detective," Steve tells Torchy. His further comment, "Maybe she'll feel better if I take her out and feed her," is tantamount to a marriage proposal, and they kiss as the film fades to black.

The General Federation of Women's Clubs (West Coast), recommending the film for a "mature audience," proclaimed:

> The direction is consistent and convincing, the settings appropriate, the large cast satisfactory with the work of Glenda Farrell most commendable.[2]

When Bernarr Macfadden, publisher and famed "Father of Physical Culture," stopped in Los Angeles during a speaking tour, *Photoplay* held a star-studded party in his honor. Glenda, who maintained her fitness by bicycling, playing tennis and chasing croquet balls around her lawn, attended with Tom Brown, Richard Dix, Madge Evans, Olivia de Havilland, June Lang, Marian Marsh, Una Merkel, Tyrone Power, Martha Raye, Cesar Romero, Anne Shirley and others.

The success of *Smart Blonde* cemented Warner Bros.' plans to feature Glenda in a Torchy Blane series, and the second installment, *Fly Away Baby*, also directed by Frank MacDonald, was released on June 19, 1937. This time around, Frederick Nebel's character became the protagonist in a story idea by Dorothy Kilgallen, who had participated in an around-the-globe airplane race by two male newspaper reporters. Quite innovative for a Foy B-unit project, the screenplay (another Kenneth Gamet and Don Ryan collaboration) treads close to those for the more ambitious Blondell-Farrell films, and would remain one of the best in the Torchy series.

"She's insane!" shouts "Maxie" (Raymond Hatton), Torchy's editor, as her behavior again is the talk of the newsroom. Another murder has occurred, leaving Lieutenant Steve McBride (Barton MacLane) and his "baboon," Gahagan (Tom Kennedy), scratching their heads. To expose the killer of jeweler Milton Deveraux and recover a cache of diamonds, Torchy proposes going

Fly Away Baby (Warner Bros., 1937; directed by Frank MacDonald). **Maxie Monk-house (Raymond Hatton), Torchy Blane (Glenda) and [seated] Colonel Higgam (Harry Davenport).**

up against two rival newspaper reporters, "Sonny" Croy (Gordon Oliver) and Hughie Sprague (Hugh O'Donnell), who are planning a global air race. Maxie gives Torchy his full support. "A woman doing anything is good copy," he announces.

Torchy initially suspects Croy of the crimes, but when he turns up dead aboard a zeppelin bound for Frankfurt, she and Steve discover that he was trying to use fake jewels to pay off a debt to the actual killer, Guy Allister (Joseph King), who plummets to his death when his parachute fails to open. Once again, Torchy chalks up another win for womanhood, and Maxie promises her a substantial bonus.

An impending wedding for Torchy and Steve is a running gag throughout the film. Again, he thwarts her attempts to eat: "Mmm, *steak*!" she declares as they enter the Globe Chop House, but soon, thanks to a clue scrawled on their menu, she is being whisked out the door.

"Running down criminals is a *man's* job," Steve insists, advising Torchy to return to the newspaper office and write "women's" stories. But Maxie knows better, throwing his diminutive self behind her plan to "beat" the men in their macho attempt to circumnavigate the planet.

"Why don't you stop trying to be a detective?" Steve asks at one point.

Dance, Charlie, Dance (Warner Bros., 1937; directed by Frank MacDonald). The one-sheet poster features Stuart Erwin, Jean Muir, Glenda and Allen Jenkins.

Glenda's razor-sharp timing sparkles as Torchy dryly answers, "Why don't you *start*?"

The initial box-office take for *Fly Away Baby* induced Warner Bros. to set Frank MacDonald to prepare the next Torchy episode, scheduled for production in late June.

In the meantime, McDonald worked with Glenda on another Warner Bros. project, *Dance, Charlie, Dance*, which began shooting in mid-January 1937. Based on George S. Kaufman's 1925 play *The Butter and Egg Man*, the film stars Stuart Erwin as Andy Tucker, an Athens, Illinois, tenderfoot who travels to New York to invest in a Broadway show in the hope of making enough money to buy a hotel in his hometown. Naturally he meets up with fly-by-night producers attempting to grab enough loot to put on an awful "musical melodrama," *Dance, Charlie, Dance*.

Allen Jenkins is ex-vaudevillian Alf Morgan, one-half of "Morgamac Productions," and Glenda is his wife, Fanny, an ex-fan dancer pulled "out of a Texas honky-tonk" by her husband. After Alf and his partner, MacArthur (Charles Foy), are unable to drain Fanny's bank account, they rook Tucker and have a disastrous tryout in the sticks. However, they go ahead with their Broadway plans, and the show is so bad it becomes a hit comedy. Slapped with a plagiarism suit, Tucker is able to trick Morgan into buying back the property. Accompanied by Alf's former secretary Mary Mathews (Jean Muir) and Alvin Gussett (Chester Clute), a local hotelier, Tucker returns to Illinois with enough profit to buy his dream business.

Throughout the film, Glenda is at her wisecracking best, sarcastically but honestly providing commentary on the fraudulent show-business practices of Morgan and MacArthur. At one point, Fanny, returning from her bank, bursts into the door of the Morgamac office to call her husband a "four-flushing bunco-steerer!"

During 1937, Warner Bros., in an effort to use the company's funds held in Great Britain, announced a schedule of "quota pictures" to be shot at London's Teddington on the Thames studio. For *You Live and Learn*, directed by Arthur B. Woods, Glenda, accompanied by her stand-in Frances Waverly, sailed to England aboard the *Queen Mary* on March 10, anxious to appear in a British film, the first on the company's docket.

Rare large-format portrait of Glenda done in the Carbro process (1937).

En route to the steamship, Glenda arrived at Grand Central Station to find an enormous crowd waiting for her. Commuters on the way to their jobs literally were swept away by the tide of people hoping to get a glimpse of Glenda.

She had intended to sail aboard the *Berengaria* on March 3, but her father, in serious condition at a Los Angeles hospital following major surgery, took precedence over the voyage. When Charles Farrell passed away, Anne Nagel kept rallying Glenda's spirits. Plans to take Anne on the European trip fell through when her work responsibilities intervened.

Warner Bros. production head Irving Asher intended to familiarize American audiences with British performers, hoping to make them stars in Hollywood. (He already had discovered Errol Flynn and Ian Hunter.) In *You Live and Learn* (shot under the title *Have You Come for Me*), Claude Hulbert was teamed with Glenda, a pairing intended to pave the way for major Warner Bros. stars like Paul Muni and Kay Francis to be cast with British counterparts.

Glenda remained in Britain for 10 weeks. She also visited the continent, especially enjoying her time in Italy. On May 12, 1937 Glenda represented Warner Bros. at the coronation ceremonies of King George VI and Queen Consort Elizabeth at Westminster Abbey. She and Frances returned to New York aboard the French liner *Normandie* on May 31. During the voyage from Southampton, their fellow passengers included several Hollywood folks, including Gloria Swanson, Neil Hamilton and Nat Levine, as well as Gloria Vanderbilt and her sister, Lady Thelma Furness.

In the July 29, 1937 *Film Daily*, Glenda was quoted regarding her interest in playing a femme fatale part:

> I have a preference for shady women's roles. There's more scope for character. And we're more interested in women with a bit of mystery wrapped around them.[3]

Returning to Hollywood, Glenda was loaned to RKO for *Here Comes the Groom*, which was in production from mid-July to August 16, 1937. Once again playing a fast-talking, gold-digging girlfriend, her Carol Wallace twice goes to the altar with irresponsible steamship company heir Jonathan Blair (Herbert Marshall), who ultimately marries Valentine Ransome (Barbara Stanwyck), whom he met during a drunken night out. (Released as *Breakfast for Two*, the film was Stanwyck's first since *Stella Dallas* [1935], for which she was nominated for the Best Actress Academy Award.)

Breakfast for Two (RKO-Radio, 1937; directed by Alfred Santell). Butch, the valet (Eric Blore), Jonathan Blair (Herbert Marshall) and Carol Wallace (Glenda).

Torchy Blane, the Adventurous Blonde (Warner Bros., 1937; directed by Frank MacDonald). **The dimwitted, lovable Gahagan gets the wink from Torchy (Glenda).**

This madcap screwball comedy includes blackout hangovers, strange women in the shower, male-female boxing "bouts," an overly friendly Great Dane (in a hilarious scene with Etienne Girardot), and the requisite bumbling butler (Eric Blore). Seven writers contributed to the script, which occasionally includes some humorous moments. At her second "wedding," Carol, told that Blair is already married (to Valentine), shouts, "This is *bigotry!*"

On October 2, 1937, MGM released *Sunday Night at the Trocadero*, a 21-minute short filmed by director George Sidney at the famous Los Angeles nightclub. The film interspersed various performers with about two-dozen Hollywood luminaries in the crowd, including Glenda, Dick Foran, Chester Morris, Robert Benchley, Sally Blane, Norman Foster, Groucho Marx, Frank Morgan, Stuart Erwin and Frank McHugh.

Released on November 13, 1937, *The Adventurous Blonde* features a strong supporting cast, including Anne Nagel, George E. Stone, William Hopper and Raymond Hatton. Unfortunately, David Diamond and Robertson White's screenplay, involving a faked murder gag that backfires, is vastly inferior to Gamet and Ryan's work on the earlier Torchy Blane films. The foiled marriage shtick begins to wear thin during this episode, in which Torchy and

Hollywood Hotel (Warner Bros, 1938; directed by Busby Berkeley). In her final appearance for Busby Berkeley, Glenda plays "Jonesy," personal assistant to histrionic actress Mona Marshall (Lola Lane). The real stars of the film are the Benny Goodman Band and the songs of Johnny Mercer.

Steve (Barton MacLane) are made the object of a "friendly" practical joke hatched by a group of reporters (including Stone and Hopper) that ends in a real murder.

Criticized by his boss Captain McTavish (Frank Shannon) for favoring Torchy over reporters at rival newspapers, Steve asks, "What do you want me to do—marry *the boys*?" Again, Torchy bests all the males, going so far as to defy the police to track down Mortimer Gray (Charles C. Wilson), the murderer of ham actor Harvey Hammond (Leland Hodgson).

In between films, Glenda kept busy on the airwaves. She joined Lee Tracy for a one-act *Silver Theatre* drama broadcast on the CBS radio network.

Glenda made her final appearance for Busby Berkeley in *Hollywood Hotel* (1938), a Warners comic musical extravaganza, shot from early August to early November 1937, based on the popular CBS radio program. Dick Powell again stars (as movie newcomer Ronnie Bowers), supported by Lola and Rosemary Lane (as temperamental star Mona Marshall and her lookalike, Virginia Stanton, respectively), Hugh Herbert, Ted Healy and Glenda (as Marshall's personal secretary).

But the real stars of *Hollywood Hotel* are the songs of Johnny Mercer (including "Hooray for Hollywood," "I'm Like a Fish Out of Water" and "Let

Hollywood Hotel (Warner Bros, 1938; directed by Busby Berkeley). Mona Marshall (Lola Lane), Chester Marshall (Hugh Herbert), "Jonesy" (Glenda) and Louella Parsons (Herself).

That Be a Lesson to You") and the music of the Benny Goodman Orchestra, including Harry James on trumpet and Gene Krupa on drums. The scene featuring a virtuoso performance of Joe Venuti's "Satan's Holiday" by Goodman and his trio (Teddy Wilson, piano; Lionel Hampton, vibraphone; Krupa, drums) is one of the finest in the history of filmed jazz.

Other famous faces include Frances Langford (who performs the elaborate "Hooray for Hollywood" with Johnnie Davis) and none other than gossip columnist Louella Parsons. For the most part, Glenda frantically follows Lola Lane around the sets, her naturalism and subtle physical comedy providing the perfect counterpoint to Lane's deliberate histrionics. During the concluding production number, featuring a reprise of "Hooray for Hollywood," Glenda may be seen singing in the chorus.

In early October 1937, Glenda joined Frank MacDonald, Barton MacLane and Tom Kennedy (who now was grabbing third billing) to shoot the fourth Torchy Blane film, *Blondes at Work* (1938). Borrowing from two previous Warner Bros. releases, *Front Page Woman* (1935), starring Bette Davis, and *Back in Circulation* (1937), with Pat O'Brien and Joan Blondell, Albert DeMond's screenplay is a step up from *Adventurous Blonde*.

Steve McBride (Barton MacLane) again is in hot water with Captain McTavish (Frank Shannon), who believes the lieutenant has been leaking po-

146

Hello Again, Mr. Manager:

I'm now on my fourth sizzling front-page scoop and another one-gal feud with the Police Lieutenant -- my little Stevie-Weevie (Barton MacLane to you). We're both in "Blondes At Work" but this blonde does all the head-work even if I don't look busy. I've got all the angles figured out for very, very exciting adventure. There are plenty of angles for you too, so take my exploitips and hit the trail on the following pages.

Yours for thrills and action,

Torchy Blane

TORCHY BLANE
"BLONDES AT WORK"
GLENDA FARRELL · BARTON MacLANE
Tom Kennedy · Rosella Towne · Donald Briggs
Directed by FRANK McDONALD · A WARNER BROS. Picture

Blondes at Work (Warner Bros., 1938; directed by Frank MacDonald). **At Warner Bros., Glenda adamantly refused to show her legs in publicity photos. But if the studio couldn't get it done one way; they did it another: with artwork on the press book cover of** *Blondes at Work!*

lice information to Torchy. After the couple agrees to put an end to this conspiracy, Torchy discovers that Gahagan (Tom Kennedy) has been keeping a diary of his daily activities with Steve. Making an impression of the key to

147

the police sedan's glove compartment, Torchy soon begins reading Gahagan's entries. One of the film's most amusing moments is the revelation that the cop and would-be poet still lives with his mother.

Wealthy businessman Marvin Spencer (Kenneth Harlan) has been bumped off, and Torchy goes to any length to get the story and solve the crime, including manipulating every cop in sight. When she overhears the jury deliberating the case, she publishes the verdict before it is heard in court, ending up in the slammer for her wily efforts.

Perhaps the most humorous line of dialogue in the entire Torchy Blane series arrives when Officer Parker (perennial cop Thomas E. Jackson), assigned to make a list of the murder victim's paramours, sarcastically deadpans, "It looks like the only dame that didn't carry a torch for Spencer was the Statue of Liberty."

There are also other priceless moments, including Steve's remark, "I wish we could find *one murderer* who could give the police department a little cooperation." Having portrayed Torchy landing in jail for her surreptitious behavior, Glenda chose not to cooperate with Warner Bros. any longer. After completing this Torchy film, she did not renew her contract.

Glenda spent late December 1937 through early February 1938 at Paramount, shooting *Stolen Heaven*, a musical melodrama featuring an excellent supporting cast and stunning production numbers choreographed by William Prinz and photographed by William C. Mellor. Unfortunately Gene Raymond is miscast in the lead role as Carl, a jewel thief, who aids the infamous "Will o' the Wisp" (Olympe Bradne, in her first starring role) in her larcenous activities.

Bradne makes up for the unconvincing plot with her singing and dancing, and Lewis Stone is superb as an aging concert pianist, doing well in his miming of several great keyboard classics, including Franz Liszt's "Liebestraum," "Second Hungarian Rhapsody" and "Sixth Hungarian Rhapsody"; Frederic Chopin's "C Sharp Minor Valse" and "Fantasie Impromptu"; Edward Grieg's "Nocturne" and others. Glenda (who looks quite stunning in her publicity photos), Porter Hall and Joseph Sawyer all acquit themselves well as members of the criminal gang.

After completing her work on *Stolen Heaven*, Glenda retreated to New York, where *Times* reporter B.R. Crisler caught up with her. In his April 3, 1938, column on film people, he wrote:

> We found Glenda Farrell on a lovely spring day nursing a vicious Manhattan head cold and a grudge against the fate, which had caused her to get it the moment she arrived in town. She took a satanic pleasure, however, in reflecting that shortly after she made her getaway from Hollywood, Paramount began frantically calling her to do retakes on *Stolen Heaven* ...

Glenda received Paramount's glamorous treatment for this publicity portrait used to promote *Stolen Heaven* (1938).

Prison Break (Universal, 1938, directed by Arthur Lubin). "Big Red" Kincaid (Ward Bond) menaces Jean Fenderson and Joaquin Shannon (Glenda and Barton MacLane, a film couple once again).

> Miss Farrell is now a freelance and has already signed for two pictures ... at Universal ...[4]

On April 16, Glenda gladly joined a celebration in Miami Beach to attend her friend, Ziegfeld girl Hazel Forbes, at her wedding to actor-singer Harry Richman. 20th Century-Fox chairman Joseph Schenck served as best man. It was the second marriage for Richman and third for Forbes. (Their union would end in divorce in 1941.)

Glenda participated in a 15-minute interview with WOR radio's Radie Harris on the evening of May 14, 1938. Two weeks later, she joined Lyle Talbot and Alan Dinehart for the "Greater New York Fund Sketch" on WABC radio. In June, Tom McAvity of the Lord and Thomas advertising agency conferred with New York radio producers about creating a *Torchy Blane* series. Warner Bros. proposed a 26-week production to star Glenda, Barton MacLane and Tom Kennedy, but several issues, including contractual problems, torpedoed their plans.

Directed by Arthur Lubin, *Prison Break* (1938) had three working titles (*State Prison*, *Prison Walls* and *Walls of San Quentin*) prior to its release on

July 15, 1938. Initially planned as the first of four Universal projects to costar Glenda and Barton MacLane, *Prison Break* was the only film actually produced; and by time it hit theaters, the pair already had appeared in two of the Torchy Blane installments (*The Adventurous Blonde* [1937] and *Blondes at Work* [1938]) at Warner Bros.

Ward Bond's career criminal, "Big Red" Kincaid, provides the only real physical presence in *Prison Break*. Inexpensively shot on cramped sets, with stock footage providing its only spatial sense, the film benefits little from Lubin and cinematographer Harry Neumann's use of shadows, but much from Bond's athletic build and menacing, though understated, performance. He had to do very little to convey power, and here he is a stone killer who looms as a legend in the minds of all the yard birds, except for Joaquin Shannon (MacLane), a Portuguese-Irish tuna fisherman, sent to the Big House after being framed for a manslaughter rap by the bigoted father (Victor Kilian) of his fiancée, Jean Fenderson (Glenda, in a sincere performance).

Barton MacLane was no physical slouch, but his fight scenes are so badly staged that no viewer could believe Shannon actually contributes to someone's death (he takes the rap for his brother-in-law, who didn't do it, either!) or knocks out Big Red in the climactic scene. He and Glenda proved their collective acting prowess by giving good performances while saddled with the clumsy dialogue of screenwriter Dorothy Reid, who adapted Norton S. Parker's story "Walls of San Quentin." However, in the best tradition of *I Am a Fugitive from a Chain Gang*, she was able (without becoming preachy) to work in a few swipes at antiquated criminal laws.

THURSDAY, JAN. 27, 1938

OUTSTANDING EVENTS ON ALL STATIONS

7:15-7:30 P. M.—"A Liberal Views Business," Senator James P. Pope of Idaho, at Williston Academy Dinner, Hotel Ambassador—WOR.

8:00-9:00 P. M.—Vallee Varieties: Sketch, "Manhattan Latin," With Glenda Farrell; Sterling Holloway, Comedian, and Others—WEAF.

8:00-9:00 P. M.—Variety Show, Kate Smith, Director; Sketch, "Night Is Never Dark," With Margo, Actress, and Others—WABC.

8:45-9:30 P. M.—Rochester Philharmonic Orchestra Concert—WJZ.

9:00-10:00 P. M.—Good News of 1938: Robert Taylor, Master of Ceremonies; Florence Rice, Actress, and Others—WEAF, WHN.

9:00-10:00 P. M.—Amateur Hour, Major Bowes, Director—WABC.

9:30-10:00 P. M.—Sinfonietta, Alfred Wallenstein, Conductor—WOR.

9:30-10:30 P. M.—America's Town Meeting: "Struggle for Power in the Mediterranean," Major James Strachey Barnes of England; S. K. Ratcliffe, Lecturer; Quincy Howe, Author—WJZ.

10:00-11:00 P. M.—Bing Crosby, Songs; Jan Smeterlin, Pianist; Madeleine Carroll, Actress; Trotter Orchestra, and Others—WEAF.

Glenda appeared on the radio program *Vallee Varieties* in the sketch "Manhattan Latin" on Thursday, Jan. 27, 1938.

The Road to Reno (Universal, 1938; directed by S. Sylvan Simon). In this publicity portrait, Randolph Scott is obviously enjoying being bookended by Glenda and Hope Hampton.

Shot during June and July 1938, Universal's *The Road to Reno* (1938), based on a *Saturday Evening Post* story by I.A.R. Wylie, is naturally about d-i-v-o-r-c-e. An odd combination of comedy and cowboy elements with *opera* (Puccini's *La Boheme*), the film stars Randolph Scott as Steve Fortness, the estranged husband of singer Linda Halliday (Hope Hampton in her film debut), and Glenda as Sylvia Shane, a professional divorcee on her way to Nevada for a fourth tie-breaker. Directed by S. Sylvan Simon, this potboiler includes an appearance by one of Universal's most ubiquitous "usual suspects," Samuel S. Hinds, as Sylvia's attorney.

In *Exposed* (1938), the third picture in her deal with Universal, Glenda plays, not a reporter, but a *Flash* magazine photographer named Claire "Click" Stewart. Directed in breakneck fashion by Harold Schuster, the film features Click snapping a photo of a bowery bum that eventually results in the arrest of racketeers and the personal and professional rejuvenation of William Reardon (Otto Kruger), a down-and-out attorney (who gets Glenda in the final fadeout).

Glenda was persuaded to return to Warner Bros. after *Torchy Blane in Panama* (1938), a William Clemens-directed entry pairing Lola Lane with Paul Kelly, bombed at the box-office. Rejoining Tom Kennedy as the ever-dim-witted Gahagan in mid-July 1938, Glenda and Barton MacLane brought the series back on track with *Torchy Gets Her Man*, although the small budget had

Exposed (**Universal, 1938; directed by Harold Schuster**). **Down-and-out attorney William Reardon (Otto Kruger) and magazine photographer Claire "Click" Stewart (Glenda).**

William "One-Shot" Beaudine in the director's chair on this occasion. Warner Bros. also economized by shooting the racetrack scenes at Inglewood's Hollywood Park, in which the studio had financial interests.

Fortunately, Albert DeMond's clever, witty screenplay compensates for Beaudine's typically pedestrian pace and lack of visual inventiveness. When Steve McBride becomes involved in a phony "Secret Service" operation to capture the notorious counterfeiter Gilbert, aka "$100 Bailey" (Willard Robertson), Torchy and Gahagan, aided by a cunning German Shepherd named Blitzen, help him solve the case.

The comic elements are consistently entertaining, masterfully delivered by Glenda and Tom Kennedy. While Torchy (borrowing the creosote maneuver from Sherlock Holmes in Arthur Conan Doyle's *The Sign of Four*) attempts to learn German in order to communicate with the dog, Gahagan demonstrates his foolproof system of picking winning horses at the track by utilizing his complete ignorance of mathematics! "Six times six is 37" becomes a running gag for Glenda.

The script is loaded with crafty dialogue. Torchy's "persistent pursuit" leads one of Bailey's goons to admit, "I don't like any dames what goes *gumshoein'* around!"

Torchy Gets Her Man (**Warner Bros., 1938; directed by William Beaudine**). **Tom Kennedy, Glenda and Barton MacLane are featured on this herald used to promote the film**

After the gang kidnaps Torchy and Gahagan, the obtuse copper, referring to the Secret Service, unleashes an unforgettable gem: "Those feds must be *dumb dicks*!" Depressed by their captivity, Torchy adds, "Maybe I should have married Steve and had babies."

Some visual gags also pay off. Maxie (Joe Cunningham), having given his usual support to Torchy's reporter-sleuth plan, receives two lipstick coated kisses in return. In another scene, Torchy, speeding after Bailey (not in a taxi nor a police sedan, but driving a Ford "suicide door" deuce coupe this time around), is fooled by a bogus detour sign and ends her journey in the middle of a stream.

Torchy's love of steak actually aids Steve in unmasking Bailey, who has been masquerading as Secret Service Agent Gilbert. When the phony fed shoots off his mouth about her culinary preference, Steve realizes that he obtained this information from Torchy herself.

With the unswerving Blitzen leading the way to the gang's rural hideout, Steve arrives in the nick of time, discovering Torchy and Gahagan bound and gagged, as one of his officers quickly tosses a time bomb out the window! All's well that ends well, thanks to lines like, "Steak! You must have known I was coming."

An admirer of the *Torchy Blane* series was young writer Jerry Siegel, who later collaborated with illustrator Joe Shuster in creating the comic book character of Superman. Siegel explained:

My wife, Joanne, was Joe's original art model for Superman's girlfriend, Lois Lane, back in the 1930s. Our heroine was, of course, a working girl whose priority was grabbing scoops. What inspired me in the creation was Glenda Farrell, the movie star who portrayed Torchy Blane, a gutsy, beautiful headline-hunting reporter, in a series of exciting motion pictures. Because the name of the actress Lola Lane (who also played Torchy) appealed to me, I called my character Lois Lane.[5]

William Beaudine now had the Torchy series running full throttle, shooting the series entries back-to-back. As soon as he wrapped *Torchy Gets Her Man* on August 17, 1938, he began production on *Torchy Blane in Chinatown*, a remake of *Murder Will Out* (1930), a First National adaptation of Will Jenkins' short story "The Purple Hieroglyph," starring Jack Mulhall and Lila Lee.

The hoary plot used by writer George Bricker also bears similarity to an earlier film, *The Unholy Night* (1929), directed by Lionel Barrymore for MGM. Several men are murdered according to a schedule, in this case when the clock strikes midnight, but in the end all are exposed as criminals, quite alive and anxious to collect a bag full of extorted cash.

Torchy Blane in Chinatown uses Chinese as the fall guys, complete with racial profiling and the expected "ethnic" references. The stereotypes are brief-

Torchy Blane in Chinatown (Warner Bros., 1939; directed by William Beaudine). Half sheet poster used to promote the film.

155

ly abated, however, during a scene in which McBride (Barton MacLane) meets with Lem Kee (Tetsu Komai), a community leader who presents the situation from the Chinese point of view. The initial murder, during which the victim has "his head shot off," is seen as revenge for the man's plundering of ancient burial tablets in China; but Lem explains that the family has 4,000 members in the United States, all of whom can be viewed as suspects!

Glenda is introduced when Torchy is slammed in the rear end by the office door of Captain McTavish (Frank Shannon), and she is treated in a similar manner throughout much of the film. "You ain't no lady," Gahagan (Tom Kennedy) claims. "You're a *reporter*."

William Beaudine's characteristically moribund atmosphere is reflected by Steve's off-handed explanation of the initial "murder": "The guy who had his head blown off was just some stiff they picked up at the morgue."

As part of the promotional campaign for *Torchy Blane in Chinatown*, Warner Bros. issued photos of Glenda preparing food in the kitchen of her home. Accompanying an image of her placing a dessert dish into the freezer was this recipe courtesy of the Warner's publicity department:

> Glenda Farrell ... adores frozen desserts and, whenever she gets the chance, makes REFRIGERATOR MOCHA DREAM herself. The following is the recipe:
> 1 teaspoon gelatin
> ½ cup milk
> ½ cup strong coffee
> 2 eggs, separated
> ½ cup sugar
> ⅛ teaspoon salt
> 1 square unsweetened chocolate
> ¼ cup hot water
> 1 cup heavy cream, whipped
> Soften gelatin in ¼ cup of milk. Scald remaining milk with coffee. Add slowly to beaten egg yolks, mixing well; add sugar and salt; cook over hot water 5 minutes, or until mixture coats spoon, stirring constantly. Add gelatin and stir until dissolved. Melt chocolate in hot water; add slowly to coffee custard, mixing well; cool. Fold in cream and stiffly beat egg whites. Turn into mold and freeze 2 to 4 hours, or until firm, stirring twice during freezing.

Although *Torchy Blane in Chinatown* is inferior to its immediate predecessor, it performed well enough at the box-office in February 1939 to warrant a follow-up, *Torchy Runs for Mayor*, which Ray McCarey began shooting that

In this Warner Bros. publicity shot used to promote *Torchy Blane in Chinatown*, Glenda displays her delicious "Refrigerator Mocha Dream" frozen dessert.

same month. Earle Snell's screenplay depicts Torchy running a series of front-page articles exposing widespread corruption in the office of Mayor Saunders (Charles Richman), a patsy being manipulated by racketeer Dr. Dolan (John Miljan).

"She really means business," Steve observes at one point. Truly a woman on a mission, Torchy stops at nothing to "clean up the city," bugging Saunders' office, breaking into Dolan's home to steal incriminating files and finally running for mayor herself. "Nobody's going to gag me and get away with it!" she insists.

Torchy Runs for Mayor (Warner Bros., 1939; directed by Ray McCarey). Glenda and Barton MacLane get cozy on this midget window card used to promote the film.

Though predictable, *Torchy Runs for Mayor* is an improvement on *Chinatown*, featuring good performances from an interesting supporting cast, including Miljan, Richman, Joe Downing, Irving Bacon and John Harron. (Best known for his lead "romantic" role in the Bela Lugosi classic *White Zombie* [1932], Harron appears in seven of the nine Torchy episodes. His prolific screen career suddenly ended on November 24, 1939, after he contracted spinal meningitis. He was only 36 years old, but had appeared in 167 films.)

After running for mayor, Glenda again grew tired of the Torchy films and left the studio to work on a freelance basis. Although Warner Bros. had announced *Torchy in Scotland Yard*, intending to shoot in England with Glenda, Barton MacLane and Tom Kennedy, the project was dropped. The final series entry, *Torchy Blane ... Playing with Dynamite* (1939), retained only Kennedy, while teaming newcomer Jane Wyman with Allen Jenkins. Noel Smith's directorial effort effectively drowned out Torchy's celluloid parade.

Glenda left for a much-needed New York vacation on October 15, 1938. Prior to her departure, she ran for mayor *for real:* the honorary position in North Hollywood sponsored by the Junior Chamber of Commerce (Jaycees). Two days later, the absentee candidate handily won the office in a landslide: Glenda's 2,550 votes buried those of Bing Crosby (902) and Lewis Stone (738). She was making strides for women, not only on the screen, but on the ground as well—even if only in a mostly symbolic capacity. During the trip to New York, she enjoyed chatting with her *Exposed* costar, Otto Kruger, who was photographed with her lighting up a "campaign cigar."

On November 8, 1938, Glenda, back in the Big Apple, guested on a WEAF radio variety program featuring the Van Steeden Orchestra. The fol-

> **8:30-WEAF—Variety Program; Van Steeden Orch.; Glenda Farrell, Actress**
> **WOR—Gould Orchestra; Vocalist**
> **WABC—Al Jolson and Parkyakarkus, Comedians; Gluskin Orch.; Beatrice Lillie; Kate Smith. Guests**

lowing week she and 400 fellow artists, including Irving Berlin, Al Jolson, Eddie Cantor, Kitty Carlisle, Lillian Gish, Hugh Herbert, Walter Huston, George Jessel, Raymond Massey, Helen Morgan and Orson Welles, gathered at Madison Square Garden for the annual *Night of Stars* benefit show. The goal to raise $100,000 for the United Palestine Appeal was chaired by Harold Jacobi and produced by Louis K. Sidney. The "greatest lineup in the show's annuals" played to a capacity crowd.

There is Only One

★ ★ ★ ★ ★ ★ ★ ★ ★ ★ ★
★ **"NIGHT OF** ★
★ **STARS"** ★
★ ★
★ ★
★ ★ ★ ★ ★ ★ ★ ★ ★ ★ ★

The Show of the Year

WEDNESDAY EVENING
NOVEMBER 16th
MADISON SQUARE GARDEN

Representing the Contribution of Every Branch
of the Amusement Industry to a Great
Humanitarian Cause

Featuring in Person

**The Foremost Celebrities of Stage,
Screen, Radio and Opera**

Headed By

Eddie Cantor, Walter Huston, Raymond Massey, Irving Berlin, Al Jolson, George Jessel, Hugh Herbert, Lillian Gish, Glenda Farrell, Kitty Carlisle, Lou Holtz, Ben Bernie

LOUIS K. SIDNEY, Chairman, Producing Committee

BEN A. BOYAR, Associate Chairman

**Proceeds for Settlement in Palestine of
Jews of Germany, Czechoslovakia
and Other Lands**

Reserved Seats Now on Sale at 111 Fifth Avenue
Leblang-Gray's Ticket Agency and Box Office

Glenda was in stellar company during the "Night of Stars," held at Madison Square Garden on November 16, 1938.

160

Back in California on December 8, the 35th Mayor of Los Angeles, Fletcher Bowron (who would serve a total of 25 years), swore Glenda into office and she immediately put into action her plan to beautify North Hollywood. The streets were to be given a daily scrubbing, each corner would be adorned with a trashcan, and flowers would be planted in every vacant lot. Like her North Hollywood home, the town itself was receiving the Glenda touch. She later said:

> I do wish I could have dignified things written about me. When I was appointed Mayor of North Hollywood ... the gossip columnists forgot all about romances—and that was nice ... I like Hollywood. I'd be awfully foolish if I didn't. However, I'm getting so I abhor newspaperwoman roles such as Torchy Blane.[6]

Notes:

1 Bubbeo, Daniel, *The Women of Warner Brothers: The Lives and Careers of 15 Leading Ladies*. (Jefferson, North Carolina: McFarland and Company, 2001).
[2]*Motion Picture Review Digest*, December 1936, p. 120.
[3]*Film Daily*, 29 July 1937, p. 20.
[4]*New York Times*, 3 April 1938.
[5]*Time*, 30 May 1988, pp. 6-7.
[6]*Milwaukee Sentinel*, 7 September 1939, p. 4.

Warner Bros. publicity portrait (1938).

Warner Bros. publicity portrait (1938).

Chapter 11
The Talk of the Town

I was looking for a wristwatch I gave Clyde, just two weeks ago. It gives a girl a queer feeling. One night you've got a man that weighs 211 pounds, and the next day—wham—all you've got left is a medal for shot-putting.
—Regina Bush, *The Talk of the Town* (1942)

OUTDOOR FUND RALLY PLANNED FOR TODAY

Stage and Radio Stars to Aid at Old Subtreasury

The first outdoor rally of the Greater New York Fund's 1940 appeal to business firms and employe groups on behalf of its 393 affiliated voluntary social welfare and health agencies will be held from noon to 1 P. M. today on the steps of the old Subtreasury Building, at Broad and Wall Streets. Stars of the stage and radio will collaborate with child musicians in an entertainment program.

Among the stars to be present are Walter Huston, Alan Dinehart, Glenda Farrell and Lyle Talbot. Eddy Duchin will lead two bands from agencies affiliated with the fund. Winthrop Rockefeller, assistant to the chairman of the fund's campaign, will speak. He explained that no donations would be sought at the rally, which is to acquaint the financial district with the aims and purposes of the drive.

Glenda participated in many charitable causes when she was working in New York.

Every Sunday evening on CBS radio, the Screen Actors Guild broadcast a show featuring stars that volunteered their time in exchange for a $10,000 sponsor contribution to a fund for needy actors and actresses. During the spring of 1939, SAG held a lavish party at Victor Hugo's French restaurant, noted for serving the finest cuisine in Los Angeles, for performers scheduled for future broadcasts.

This was exactly the type of worthwhile Hollywood get-together that interested Glenda. She happily joined a luminous gathering including Guild president Ralph Morgan, Edward Arnold, William Bakewell, Joan Bennett, Jack Benny, Mary Brian, John Mack Brown, Joan Crawford, Louise Fazenda, Reginald Gardiner, Judy Garland, Myrna Loy, Robert Montgomery, Wayne Morris, George Murphy, Conrad Nagel, John Payne, Mary Pickford, Basil Rathbone, Rosalind Russell, Norma Shearer, Anne Shirley and Robert Young.

On April 1, 1939 Glenda was part of the "Eastern delegation" that took part in the enormous publicity campaign for Warner Bros.' mighty Technicolor Western *Dodge City* (1939), directed by Michael Curtiz and starring Errol Flynn and Olivia de Havilland. The New Yor players, executives and newspaper reporters changed trains in Chicago, while those in the film capital traveled directly to Dodge City, Kansas aboard the Santa Fe Special from Hollywood. A third group from the Midwest and South left from Memphis.

Jack Warner and Hal Wallis were joined by 150 journalists and a stellar lineup of performers: Flynn, de Havilland, Ann Sheridan, Bruce Cabot, Guinn "Big Boy" Williams and Ward Bond (all of whom appear in the film), together with Glenda, George Bancroft, George Brent, James Cagney, Marlene Dietrich, Richard Dix, William S. Hart, Hugh Herbert, Rosemary Lane and many others. A gala parade preceded the screening of the film.

Glenda and Chester Morris costarred in the 30-minute radio play, "The Man from Medicine Hat," aired by WABC on the evening of June 9, 1939. Now a freelance actress, Glenda enjoyed working in a variety of media and was very anxious about her return to the theater.

On May 15, 1939, she opened opposite a 21-year-old Steve Cochran in Edna Ferber and George S. Kaufman's *Stage Door* at the Olney Playhouse in Maryland. During July at L.A.'s Westport Playhouse, she played the title role in Eugene O'Neill's *Anna Christie* to enthusiastic reviews. Soon after the play closed, she joined Douglass Montgomery for a touring production of S.N. Behrmann's *Brief Moment*. During its stop in Wisconsin in early September, Glenda received all the praise the *Milwaukee Journal* had to offer:

> In the present unveiling … the play seems rather grievously dated … Never mind that. The important point to consider is that Miss Farrell is a vivacious, gifted and exceedingly busy exponent of the smart school of acting … when she arrives to take charge the comedy is bright and brisk. Toward the end it is even dramatic and all the credit goes to the star.[1]

Nerves among the company were tense. On September 1, Adolf Hitler's troops had stormed into Poland with orders to murder, in an ethnic cleansing campaign, every man, woman and child of the Poles' "inferior race." When queried about the international political situation by a reporter for the *Milwaukee Sentinel*, Glenda replied:

> I remember the last war … and the condition in which it left my husband, whom I married a few years later, left me with an indelible horror of war.
>
> I've been extremely worried the past few weeks about European affairs. Of course now my boy is too young to fight, but if this conflict is anything like the last one and is to last as long—oh, I just shudder at the thought.[2]

much lighter note, Warner Bros.' annual "Warner Club" dinner and
s held at the Los Angeles Biltmore Hotel. Studio employees and their
all gathered to celebrate another successful year and enjoy the new
on "blooper reel," in this case "Breakdowns of 1939," in which Glenda and Barton MacLane appear in several humorous outtakes from *Torchy Gets Her Man.*

The August 24, 1931 issue of the *Corona Daily Inde-pendent* reported Glenda's appearance in *On the Spot* at the Belasco Theater in Los Angeles.

At another celebration, the honorary mayors of the San Fernando Valley, including Glenda, Al Jolson, Mischa Auer, Hugh Herbert, Richard Arlen, Bing Crosby and Marian Marsh, were all invited to Universal's special preview of *Tropic Fury*, starring Arlen and Andy Devine, at Van Nuys on September 27, 1939. This "Rt. Hon. Preview" particularly pleased Devine, who was honorary mayor of Van Nuys.

On November 22, Glenda costarred with Franchot Tone in the 30-minute radio play "Candle Light," broadcast on WABC. The following month, the *New York Times* announced an upcoming production of *Thanks for My Wife*, to open in Portland, Oregon, on January 4, 1940, and tour to Seattle, Minneapolis, St. Paul and Milwaukee, hitting Chicago on February 5. Glenda was cast with Alan Dinehart and her old Warner Bros. colleague and pal Lyle Talbot. The successful tour eventually closed in Chicago in mid-March.

Later that month, Glenda began starring in Joseph Carole and Alan Dinehart's comedy *Separate Rooms*, which ran for 613 performances at three Broadway theaters: Maxine Elliot's, the Mansfield and the Plymouth. The cast also included Dinehart, Jack Smart and Lyle Talbot. On April 27, Glenda also managed to squeeze in a morning radio drama, "Lincoln Highway," on station WEAF.

On May 16, Glenda joined Dinehart, Talbot and Walter Huston at the first outdoor rally of the Greater New York Fund's 1940 appeal to "business firms and employee groups on behalf of its 393 affiliated voluntary social welfare and health agencies." Held on the steps of the old Subtreasury Building at Broad and Wall Streets, the event also featured music by two orchestras conducted by Eddie Duchin and a speech by campaign chairman Winthrop Rockefeller. The rally was held, not to collect donations, but to acquaint the New York financial district with the aims of the drive.

That same day, Glenda maintained a busy social schedule by taking part in the judging of a fashion show at Saks 34th Street. The "Him and Her" fashion parade showed off couples donning complementary ensembles for four different phases of marriage: honeymooning, sports, business activity and evening gayety. Glenda took part in the nightlife "romance wardrobe" event, joining fellow judges Anne Hirst, Jane Pickens and Bea Wain. Cool evening jackets in light colors for men were the "outstanding innovation."[3]

During September 1940, Glenda became involved with the 1,410 female members of the Committee to Defend America by Aiding the Allies. The group's campaign to call every housewife in New York's five boroughs (735,488 residential numbers) was waged in the hope of enrolling them as "Minute Americans." During her visit to the Bell System Exhibit at the World's Fair, Glenda, officially opening the drive, phoned Constance Bennett in Hollywood. Bennett vowed to ask her Congressional representatives to support the committee's principles, as established by chairman William Allen White.

During the run of *Separate Rooms*, Glenda, thanks to a sore throat, met Dr. Henry Ross, a West Point, University of Rochester and Harvard Medical School–educated diagnostician. Ross practiced at Doctor's Hospital and served as house physician at several Manhattan hotels including the Hilton, Lexington and Essex House.

Glenda *almost* costarred with Bob Hope, Bing Crosby and Dorothy Lamour in Paramount's *Road to Zanzibar* (1941), the second entry in the popular musical-comedy series, which was shot by director Victor Schertzinger in November and December 1940. Though she was announced for the role of Julia Quimby, Una Merkel eventually was cast.

She did, however, "costar" with her friends Mary Brian and Lyle Talbot at the 21st Annual Charity Dinner and Dance of Motion Picture Associates held at the Hotel Astor on November 20. Several other Warner Bros. veterans, including Marian Marsh and Claire Trevor, were also on hand to help the studio promote *Knute Rockne—All American* (1940), the new biopic starring Pat O'Brien, Gale Page, Ronald Reagan and Donald Crisp.

Glenda's love of felines was on exhibit in the Village Room of Manhattan's Hotel Taft on January 10, 1941. Ray Perkins and frequent collaborator Alan Dinehart joined her in presenting awards and prizes to finalists at the Atlantic Cat Club's 39th annual championship cat show. Categories for Siamese,

Glenda and Dr. Henry Ross pictured on their wedding day (January 19, 1941).

Domestic Short Hairs, Manx, Household Pets and Indian were included, as well as awards for individual animals. Best in Show was awarded to "Eiderdown Hoga-Baba," a red male Persian owned by Mary B. W. Smith of Pitman, New Jersey.

On January 19, Glenda and Dr. Ross were married by Police Judge Michael Andrus at the home of the groom's friend, Dr. Irving H. Saxe, in Passaic, New Jersey. Mary Brian was Glenda's maid of honor. Another Ross pal, Nat Rosoff, stood up as best man.

When not appearing in *Separate Rooms*, Glenda began to settle into her new husband's Park Avenue apartment and 50-acre estate in Brewster, New York. In the coming year, she sold her San Fernando home to B-Western icon George "Gabby" Hayes. Tommy Farrell said of Ross, "He was the kind of man you had to admire: so bright, so brilliant and such a sweet person."[4]

On June 23, 1941, Glenda turned in her withdrawal notice to the *Separate Rooms* company, to take effect on July 5, when she was scheduled to leave for Hollywood. She had been hired by her friend Mervyn LeRoy to appear in his MGM film *Johnny Eager*, slated to begin shooting on September 2. Held over in the play for a few extra performances, Glenda finally left for the West Coast on July 14.

The *Johnny Eager* shoot wrapped on October 28, 1941. LeRoy kept the principals, including Robert Taylor, Lana Turner and Van Heflin, busy for nearly two months, but Glenda's one-scene role was shot very quickly. Johnny Eager (Robert Taylor) is an ex-con who drives a taxi but moonlights as a racketeer intent on opening a new, lavish gambling joint. A heartless, selfish heel, he makes the mistake of falling in love with society girl Lisbeth Bard (Lana Turner), a move that leads to his downfall in a hail of bullets in the middle of a lonely street.

Glenda's brief turn as Johnny's former girlfriend, Mae Blythe, now happily married to a police officer, is quite poignant. Her husband, Officer No. 711 (Byron Shores), was moved to a distant beat, due to Johnny's racketeering activities; but now she asks Eager if he can use his influence to get hubby transferred closer to home. Johnny refuses. His only friend, cynical alcoholic Jeff Hartnett (Van Heflin), tries to prod him into an honest life, but ultimately ends up in the street, tearfully cradling the dying man in his arms. The officer reporting to the crime scene is wearing badge 711.

Van Heflin brilliantly steals the film. Receiving enthusiastic reviews, he also won a Best Supporting Actor Academy Award for his performance. In "The Role I Liked Best," a February 1947 article for *The Saturday Evening Post*, Heflin cited Jeff in *Johnny Eager*.

Following *Johnny Eager*, Glenda went to work on

Johnny Eager (Metro-Goldwyn-Mayer, 1942; directed by Mervyn LeRoy). **Three-sheet poster used to promote the film.**

Director Mervyn LeRoy, Henry O'Neill and Glenda chat on the set of *Johnny Eager.*

Twin Beds, shot for Edward Small Productions by director Tim Whelan from late September to late October 1941. A tried and true bedroom farce, the familiar material is enlivened by a fine cast, including Glenda, her Warner Bros. colleague George Brent, Joan Bennett, Mischa Auer, Una Merkel and Ernest Truex. Particularly praising the comic contributions of Auer, *Film Daily* reported:

> Joan Bennett vies for feminine first place with prodigal, Glenda Farrell, whose tough wife role is a standout.[5]

On October 27, members of the Theatrical, Motion Picture and Radio Division of the Citizens Committee for the Re-Election of LaGuardia, McGoldrick and Morris gathered for a campaign luncheon in the grand ballroom of Manhattan's Hotel Astor. The three-dais event, at which Mayor LaGuardia spoke, drew 70 notables, including Glenda, Tallulah Bankhead, Ethel Barrymore, Irving Berlin, Burgess Meredith, Eddie Cantor, Helen Hayes, Ben Hecht, Al Jolson, Elia Kazan, Oscar Levant, Paul Lukas, Clifford Odets, Cole Porter, Bill Robinson, Luise Rainer, Lyle Talbot and Billy Rose.

When the United States declared war on Japan in December 1941, Dr. Ross enlisted in the Army, training as a flight surgeon at San Antonio. After serving as resident flight surgeon at West Point and the head of the Stewart Field hospital, he was ordered to join General Dwight D. Eisenhower's health mission to France. He eventually attained the rank of colonel, and was one of the first high-ranking medical officers to inspect the Nazi concentration camps. He reported to Eisenhower on the appalling conditions of the camps and organized the French and German medical personnel to treat the survivors.

On April 29, 1942, Glenda opened in William Roos' comedy *The Life of Reilly* at the Broadhurst Theatre. After its first preview five days earlier, Glenda spent some time being interviewed by a group of 100 high school newspaper editors. By May 2, after only five performances, the Broadway "run" was over. The disappointed cast also included fellow Warner Bros. veteran Polly Walters, who so adeptly played dumb blondes during the early 1930s.

During the World War II years, Glenda toured summer theaters in the East. Tommy, then a student at the University of Arizona, acted as his mother's "advance man" and learned his own craft as an actor by rehearsing her parts with the rest of the cast, and making certain that the lighting was just right. When show time arrived, Glenda would take the stage, using her prodigious talent for memorization to deliver a spot-on performance. Tommy described her process for developing a role:

Corporal Tommy Farrell, U.S. Army, and his proud mother relax at the Stork Club, New York City (1942).

She didn't just get a script, learn the words, then get up and do it. She read the script entirely, everyone's parts, to see what everyone's connection was, and that's what she taught me to do. When she approached a part, she would read it, think about it and then she would say, "Let's see what we can do with this lady." Then, she'd go to work![6]

Tommy, who attained the rank of corporal in the U.S. Army Air Corps, was hired by George Abbott to appear in two Broadway shows, *Strip for Action* (1942-1943) and *Winged Victory* (1943-1944). The latter was adapted for a 1944 film version in which Tommy made his big-screen debut. He also teamed up with song-and-dance men Jack Williams, Kenny Roberts and Red Buttons to form a musical comedy group that toured throughout Europe, entertaining the troops.

George Stevens' delightful *The Talk of the Town*, shot at Columbia from January 19 through April 8, 1942, went through a series of 12 working titles before a final decision was made. A masterful blend of comedy, drama and murder mystery, the film is one of the finest in which Glenda appears. (Claire Trevor was originally announced for her role of beauty parlor proprietor Regina Bush.)

"Strip for Action," a new comedy from the typewriters of Howard Lindsay and Russel McKinley Crouse, opens tonight at the National under the sponsorship of the authors and Oscar Serlin, the same trio who were responsible for "Life With Father." The action of the show revolves around the misadventures of a burlesque troupe which enters a military camp for the unauthorized purpose of entertaining the troops.

Keenan Wynn, Eleanor Lynn, Joey Faye, Jean Carter and Murray Leonard are featured in the cast of forty-nine players that also includes Billy Koud, Boo La Von, Harry Bannister, Tommy Farrell, Leslie Barrie and Paul Huber. Bretaigne Windust is the director and Raymond Sovey designed the sets. Tickets for tonight are scaled from $5.50 to $1.65; thereafter, from $3.85 to $1.10. Tonight's curtain will rise at 8:40.

New York Times, Sept. 30, 1942

Cary Grant, Jean Arthur and Ronald Colman are the dream cast in this endlessly entertaining romp written by Dale Van Every, Irwin Shaw and Sidney Buchman from a story by Sidney Harmon, with an exciting and atmospheric opening jailbreak scene worthy of a classic suspense thriller, all beautifully rendered by ace cinematographer Ted Tetzlaff. One working title, *Mr. Twilight*, was dropped after Grant, fearing that he'd be overshadowed by his esteemed colleague, suggested that it might lead audiences to believe that the film was about only one male character, namely Colman's.

Grant is Leopold Dilg, a local agitator accused of torching a woolen mill and incinerating the foreman, Clyde Bracken (Tom Tyler), whose only "re-

The Talk of the Town (Columbia, 1942; directed by George Stevens). Andrew Holmes (Charles Dingle, left, behind man with camera), Regina Bush (Glenda), Jake (Dewey Robinson, center), Sam Yates (Edgar Buchanan), Professor Michael Lightcap (Ronald Colman) and Nora Shelley (Jean Arthur).

main" is a charred shot-put medal. After busting out of the slammer, Dilg hides in the attic of a house rented out by schoolteacher Nora Shelley (Jean Arthur). The current tenant, law professor Michael Lightcap (Ronald Colman), arrives early, setting into motion a series of madcap events culminating with his appointment to the Supreme Court of the United States and the union of Leopold and Nora.

Lightcap is so intent on wooing Miss Regina Bush (Glenda), the girlfriend of the "late" Bracken, into revealing the truth about the fire and "murder" that he shaves off his beloved beard of 15 years. Rex Ingram, as Lightcap's "man" Tilney, weeps as his boss performs the shearing.

The scene then dissolves to Regina's beauty parlor, where she finishes giving the Professor a manicure. "You have beautiful hands," she tells him, "scholarly. Clyde had hands you could use to knock in spikes with."

"Who is Clyde?" asks Lightcap.

"Who *was* Clyde would be more accurate," Regina emphasizes, pulling out a black handkerchief. "I'm in mourning. It's a great hardship, because I'm the type of girl who loves to get around." As she rings the cash register, she

The Talk of the Town (Columbia, 1942; directed by George Stevens). **In this rare candid, director George Stevens describes the beauty parlor scene to Glenda and Ronald Colman.**

continues, "Gee, I wish he wasn't dead—at least for one night. I sure would love to go dancing tonight."

"Miss Bush," Lightcap graciously replies, "I wonder if I might have the pleasure of taking you dancing tonight?"

Stevens cuts to a close-up of Glenda, as the surprised Regina responds, "The ple*aaaa*-sure? Well, say, now that's really something. I don't know what to say. It takes my breath away." Giving him a long glance, she compliments, "Why, you're *real* cute. Listen, you blow your horn tonight at seven, right outside—Sonny." ("Sonny" is the dreaded law school nickname that prompted him to grow his trademark beard.)

"You dance divinely, Miss Bush," Lightcap tells her that evening. "Your physical coordinations are—remarkable."

"I thought I'd heard them all," she replies, "but your line's brand new."

A furious jitterbug sends them retreating to a table for some champagne. "You know, you're definitely a superior person, Miss Bush," says Lightcap. "Far too superior for this kind of exhibition."

"Ah, you're cute," she responds, revealing some tipsiness. "You know what? If I was free, I would take you very, very seriously."

The Talk of the Town (Columbia, 1942; directed by George Stevens). Glenda and Ronald Colman in another rare candid shot on the beauty parlor scene.

"Oh, but you *are* free, aren't you?" he inquisitively reminds her. "Your gentleman friend is, a—he's dead, isn't he?"

"That's the *general impression*," she answers, continuing to sip her champagne.

As Lightcap continues his flattery, Regina asks for another dance, then a kiss, and finally pulls from her purse a letter written by the "dead" Clyde Bracken.

The sweet talk goes on, but when Lightcap offhandedly mentions Bracken's "moronic handwriting," noting the scrawled return address on the envelope, Regina, even in her slight alcoholic haze, realizes the whole date was a carefully planned deception. "Help! Help!" she yells to the other club patrons. "Throw this guy out!" Angrily turning back to the Professor, she accuses. "You dirty double-crosser! Get him out of here!"

The mystery solved, now Lightcap, Dilg and Nora are able to retrieve the in-hiding Bracken and prove Leopold's innocence. With the whole town up in arms, ready to lynch him, Leopold and Lightcap make certain he gets a fair hearing. The Professor's eloquent exposition proves he is worthy of sitting on the Supreme Court.

Glenda is perfectly cast in a cleverly written film loaded with superlative contributions from all concerned. *The Talk of the Town* was nominated for sev-

The Talk of the Town (**Columbia, 1942; directed by George Stevens**). **Regina Bush (Glenda) trips the light fantastic with the elegant Professor Michael Lightcap (Ronald Colman).**

en Academy Awards: Best Picture; Best Writing, Story; Best Writing, Screenplay; Best Cinematography, Black-and-White; Best Art Direction—Interior Decoration, Black-and-White; Best Film Editing; and Best Music, Scoring of a Dramatic or Comedy Picture. Incredibly, none of the stellar performers received a nomination.

Glenda celebrated her 38th birthday (actually her 41st) on June 30, 1942. Always the perfect host, she decided to bake a separate small, personalized cake for each family member, an act publicized by General Mills, whose "Betty Crocker" columnist wrote:

> Everybody has fun at Glenda Farrell's parties. That's why she's one of Hollywood's most popular hostesses, and why invitations to her home are enthusiastically welcomed by her numerous friends and relatives. The secret of Glenda's success as a hostess can be explained by the fact that, in addition to her warm Irish charm, she has an inborn ability to know how to please the other fellow. One of her pet theories is that everyone appreciates individual attention, and she applies that practice to her parties.

The syndicated column included recipes for Glenda's creations, including Lemon Snow Cake, Baby Baltimore Cakes and Chocolate Pecan Cake.

Glenda's next feature, *City Without Men*, was an independent effort for Samuel Bronston Productions directed by Sidney Salkow from August 20 to September 26, 1942. Released by Columbia in January 1943, the film, set five months prior to the attack on Pearl Harbor, deals with Tom Adams (Michael Duane), a U.S. Navy man wrongfully convicted of collaborating with Japanese saboteurs. His fiancée, Nancy Johnson (Linda Darnell), fighting to exonerate him, moves into a boardinghouse near Blackport Prison where she rooms with other prisoners' wives, including Billie LaRue (Glenda, who replaced Claire Trevor), a tough-talking former burlesque queen.

The women work together at a laundry six days each week, with Sunday reserved for visiting the prison. Even though Adams' advocate, Judge Michael Malloy (Edgar Buchanan), proves to be a drunken fraud, he eventually pleads the case to his brother, Senator Malloy (Boyd Davis), head of the parole board. Set free, Adams, back in uniform, is reunited with Nancy.

The film's bow to the war effort is clumsily shoehorned into the final scenes, when Malloy preaches to his brother about Tom's patriotism and how it ties into the United States' effort to combat global oppression. Meanwhile, an attempted prison break is foiled at the last minute, and Billie swears she's

City Without Men (**Columbia, 1943; directed by Sidney Salkow**). **Nancy Johnson (Linda Darnell, second from left), Billie LaRue (Glenda) and Mr. Peters (Don De-Fore**).

A Night for Crime (**Producers Releasing Corporation, 1943; directed by Alexis Thurn-Taxis). Detective Hoffman (Ralph Sanford) and Susan Cooper (Glenda).**

giving up on her husband, Monk (Sheldon Leonard). However, this wartime version of Glenda's sarcastic, brassy broad returns to the boardinghouse to announce, "Somebody's got to keep you dames from going off the deep end."

Teaming with old pal Lyle Talbot, Glenda received top billing in *A Night for Crime*, a Poverty Row mystery directed by Alexis Thurn-Taxis for PRC in late June and early July 1943. Including appearances by real-life columnists Jimmy Starr, Erskine Johnson, Edwin Schallert and Harry Crocker, the film, set in a blackout, features Glenda as Susan Cooper, a newspaper reporter, and Talbot as her boyfriend, Joe Powell, publicity director for Motion Picture Associates Studio, as they investigate a fatal strangling that occurs in the apartment across the hall.

Lina Basquette, whose last film appearance was for John Ford in *Four Men and a Prayer* (1938), made a brief return to the screen, playing movie star Mona Harrison, whose disappearance also plays a part in the investigations. Ruby Dandridge (mother of Dorothy) also appears in a small role.

In late August 1943, the Providence Playhouse ended its 10-week summer program. Unfortunately, attendance was down from previous years, due to an extended heat wave and the Office of Price Administration's ban on the use of automobiles, which particularly affected out of town patrons' ability to attend the performances. Noted film stars, particularly Constance Bennett and Glenda, topped the list of box-office draws.

On September 30, 1943, Glenda was in New York for "United Nations Day." An enormous War Bond rally was held in Victory Square, attended by individuals who purchased bonds at values of $100 to $1 million. Emcees Ed Sullivan, Bert Lytell and Lt. Rudy Vallee welcomed a who's who of the film and radio worlds, including Glenda, Frank Sinatra, Perry Como, Walter Pidgeon, Lana Turner, Allan Jones, Billie Burke and the Ink Spots. Prior to the rally, the Entertainment Committee of the Treasury's War Finance division already had made $2 million in advance sales.

Fatigued from touring in stage work, Glenda accepted a supporting role in Columbia's *Klondike Kate* (1943) after her agent promised that the assignment wouldn't prove too taxing. When she arrived at the studio, however, director William Castle revealed that she would have to *dance* in two major production numbers. Since Glenda wasn't a dancer, the routines, including a can-can, proved one of the great challenges of her film career. The *Pittsburgh Press* reported:

> If you want to make a hit with Glenda Farrell these days, don't send her flowers or perfumes, or even a pair of nylons—bring her a bar of candy.
>
> Glenda, who dropped 20 pounds on a recent road tour, has been trying everything to regain weight. The other day Glenda received a letter on the set of *Klondike Kate* from her husband, Major Henry Ross, who is a flight surgeon at West Point.
>
> "The Army has found," wrote Glenda's favorite doctor, "that candy has proven more beneficial in putting on weight than even vitamin tablets."

Klondike Kate (**Columbia, 1943; directed by William Castle**). **As Molly, the manager of a dance troupe, Glenda, required to perform in two production numbers, faced one of the great challenges of her career.**

"But," moans Glenda, "where can a civilian like me get candy?"[7]

For the first time in seven years, Glenda and her friend Hugh Herbert shared the silver screen, in *Ever Since Venus*, shot at Columbia from May 19 to June 7, 1944. Directed by Arthur Dreifuss, who co-wrote the screenplay with McElbert Moore, this musical comedy involving "hamburger slinger" and aspiring songwriter "Tiny" Lewis (Billy Gilbert) and his efforts to sell a new number to the "all-girl" orchestra headlining the annual trade show of the American Beauty Association, provided the first major feature film role for bandleader Ina Ray Hutton. Glenda plays Babs Cartwright, Hutton's assistant,

180

Ever Since Venus (Columbia, 1944; directed by Arthur Dreifuss). This one-sheet poster was used to promote the film that reunited Glenda with Hugh Herbert for the first time in seven years.

who uses her feminine wiles to outwit the scheming J. Webster Hackett (Alan Mowbray), president of the Milo Cosmetics Company.

Herbert again performs his shtick as an eccentric businessman, in a cast also including Ann Savage, Ross Hunter, Marjorie Gateson, Thurston Hall and Fritz Feld. The excellent score includes songs by Sammy Cahn and Saul Chaplin ("Do I Need You?"), Lester Lee and Harry Harris ("Glamour for Sale," "Rosebud, I Love You") and Bernie Wayne and Ben Raleigh ("Wedding of the Boogie and the Samba"), all performed by Hutton and her band. The soundtrack also features the melody from Harold Arlen's classic "Let's Fall in Love."

In 1946 Glenda recorded a children's book, *Adventures of Buzzy Bear and Peggy Penguin.*

Glenda's next Broadway role, Judith Bancroft in Vincent Lawrence's drama *The Overtons*, ran for a total of 175 performances (at the Booth, Forrest and National Theatres) from February 6 to July 7, 1945. Directed by Elisabeth Bergner, the play costarred Arlene Francis, Charles Lang, Mary Lawrence and Jack Whiting. Following the premiere, the *New York Times'* Lewis Nichols, claiming that the cast "carr[ies] on like a drunken jazz band after hours," added that Glenda's character "has more than a pinch of Tallulah Bankhead."[8]

When not performing on stage, Glenda enjoyed keeping her presence on the airwaves. On Saturday, March 10, she starred in *Theatre of Today*, a 30-minute program broadcast on WABC radio. On June 17, she returned to Hollywood and was succeeded in her *Overtons* role by June Knight. During her trip, she studied the script for a new play, John Cecil Holm's *Growing Weather*, which she considered appearing in during the summer.

Notes:

[1]*Milwaukee Journal*, 12 September 1939, p. 7.
[2]*Milwaukee Sentinel*, 7 September 1939, p. 4.
[3]*New York Times*, 17 May 1940.
[4]Tommy Farrell, in Dan Van Neste, "Glenda Farrell: Diamond in the Rough," *Classic Images*, Vol. 275, May 1998.
[5]*Film Daily*, 21 April 1942, p. 10.
[6]Tommy Farrell, in *Classic Images*.
[7]*Pittsburgh Press*, 21 April 1942, p. 10.
[8]*New York Times*, 7 February 1945.

COLUMBIA
PICTURES
presents

Franchot · Janet
TONE · BLAIR

I LOVE TROUBLE

with JANIS ADELE GLENDA STEVEN TOM
CARTER · JERGENS · FARRELL · GERAY · POWERS

An S. SYLVAN SIMON Production

Screenplay by ROY HUGGINS from his novel, "THE DOUBLE TAKE"

Produced and directed by S. SYLVAN SIMON

Chapter 12
Live from New York ...

Paul could write *Madame Butterfly* and it wouldn't even get
me a girdle.
—Lucille Sears, "June Moon," *Studio One* (1949)

On January 4, 1946, Thomas Richards passed away, just four days short of his 47th birthday. Tommy Farrell recalled seeing his father a total of four times. During his time working at Warner Bros., Richards edited many excellent films, including *Dangerous* (1935), with Bette Davis, *Each Dawn I Die* (1939), with James Cagney and George Raft, *They Drive by Night* (1940), with Raft and Humphrey Bogart and *The Maltese Falcon* (1941), with Bogart. (He also worked as an editor on two of Glenda's films, *The Big Shakedown* and *Gold Diggers of 1937*.)

On the evening of June 8, 1946, Glenda and Henry Morgan performed on WOR radio's 30-minute program *Leave It To the Girls.* On September 3, she was the special guest on producer Ray Green's *Hollywood Open House*, a 30-minute transcribed radio program featuring top stars and comedians in adaptations of hit films. In her installment, Glenda joined Jan Murray, host Jim Ameche and the Enric Madriguera Orchestra. Previous stars on the program included Marlene Dietrich, Luise Rainer, Allan Jones, Ruth Chatterton and Ann Rutherford.

In November 1946, Glenda and Tommy provided information to the Brooklyn District Attorney's Office in the Mergenthaler Linotype Company embezzlement case. Joseph Millstein, a 45-year-old man of "agile mind," had devised a swindle that made possible an enormous increase in income for Mergenthaler cashier William Arthur Nickel, who had been arrested in Miami. The *New York*

Glenda Farrell, stage and movie actress, and her son, Tom, who was said to be about 17 years of age, called at the District Attorney's office early last night and gave information bearing on the investigation.

She called the District Attorney's office at 6 P. M. and told Assistant Chief Clerk William Kelly that she believed she had information that would clarify some points in the case. Mr. Kelly invited her and her son to visit the District Attorney's office, and they arrived there at 7:30 P. M.

Both had a talk with Mr. McDonald.

"Both talked to us and gave us information," Mr. McDonald said later. "They answered questions which were very helpful."

New York Times, Nov. 4, 1946

In November 1946, Glenda and Tommy Farrell provided information to the Brooklyn District Attorney's Office in the Mergenthaler Linotype Company embezzlement case. Here they are pictured with Harry States, a detective assigned to the investigation.

Times reported that Glenda and Tommy both met with ADA Miles McDonald and "answered questions which were very helpful."[1]

Glenda again worked for director S. Sylvan Simon, in Columbia's *The Double Take*, shot from May 14 to June 19, 1947. This B-film noir, released as *I Love Trouble* in January 1948, stars Franchot Tone as private eye Stuart Bailey, who becomes involved in an investigation that leads him from Los Ange-

I Love Trouble (Columbia, 1947; directed by S. Sylvan Simon). **Private eye Stuart Bailey (Franchot Tone, right) is aided by his rod-packing secretary, Hazel Bixby (Glenda).**

les to Portland, Oregon. Hired by politician Ralph Johnston (Tom Powers) to investigate the background of his wife (Lynn Merrick), Bailey is aided by his trusty secretary, Hazel Bixby (Glenda). This entertaining crime drama features an excellent supporting cast, including Janis Carter, John Ireland, Eduardo Ciannelli, Robert Barrat and Raymond Burr.

From late July to early August 1947, Lewis D. Collins directed *Heading for Heaven* for Ace Pictures, to be released through Producers Releasing Corporation. Glenda was cast as Nora, wife of Henry Elkins (Stuart Erwin), who steadfastly refuses to sell a 100-acre tract of land that has been in his family

Heading for Heaven **(Eagle-Lion Films, 1947; directed by Lewis D. Collins). Nora Elkins (Glenda) and her befuddled husband, Henry (Stuart Erwin).**

for three generations. Nora, wanting the windfall the sale would bring, gullibly falls for a scam hatched by a fake swami (Russ Vincent) to procure the land for National Transit Airways of Chicago.

Much of the film consists of the family squabbling over the fate of the land, including Henry's intention to keep the tract for the building of Elkins Eastern Acres, an affordable housing development. The shenanigans result in Nora leaving Henry, his supposed suicide and subsequent appearance in "spirit form" at a séance. In the end, the family reunites after NTA buys the land for an airport and the development, which will provide housing for the construction workers.

The Poverty Row, B-film situations, particularly the swami's "séances" and other scenes of forced comedy, are below the talents of the cast, including Glenda and prolific character actor Milburn Stone, who plays NTA agent Harding. Henry's command, "Sit down, you *swami salami!*" is an example of the ludicrous dialogue rampant in Lewis Collins and Ralph Mugge's screenplay. Nevertheless, Glenda remains sincere throughout.

In the B-musical *Mary Lou*, filmed in just nine days (September 5-13, 1947) by director Arthur Dreifus for release by Columbia, Glenda receives third billing behind Robert Lowery and Joan Barton. The Frankie Carle band is the real "star" of the film, as all concerned attempt to make airline stew-

Lulu Belle (**Columbia, 1948; directed by Leslie Fenton**). **Harry Randolph** (**Otto Kruger**), **Lulu Belle** (**Dorothy Lamour**) **and Molly Benson** (**Glenda**) **observe a violent brawl.**

ardess-cum-vocalist Ann Parker (Joan Barton) their new "Mary Lou" after the current canary (Abigail Adams) splits the scene in favor of a Hollywood screen test. Trouble ensues when the disillusioned would-be starlet wants to return to the band, filing a lawsuit over who can use the "Mary Lou" moniker. J. Russell Johnson, Abe Lyman and George Waggner (director of *The Wolf Man* [1941] and numerous other classic feature films and television shows) wrote the title song for the score.

Director Leslie Fenton shot *Lulu Belle*, starring Dorothy Lamour and George Montgomery, for Benedict Bogeaus Productions from October 27 to December 13, 1947. The project, originally intended for Paramount, had been delayed for more than a year due to objections from the Production Code Administration, which claimed it was based on "a story of adultery and illicit sex without the proper compensating moral values" (the Charles MacArthur–Edward Sheldon play *Lulu Belle*, produced by David Belasco on Broadway in 1926). The completed version of the film was released by Columbia in August 1948.

"New York, at the turn of the century" presents Lulu Belle (Dorothy Lamour) in her spectacular stage show. Just after she heads for her dressing room, a man bursts into the theater and shoots her and wealthy suitor, Harry Randolph (Otto Kruger), leaving them both in a coma. Though no one else witnessed the

189

Clancy Cooper and Glenda Farrell in *Lulu Belle*

shooting, the police arrest George Davis (George Montgomery), her ex-husband, who proclaims his innocence.

The film dissolves into a flashback as Davis tells his story to Commissioner Dixon (Addison Richards). In a Natchez joint, after Lulu Belle finishes a song, her friend Molly Benson (Glenda, using a Southern accent and wearing an enormous blonde wig) approaches Davis at the bar. But he gradually becomes more interested in the singer, whom he marries after selling his law practice. He soon becomes jealous, since Lulu Belle is not able to give up her wanton ways.

Molly is called in for questioning, and another flashback ensues. While performing in the New Orleans club owned by gambler Mark Brady (Albert Dekker), Lulu Belle meets Harry Randolph, who wants to take her to New York. Tired of being taunted by Butch Cooper (Greg McClure), another of his wife's boyfriends, George, who has been sitting with Molly, gets into a (very unconvincing) fistfight. Beaten badly, George grabs a fork and stabs Butch in the eye.

In New York, Randolph courts the divorced Lulu Belle, while George, having been on the lam for two years and in prison for three, is once again a free man. Lulu Belle tries to reconcile with George but none of her suitors will leave her alone.

Randolph regains consciousness, whispering to the Commissioner, just before he dies, that his wife fired the shots. Assured that Lulu Belle will recover, George leaves for Natchez.

Amidst a pedestrian pace and generally artificial trappings, Glenda, enjoying a lot of screen time, does her best to bring some naturalism to her characterization. Unlike some of her earlier films, particularly at Warner Bros., in which she was required to *appear* to smoke, here she turns down a cigarette offered by Addison Richards.

On January 3, 1949, Glenda, paired with old buddy Guy Kibbee, made her television debut in "The Mirror and the Manicure" on NBC's *Chevrolet Tele-Theater*, which had made its first series broadcast the previous September. On June 22, she starred in the Jazz Age satire "June Moon" on *Westinghouse Presents Studio One*, broadcast by CBS. (First aired on November 7, 1948, the acclaimed series ran until September 29, 1958.)

Directed by Walter Hart, "June Moon" was adapted from the George S. Kaufman and Ring Lardner play by Gerald Goode. Glenda plays Lucille Sears, the long-suffering wife of songwriter Paul Sears (Edward Andrews), who has grown tired of trying to scrape by on a few royalties earned from silly, dull popular ditties. Paul hooks up with naïve young lyricist Fred Stevens (Jack Lemmon), who has just arrived in New York City from Schenectady in the hope of collaborating on a new hit song. Although Fred meets a beautiful dental assistant (Eva Marie Saint) on the train, he gets played for a sucker by Lucille's brash, gold-digging sister, Eileen (Jean Carson), who soon helps deplete his savings and nearly drags him to the altar.

With her "running commentary of the vicissitudes of the songwriting business," Lucille is at the very core of Kaufman and Lardner's cynical view of commercial tunesmiths in 1929.[2] Glenda receives top billing in a fine cast that includes Lemmon and Saint, two superb actors during the early years of their respective careers.

Referring to the magnitude of advance royalties that her husband has wangled from publisher Joe Hart (Henry Lascoe), Lucille admits, "Paul could write *Madame Butterfly* and it wouldn't even get me a girdle."

Unlike some actors who looked down on the new medium, Glenda enjoyed working in television. In his production summary for a restored release of the *Studio One* program, Larry James Gianakos wrote:

> "June Moon" is ... bolstered by a superior performance from silver screen veteran Glenda Farrell, who was born to play the caustic Lucille Sears ... Farrell became a television staple, delving into the medium's huge tapestry of available characters during the live anthology period. Afterwards, she performed many memorable filmed television roles ...[3]

Opens **TONIGHT 8:00 Sharp**
GEORGE ABBOTT presents a New Comedy
MRS. **GIBBONS' BOYS**
by WILL GLICKMAN & JOSEPH STEIN
with LOIS   GLENDA   FRANCIS
BOLTON   FARRELL   COMPTON
Staged by Mr. Abbott
MUSIC BOX THEA., 45th St. West of B'way
TONIGHT $6.00 to 1.80. Eves. thereafter $4.80
to 1.80. Mats. Sat. & Wed. $3.60 to 1.20 (tax incl.)

Glenda looked for a variety of dramatic and comic roles on television and had the luxury of choosing only those scripts that included a character she really wanted to play. She freely admitted that being married to a successful professional allowed her to turn down material she didn't like, and some of the sponsor-driven, mundane television stories didn't appeal to her. Though she eventually was offered several Hollywood television series, she turned down all of them, because rehearsing and shooting in California on a 39-week schedule would have taken her away from her New York homes and the Broadway stage for too long.

From May 5-7, 1949 Glenda unfortunately appeared in another Broadway flop, Will Glickman and Joseph Stein's comedy *Mrs. Gibbons' Boys*, produced and directed by George Abbott at the Music Box Theatre. As Myra Ward, Glenda saw Edward Andrews, Royal Dano and Ray Walston support her and the fine cast.

Glenda returned to CBS on February 13, 1950, for "The Gaudy Lady" episode of *The Silver Theatre*, hosted by Conrad Nagel. CBS also produced a small-screen version of Harry Leon Wilson's popular play *Ruggles of Red Gap*, aired on February 27, 1951. This *Prudential Family Playhouse* presentation costarred Glenda, Walter Abel, Eva Condon, Henry Jones and Cyril Ritchard. The following week, Glenda was at ABC, for the March 3 broadcast of "Fountain of Youth" on the short-lived series *Faith Baldwin Romance Theatre.*

On May 15, 1951, Glenda was honored at the monthly breakfast of New York's Twelfth Night Club, located at 21 West 47th Street. Two weeks later, she joined Nils Asther, Melville Cooper, Jack Albertson and Jean Stapleton for the CBS television episode "The Come-Back," written by Eric Hatch and directed by Curt Conway for the *Starlight Theatre.* Following a year-long hiatus from the small screen, she returned on April 15, 1952, for writer-actress Kay Arthur's "The Darkroom" on NBC's *Armstrong Circle Theatre,* supported by Louise Allbritton, Walter Matthau and John Newland. Of working on live television, she said:

> It's tough work … but I love it. It's not easy for movie people, because they have to remember all their lines. Also, they have to learn to conserve their energy so they can sustain their performance for an hour. That's something you don't learn in pictures.[4]

Notes:

[1]*New York Times*, 4 November 1946.
[2]Larry James Gianakos, *Studio One Anthology*, 6-DVD set book (KOCH Entertainment, 2008), p. 29.
[3]Larry James Gianakos, p. 29.
[4]*Pittsburgh Post-Gazette*, 19 June 1952, p. 18.

Chapter 13
Glenda Goes Gunslinger

Hey, I've got a bottle of eight-year-old stashed away. Get that
cup over there and we'll drink a toast to those good old days.
To Peso, the gayest, the most gallant, the most *man* man in
this whole cockeyed world!
—Fanny Webson, *Apache War Smoke* (1952)

During the shooting of *Apache Trail*, her first Hollywood film in five years,
Glenda spoke about her preference for the East Coast and stage work:

> Whenever things get dull, I can always do television or a play.
> I don't miss my old pals, because I see more of them in New
> York ... You go to a restaurant in Hollywood and you don't
> see anybody but agents and producers.
>
> There's no social life here anymore. The only time you
> see people is when someone throws a big party, and they can't
> afford to do that anymore.
>
> I went through the mill here ... Sometimes I would be in
> three pictures that were shooting at the same time. It was good
> experience. But I preferred to go back to the stage.[1]

Glenda hadn't given up on filmmaking, however. She still sought out roles
that differed from the types of fast-talking characters she played while at Warner Bros. during the 1930s. Although she appeared in fewer feature films as
time went on, she always enjoyed the experience of acting in them. The major
difference between developing a character for the stage or live television and
a motion picture was one of continuity: Whereas she could logically build the
persona and actions of a "live" character as the play progressed, the primarily
out-of-sequence nature of filmmaking didn't allow as many opportunities for
this process.

Director Harold Kress began shooting *Apache Trail* for MGM in late May
1952. Working on a tight, two-week schedule, the crew filmed many of the exteriors in Soledad Canyon, near Monterey, California. Other footage was taken
from *Apache Trail* (1942), an earlier adaptation (codirected by Richard Thorpe
and Richard Rosson, and starring Lloyd Nolan and Donna Reed) of the story
"Stage Station" by Ernest Haycox. (Haycox's story "Stage to Lordsburg" was
used by John Ford and Dudley Nichols as the basis for the celebrated *Stagecoach* [1939].)

Apache War Smoke (**Metro-Goldwyn-Mayer, 1952; directed by Harold Kress**). **Madre (Argentina Brunetti) examines the two pistols that Fanny Webson (Glenda) carries in her suitcase.**

Gilbert Roland stars as Peso Herrera, an infamous bandit intent on robbing gold from the strongbox of a Wells Fargo stagecoach. His estranged son, Tom (Robert Horton), head of the Tonto Valley stage station, is busy preparing for an attack by Apaches seeking vengeance against a devious white man who murdered some of their people in cold blood. Assuming the killer to be Peso, Tom confiscates his two pistols, while several passengers arrive on the incoming stagecoach. One of the travelers is Fanny Webson (Glenda), an old "friend" of Peso's on her way to San Francisco to open a new gambling establishment. Following a fierce battle with the Apaches, Peso identifies the real killer, a local sidewinder named Pike Curtis (Myron Healey), changes clothes with him, and then sends him riding out to be dealt with by the Native American horde.

In this leisurely-paced Western, Glenda shares several excellent scenes with the devilishly charming Gilbert Roland. When they first become reacquainted, Peso sneaks through the window into Fanny's bedroom and swats her rear end with his hat. They share a drink and she sits on his lap as they reminisce. Toting two pistols (Glenda twirls one of them), she gives them to Peso. Later, for moral support, Fanny pours two more drinks of "Golden Delight" whiskey. When Peso mentions the dire circumstances he may be in, she replies, "Don't talk like that. You'll have me crying in my booze." During a second Apache attack, Fanny is still drinking whiskey as she fires a rifle out the window of the station, killing one of the marauders.

With the tribe avenged, the film, released as *Apache War Smoke*, ends with Peso riding after the stagecoach, presumably to join Fanny. However, the box of gold is still aboard and another of his sons, Luis (Robert Blake), is driving the team.

In late September 1952, Universal began shooting locations on New York's lower East Side and in Brooklyn for *Night Flowers*, screenwriter Ray Buffum's melodrama of slum life starring Joyce Holden, Patricia Hardy, Harvey Lembeck and Glenda, again cast in a limited mother role. However, her motherly input also involved her son, Tommy, who appears in a small supporting part. Under the direction of Jack Arnold, filming wrapped in November for a January 1953 release under the title *Girls in the Night*.

Glenda plays Alice Haynes, who longs to move her family out of the ghetto to Long Island. Her husband, Charlie (Anthony Ross), having just received a promotion, intends to honor her wish but is injured by a speeding car after leaving a neighborhood bar. Alice has her hands full dealing with her children's entanglements in their rough area of the city, culminating with a murder

Girls in the Night (Universal, 1953; directed by Jack Arnold). Alice Haynes (Glenda), her son, Chuck (Harvey Lembeck), and daughter, Hannah (Patricia Hardy).

charge against her son, Chuck (Harvey Lembeck), who has been framed by young hoodlum Irv Kelleher (Don Gordon) for the shooting of Blind Minosa (Paul E. Burns), a local beggar.

Chuck did steal some hidden money from Minosa's shack, but failed to see his already dead body during the burglary. The plot thickens as the Haynes teens and their friends all become involved in the case, but the real killer is identified after Kelleher's criminal activities get the best of him and he is accidentally killed while running away from Chuck and the police. The stolen money is returned and the Haynes family moves out of the slum. Though strictly a low-budget affair, this example of the 1950s teen exploitation genre benefits from cinematographer Carl Guthrie's gritty location work.

The live science-fiction anthology series *Tales of Tomorrow* premiered on ABC on August 3, 1951, and ran for two seasons, featuring such guest stars as Boris Karloff, Lon Chaney, Jr., Chester Morris, Bruce Cabot, Thomas Mitchell and Rod Steiger. On February 6, 1953, Glenda appeared in the 30-minute episode "The Build-Box." On April 14,  she returned to NBC's *Armstrong Circle Theatre*, in Hamilton Benz's "The Straight and Narrow," which paired her with a 32-year-old Walter Matthau.

Glenda's cousin Jerry Hopper cast her with Charlton Heston, Robert Young, Nicole Maurey and Thomas Mitchell in the Technicolor adventure epic *Legend of the Incas*, shot on location at Cuzco and Machu Picchu, Peru, from mid-October to early December 1953. The opening credits of the film, released as *Secret of the Incas* in June 1954, include an apt description of its content:

> In the high Andes of Peru—where much of this picture was filmed—the descendants of the Inca have searched for centuries for the symbol of their past glories—a fabulous golden disc encrusted with jewels—there are others—who search—but only for gold.

The excellent supporting cast includes Michael Pate, Leon Askin, William Henry and Kurt Katch. Yma Sumac, a singer of Indian-Spanish descent,

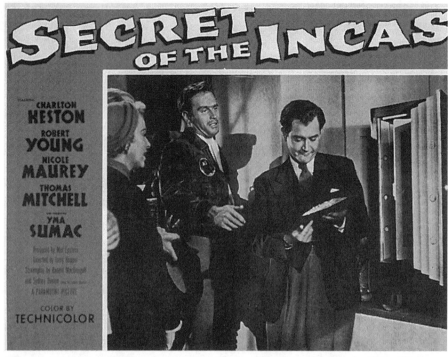

CHARLTON
HESTON

ROBERT
YOUNG

NICOLE
MAUREY

THOMAS
MITCHELL

YMA
SUMAC

COLOR BY
TECHNICOLOR

Secret of the Incas (**Paramount, 1954; directed by Jerry Hopper**). **Mrs. Winston (Glenda), a married tourist, is quite enamored with Cuzco guide and adventurer Harry Steele (Charlton Heston, center).**

made her debut in the film, after Sidney Boehm met her at a party and developed the idea for the screenplay, which he co-wrote with Ranald MacDougall. Five-hundred native Indians were used as extras. Dr. Albert A. Giesecke, former president of the University of Cuzco, and Cesar Miro served as technical advisors.

Glenda plays Mrs. Winston, a married tourist enamored with Cuzco guide Harry Steele (Charlton Heston), who seeks the jewel-encrusted sunburst disc that weighs "30 pounds—pure gold." In the meantime, Steele meets Elena Antonescu (Nicole Maurey), a Romanian fugitive trying to make her way to Mexico, thus having a chance to get to the United States. For a price, he agrees to help, but takes her by way of Machu Picchu, where they run into an archaeological expedition led by Dr. Stanley Moorehead (Robert Young).

Heston was beginning to make his mark as the star of historical and adventure spectacles. In the past year, he had appeared in *Pony Express* (1953), *The President's Lady* (1953) and *The Naked Jungle* (1954), and soon would play William Clark in *The Far Horizons* (1955) and Moses in *The Ten Commandments* (1956).

Precious little of the 101-minute running time is devoted to the hunt for the priceless disc, while the meandering plot too often focuses on the formulaic romantic triangle involving Heston, Young and Maurey. In the end (in

Secret of the Incas (**Paramount, 1954; directed by Jerry Hopper**). **Mrs. Winston (Glenda) flirts with Harry Steele (Charlton Heston).**

the tradition of films about treasure), Ed Morgan (Thomas Mitchell) tells the members of the expedition that the sunburst is nothing more than a stone.

But Steele knows better, discovers the actual golden disc and then loses it to Morgan, who is chased by a tribe of Indians into the mountains. After struggling with Steele, Morgan plummets to his death, and the tour guide returns the sunburst to the natives, who place it back in the Temple of the Sun, from which it had been stolen centuries earlier. (Steven Spielberg "borrowed" heavily from these scenes for his *Raiders of the Lost Ark* [1981].)

In mid-December 1953, Glenda began working with director Frank Tashlin at RKO. Though Steve Fisher and Alex Gottlieb's play *Susan Slept Here* had yet to be published or performed (it eventually ran for a mere 16 performances in 1956), Howard Hughes nonetheless green-lit the film adaptation.

The title role, a 17-year-old "juvenile delinquent" who is presented as a Christmas "gift" from Police Sergeant Sam Hanlon (Herb Vigran) to struggling screenwriter Mark Christopher (Dick Powell) as impetus for a new script, went to 21-year-old MGM loan-out Debbie Reynolds. Dan Dailey had been announced for the Christopher role, but a prior commitment to 20th Century-Fox made him unavailable. Mickey Rooney and Robert Mitchum also had been considered, but the part ultimately fell into the capable hands of the 49-year-old Powell, who made his cinematic swansong in the film (which also marked his fourth and final screen collaboration with Glenda).

Glenda with Debbie Reynolds and Alvy Moore in *Susan Slept Here*.

The age difference between the lead characters (Christopher is depicted as 35) raised some eyebrows with censors in Chicago, but the film did not meet with opposition from the Production Code Administration. Anne Francis, then 23, was cast as Christopher's frustrated girlfriend, Isabella Alexander. Receiving fourth billing, Glenda, at 52, was three years older than Powell, and their characters' mature relationship provides the comic center of the film.

Christopher's longtime private secretary, Maude Snodgrass (Glenda), is also qualified as a mother because she "happened to have typed the script for *Stella Dallas*." Maude holds the entire crew, including Christopher's "assistant," Virgil (Alvy Moore), together, and is largely responsible for her boss' decision to remain married to Susan (after he weds her in Las Vegas "to keep her out of jail" on a vagrancy charge).

Maude's devotion to Christopher knows no bounds, and the scene in which Glenda types the new script while wearing mittens and cozying up to the fireplace is a comic high point. In the closing scene, Maude finally finds happiness by accepting the marriage proposal of her dream man, "Oswald from North Dakota" (Red Skelton, who makes a surprise cameo).

Susan Slept Here received two Academy Award nominations, one for Best Sound Recording and another for Best Song, Jack Lawrence and Richard Myers' "Hold My Hand," performed by Don Cornell and played on a phonograph in the film.

Of her stage work, Glenda again emphasized:

> There's something more satisfying about working in a play. You get that immediate response from the audience, and you feel that your performance is your own. In pictures you get frustrated because you feel you have no power over what you're doing.[2]

In Walter Macken's *Home is the Hero*, she played Daylia, the long-suffering wife of Dovetail, a braggart played by J. Pat O'Malley. Running for 30 performances at the Booth Theatre during September and October 1954, Worthington Miner directed the drama that costarred Frances Fuller, Peggy Ann Garner and Christopher Plummer.

Glenda also continued her frequent television work. She was reteamed with Frank McHugh for the "House of Hatred" episode of *Justice*, broadcast February 17, 1955 on NBC. Sidney Lumet directed her in a cast including John Cassavetes, Will Kuluva, Robert Preston and Mark Rydell for Reginald Rose's "Crime in the Streets," which aired March 8 on ABC's *The Elgin Hour*. Later in the year, Don Siegel made a feature film version, also featuring Cassavetes, Kuluva and Rydell, as well as Sal Mineo and James Whitmore.

Studio One welcomed Glenda back on March 21, 1955, for an adaptation of Howard Rodman's "Miss Turner's Decision," costarring Edward Andrews and Nina Foch. On June 1, she returned to Hollywood to begin working on the feature film *The Girl in the Red Velvet Swing*, which was in production until mid-July.

The Girl in the Red Velvet

The Girl in the Red Velvet Swing (20th Century-Fox, 1955; directed by Richard Fleischer). Glenda plays the mother of the tragic Evelyn Nesbit (Joan Collins) in this lavish drama based on the 1906 Thaw-White murder case. She receives sixth billing on this one-sheet poster.

Swing opens with the following written prologue:

In 1906, the Thaw-White murder case rocked America. Because it involved a man of great consequence, another of great wealth and a girl of extraordinary beauty, it remains unique in the annals of crime ... What follows is taken from actual reports of the trial, and from personal interviews with Evelyn Nesbit.

Picture Material

"The Girl in the Red Velvet Swing," the story of Evelyn Nesbit Thaw and the sensational murder of architect Stanford White by playboy Harry K. Thaw, has been filmed by Twentieth Century-Fox in Cinema-Scope with De Luxe color and opens today at the Lyric Theatre. Starred in the principal roles of the love triangle that made turn-of-the-century headlines are pert British import Joan Collins in the title role; Ray Milland as the debonair architect and Farley Granger, as the eccentric playboy millionaire husband.

Charles Brackett, who collaborated on the script with Walter Reisch after conferring with the original Evelyn, now a sprightly 70 years old, produced the still controversial drama with Richard Fleisher, ("20,000 Leagues under the Sea") as his director. Featured in the motion picture are many Broadway and Hollywood "big names" including Luther Adler, Cornelia Otis Skinner, Glenda Farrell, Frances Fuller, Philip Reed and Gale Robbins, moving against the lavish New York settings known to the "400" and Floradora queens of Broadway.

Newspaper article on the release of *The Girl in the Red Velvet Swing*.

The film was based on the infamous 1906 murder of architect Stanford White by millionaire Harry Kendall Thaw, who was jealous about White's past affair with his wife, chorus girl and artist's model Evelyn Nesbit. In 1901, when she was a member of the famed Floradora Girls chorus line, Evelyn had become interested in the married White. She also posed for artist Charles Dana Gibson, whose portrait "The Eternal Question," featured on the cover of *Colliers* magazine, is one of the best examples of his "Gibson Girl" series.

During her affair with White, Evelyn was named "The Girl in the Red Velvet Swing" because of a swing in his apartment in which she liked to sit. The mentally unstable Thaw married Evelyn in 1905. Obsessed by the thought that White had "ruined" Evelyn, Thaw gunned him down at the Roof Garden of the newly built Madison Square Garden. The scandalous revelations during the subsequent legal proceedings reverberated for decades.

20th Century-Fox paid Evelyn Nesbit $50,000 to act as consultant on the film, which was based partially on the 1953 book by Charles Samuels. Nesbit believed the book to be full of inaccuracies, and Samuels' name wasn't listed in the credits. However, several critics who reviewed the film questioned Nesbit's own version of events.

Marilyn Monroe was announced for the Nesbit role, but writer-producer Charles Brackett and director Richard Fleischer also considered Terry Moore and Debra Paget before selecting 22-year-old English beauty Joan Collins.

Robert Montgomery was first choice for the Stanford White role, which eventually went to Ray Milland. The Harry Thaw part went to Farley Granger. Glenda appears as Evelyn Nesbit's mother. The 20th Century-Fox pressbook includes a brief entry about her career:

> GLENDA FARRELL — *Mrs. Nesbit* — Longtime star-comedienne active in New York on Broadway and in TV for past five years, returning to Hollywood only periodically for roles that please her. Last was *Susan Slept Here*.

The Girl in the Red Velvet Swing is a sumptuous DeLuxe color Cinemascope film. Cinematographer Milton Krasner's work is exemplary, and the scene in which Evelyn gleefully soars in the swing is a dizzying ride for both Joan Collins and the viewer. After Harry is found not guilty by reason of insanity and is confined to an asylum, Evelyn, who refuses a cheap payoff from the Thaw family, takes a job in vaudeville as "The Girl in the Red Velvet Swing."

The film is well acted, particularly by Granger as the arrogant, violent Thaw, and Collins as the initially innocent and naïve Evelyn. Her American accent never falters. Glenda's Mrs. Nesbit is a hard-working, strong woman who looks out for her daughter's interests and well being, doing her best to advise her against unscrupulous males, although Evelyn disastrously doesn't pay heed.

Following *The Girl in the Red Velvet Swing* shoot, Glenda returned to the stage, in the William Marchant comedy *The Desk Set*, scheduled to open at the Broadhurst Theatre on October 13, 1955. However, during the pre-Broadway tour in Boston on September 13, Glenda chose to drop out of the production after the playwright decided to write a "new conception" for her role. Dorothy Blackburn was cast in the rewritten part.

Glenda was back on live television, again working with John Cassavetes for an October 9 *Goodyear Playhouse* broadcast of Reginald Rose's "The Expendable House." Directed by Daniel Petrie, the 60-minute production also featured Gena Rowlands, Pat Hingle, Jack Klugman, Lee Philips and Vaughn Taylor.

ANOTHER divorce coming up in the Godfrey-show-staff . . . Ava phones Frank twice daily but that isn't why Peggy Connolly flew back here . . . The Irving Berlins' daughter, Mary Ellen (Mrs. M. Barrett) expects a third image . . . Glenda Farrell will be matron-of-honor at Winchell Peggy Ann Garner's wedding to actor Albert ("Bus Stop") Salmi Friday . . .

Glenda received a mention in Walter Winchell's column on May 14, 1956.

The Alcoa Hour: "Doll Face" (NBC, March 18, 1956; directed by Sidney Lumet). Cast as an aging beauty queen, Glenda costarred in this television episode with old pal Frank McHugh and Suzanne Poulton.

On January 25, 1956, Glenda reprised her Broadway role for a television adaptation of "Home is the Hero," aired on NBC's *Kraft Television Theatre* and featuring Brian Donlevy, J. Pat O'Malley and Anthony Perkins. *Kraft* welcomed her back on February 15, with an ensemble cast including Steve Allen, Henry Jones and Murray Matheson, in "The Man on Roller Skates."

Glenda, playing an aging beauty queen alongside old pal Frank McHugh, once again worked with Sidney Lumet in Jerome Ross' "Doll Face," the

March 18, 1956, episode of NBC's *The Alcoa Hour*. On April 11, she joined a fine cast including Edward Arnold, Victor Jory and Elizabeth Montgomery, in "The Last Showdown" on *Kraft Television Theatre*.

> Glenda Farrell is an ex-beauty queen whose mistaken notions of her charms (25 years after winning her title) causes anguish for her family on the "Alcoa Hour" at 9 p.m. on (4) . . .

Following an eight-month hiatus, Glenda was back on television for "Cracker Money," the December 4, 1956, episode of NBC's *The Kaiser Aluminum Hour*. Though she didn't need to work, she continued to look for quality small-screen roles. She found another working for director Lewis Allen in "The Marriage Broker," aired June 12, 1957 on CBS's *The 20th Century-Fox Hour*. The excellent cast included Lloyd Corrigan, Lee Patrick, Harry Morgan and Ellen Corby.

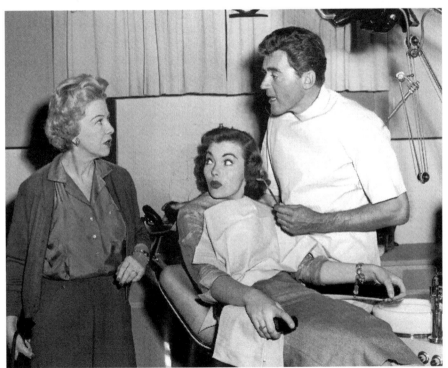

The 20th Century-Fox Hour, "The Marriage Broker," 1957 finds Glenda, Kipp Hamilton and William Bishop in a dentist's office.

A September 11, 1957, appearance in "The Old Ticket" on NBC's *Kraft Television Theatre* was followed by her work for director Paul Guilfoyle in "Federal Witness," the December 13 episode of the syndicated *Sheriff of Co-*

chise, also featuring John Bromfield, Sidney Blackmer, Joe De Santis and Roy Engel. Five days later, she was back with *Kraft* for "Polka," costarring James Gregory, Torin Thatcher and Shelley Winters.

Glenda began the New Year with another first-rate *Studio One* assignment. Theodore Apstein's adaptation of J.B. Priestley's story "The Other Place," also starring Richard Carlson, Betty Furness and Sir Cedric Hardwicke, was aired January 13, 1958 on CBS. Glenda and Betty Furness again reteamed for *Studio One* on April 28, in "The Edge of Truth," delivering a live effort alongside Paul Douglas and Barbara Pepper.

On May 31, 1958, the Brewster Garden Club held a tour of celebrities' homes called "Open House in the Brewster Area" to raise funds for a beautification project providing new flowering trees and shrubs for the rural New York community. Five residences, including those of Glenda and Dr. Ross, operatic contralto Marian Anderson, songwriter Dorothy Fields, author-actor Rex Stout, and Alieda Van Wesep (of Lord and Taylor), were on the itinerary organized by Mrs. Malcolm Edwards.

NBC's Western series *Cimarron City* ran for one season during 1958-1959. Aired on December 6, 1958, "A Respectable Girl," written by Leo Townsend and directed by James Neilson, pairs series regulars George Montgomery (whose Mayor Matt Rockford narrates during the framing story), Audrey Totter (as Beth Purcell) and John Smith (as Deputy Lane Temple) with "special guest star" Dorothy Malone and Glenda, who receives an "also starring" credit.

Borrowing *Wagon Train*'s formula of having the star (Montgomery aping Ward Bond) appear only at the beginning and end (during which he provides the voiceovers), "A Respectable Girl" features Glenda's "respectable widow" Maggie Arkins posing as the mother of Nora "Arkins" (Dorothy Malone) in order to scout Cimarron City for a possible site for a new gambling joint. In cahoots with the dreaded Sam Jethro (John Beradino), who is thrown out of town, the women pull off their ruse until Maggie is persuaded by Frank Shanley (Walter Sande) to join him in a libation at the Oklahoma Saloon.

"Ladies just don't go into places like the Oklahoma Saloon," Temple informs Nora, whose romance with the deputy is nipped in the bud by Maggie's careless female transgression. Well representing the male-centered moral code of the Old West, the episode also intertwines the subplot of cattlemen wanting to drive their herds through the town, an action that naturally results in all manner of drunken vice and violence.

The villains who aspire to keep out the cattle, going so far as to gun down both Jethro and Nora, include Harold J. Stone (typically steeled, as killer Fred Barker) and the ever-oily Hal Baylor (as the grinning, reptilian McGee). After McGee is shot off his horse, Barker meets his just reward, trampled under the hooves of a stampeding cattle herd.

Glenda's spunky "widow" sparks this uniformly well-acted episode. Dressed to the nines, Maggie causes quite a stir at the saloon, living it up as she calls out for "the bottle." Later she tells Nora that the whiskey-fueled outing provided "the only laughs I've had since Kansas City." After the smoke of the guns and the dust of the cattle settles, Maggie is the last woman standing.

Paddy Chayefsky adapted his own successful, critically acclaimed Broadway play for director Delbert Mann's screen version of *Middle of the Night*. In production from January 5 through February 15, 1959, at Gold Medal Studios in the Bronx (and shot primarily in sequence), this daringly mature film gives Glenda top support billing as Mrs. Mueller, the mother of Betty Preisser (Kim Novak), who strenuously objects to her 24-year-old daughter's serious romantic relationship with the three-decades-older Jerry Kingsley (Fredric March).

Martin Balsam, Betty Walker, Lee Philips and Effie Afton all had appeared in the Broadway version directed by Joshua Logan and starring Gena Rowlands and Edward G. Robinson, which ran for 477 performances at the ANTA Playhouse from February 8, 1956, to May 25, 1957. June Walker had played the part assigned to Glenda in the film.

***Middle of the Night* (Columbia, 1959; directed by Delbert Mann). Title lobby card used to promote Paddy Chayefsky's screen adaptation of his hit Broadway drama.**

Making the film in New York was a joy for Glenda, because, as in a Broadway play, she could return to her apartment in the evenings. Shooting the film in sequence also created a very smooth work experience for all the actors, who had rehearsed the script for three weeks before Delbert Mann rolled the cameras.

Glenda Farrell (right) as Mrs. Mueller in *Middle of the Night*

Glenda was a frequent guest star on television dramas in the 1950s.

Glenda found working with both Mann and Chayefsky a pleasant experience, as they were always approachable, willing to discuss script problems and not averse to changing dialogue or action if it would improve the performance.

Voted one of the top 10 films of 1959 by the National Board of Review, *Middle of the Night* also earned nominations for March (Golden Globe) and Mann (Cannes Film Festival). Glenda always remembered it as one of her happiest filmmaking experiences.

On March 16, 1959, Glenda appeared in Sigmund Miller's comedy *Masquerade* at the John Golden Theatre. Featuring an excellent cast including Cloris Leachman (playing Glenda's daughter) and old Warner Bros. stalwart Donald Cook, the play had the shortest run of her stage career: *one* performance. Nonetheless, *New York Times* critic Brooks Atkinson wrote:

> [Farrell] had the composed grace of a woman standing at the
> top of a pyramid of advanced civilizations.[3]

Following the flop of *Masquerade*, Glenda split her time focusing on television roles and devoting quality time to her four grandchildren. Tommy, who continued to play small roles in films and especially on television, also sought further work as a standup comedian.

April 17 found Glenda back on the small screen. "Confession of Murder," an episode of NBC's *The Further Adventures of Ellery Queen*, cast her with Lee Philips, Scott Marlowe and Wayne Morris. After sixth months of domesticity, she starred in director Mitchell Leisen's "Night Club" on *General Electric Theater*, a long-running (1953-1962) CBS series hosted by Ronald Reagan. This October 11, 1959 episode cast her with an impressive lineup including Barbara Hale, Jeanne Cooper, Amanda Blake, June Lockhart, Kathleen Freeman, Rosemary DeCamp and Hillary Brooke.

Glenda also ventured into the feature-length television movie format with *The Bells of St. Mary's* in 1959. This CBS "remake" of the 1945 film starring Bing Crosby and Ingrid Bergman cast her with Claudette Colbert, Robert Preston and Charles Ruggles.

> Steve Allen announces that he'll resume his ad-lib audience interviews starting with his NBC-TV show of Monday, Oct. 19 . . . Marc Connelly, Nancy Marchand and Glenda Farrell join Claudette Colbert, Robert Preston and Charles Ruggles in the CBS-TV production of, "The Bells of St. Mary's," set for Tuesday, Oct. 27.

Another 90-minute effort, A.E. Hotchner's adaptation of Ernest Hemingway's "The Killers," was aired on CBS's *Buick-Elec-*

tra Playhouse on November 19, 1959. In another of her many outings with reliable Frank McHugh, Glenda also was joined by Diane Baker, Dane Clark, Ned Glass, Robert Middleton, Dean Stockwell and Ray Walston.

The popular Western series *Wagon Train*, starring Ward Bond as wagon master Seth Adams and featuring a major guest star each week, made its NBC debut on Wednesday, September 18, 1957. Broadcast November 25, 1959, "The Jess MacAbee Story," written by Jean Holloway and directed by David Butler, presents Glenda and Andy Devine as an eccentric Southern married couple who haven't welcomed a single visitor to their isolated, verdant farm during their entire 20-year residence. Having appeared in several feature films with Glenda, Ward Bond, unfortunately, did not appear with her in this Robert Horton–dominated installment.

Mrs. Belle MacAbee takes care of the family and household, while Jess lies around in a hammock, rising periodically to wield a shotgun, scaring off any (fictitious) "Indians" that may be trespassing into "Paradise Valley," his sovereign territory. He is so lazy, it is difficult to believe that he has fathered five daughters, all of whom eventually are offered to Flint McCullough (Robert Horton), who is expected to choose one as his wife.

Having gone 20 years without seeing another member of the opposite sex, Belle faints upon seeing — and then touching — the handsome young McCullough. "She's never done *that* before," announces the bewildered Jess.

During dinner, none of the five girls can take their eyes off McCullough. The following morning, he helps all of them with their various field chores, as Jess unconcernedly watches from the hammock in sloth-like apathy.

When McCullough, thinking that Belle may have been held against her will, asks if she likes remaining in the valley, she explains, "Mr. MacAbee is a Southern gentleman, and a Southern gentleman always does what his lady wishes. Of course, she may not always let him know that that's what he's doing, but she has her ways of seeing that he does it."

After a friendly party of Native Americans arrive, McCullough makes a deal with them before riding to the nearest ranch for "help." Jess collapses but Belle and the five girls, all brandishing rifles, pull him through. McCullough returns with the Culpepper men, including six sons, saving himself from a problematic situation. Physical opposites as well as having completely different acting styles, Glenda and Andy Devine make a first-rate comic couple.

Notes:

[1]*Pittsburgh Post-Gazette*, 19 June 1952, p. 18.
[2]Dan Van Neste, "Glenda Farrell: Diamond in the Rough," *Classic Images*, Vol. 275, May 1998.
[3]*New York Times*, March 1959.

La irresistible Glend
Ferrell, de Warne
Brothers, con un par d
gatitos . . . ¡y con u
par de ojos!

Glenda poses with her cats for a French magazine.

Chapter 14
"The Pure Truth"

One way to confound your enemies is to tell them the truth.
Did you ever notice how little attention people pay to the truth?
—Miss Lulabelle "Looney" Watkins, "The Pure Truth," *Bonanza* (1964)

Glenda rang in the 1960s with more television roles. In the New Year-oriented "Queen of the Orange Bowl," the January 13 installment of CBS's *The U.S. Steel Hour*, she shared the small screen with a diverse cast including Johnny Carson, Anne Francis, Al Lewis, Nancy Kovack and the perennial Frank McHugh.

The April 4, 1960, NET *Play of the Week*, "A Palm Tree in a Rose Garden," featured Glenda, Barbara Barrie, Barbara Baxley and Robert Webber. Two actors who kept busy on television, Frank DeKova and Robert Ellenstein, joined her for "The Widow from Richmond," aired December 18, 1960, on ABC's *The Islanders*.

In August 1960, NBC had announced the forthcoming production of the tentatively titled "The Invincible Dude," to star George Peppard as Theodore Roosevelt and Glenda as his mother. Executive producer Mildred Freed Alberg, intending to include the "taped play" in the *Our American Heritage* series, also cast Thomas Mitchell (as TR friend and adviser Joseph Murray) and Ina Balin (as Edith Carow, TR's second wife). The finished production, retitled "The Invincible Teddy," broadcast January 13, 1961, also featured Arthur Hill and Joanne Linville. Lowell Thomas narrated Tad Mosel's teleplay, directed by Jack Smight.

Barbara Baxley and Glenda in *Play of the Week*: "A Palm Tree in a Rose Garden." (April 4, 1960)

On February 7, Glenda, Chester Morris, George Grizzard and a young Jane Fonda

212

Story of Love "A String of Beads" (NBC, February 7, 1961). Jane Fonda earned her second screen credit in this television movie costarring Glenda and George Grizzard.

appeared in "A String of Beads" on NBC's *Story of Love*. As soon as the program concluded, Glenda began memorizing yet another television script, Ranald MacDougall's "A Tale of Two Mothers," aired just 10 days later on NBC's *Westinghouse Playhouse*. The impressive cast also included Nanette Fabray, Wendell Corey and Carl Benton Reid.

The *U.S. Steel Hour* welcomed Glenda back to CBS for "Summer Rhapsody" on May 3 and "The Woman Across the Hall" on August 23. Her final television performance of 1961 was given on November 16 in *Special for Women: The Glamour Trap* for NBC.

Another Western series inspired by *Wagon Train*, *Frontier Circus* starred Chill Wills as Colonel Casey Thompson, the strong but benevolent master of a wagon caravan co-owned by Ben Travis (John Derek). Running for only one season (1961-1962) on CBS, the series, like *Wagon Train*, featured a major guest star each week. Aired April 5, 1962, "Mighty Like Rogues," directed by Alan Crosland, Jr., features Glenda as "Ma" Jukes, a colorful, rascally role she was born to play.

"He was a fine man," says Ma to her three children (who comprise her personal gang of thieves), "a wonderful husband and father—until they shot him." Inspired by his mother's words, young George Washington Jukes (Joby Baker) aspires to follow in his father's felonious footsteps.

The charm of Ma Jukes emanates from Glenda's sincere performance. Though the larcenous woman assigns specific tasks of thievery to her offspring, she believes there is nothing morally wrong with such behavior. After George enjoys helping Duffy (J. Pat O'Malley) with the show animals, he claims that working isn't so bad, prompting Ma to remark, "We'll steal you a dog sometime."

Finally, after all the children have experienced kind treatment from the troupe, they can no longer justify stealing from their new friends. Betsy Ross Jukes (Jena Engstrom), too, has enjoyed pleasant personal moments with Ben, who had overlooked her "borrowing" of another woman's dress.

"You *squealed* on your ma," Ma Jukes concludes, but is offered a "deal" by Casey, who develops a plan for the entire family to work for the Thompson-Travis Circus. "You're the *crookedest* woman I ever ran across," he tells her.

Two days after she was a Mighty Rogue, Glenda became involved with "The Naked Heiress" on CBS's *The Defenders*, directed by Jack Smight and costarring E.G. Marshall, Robert Reed and Salome Jens. Then came "The Inner Panic," another episode of *The U.S. Steel Hour*, featuring Glenda, Simon Oakland, Tommy Sands, George Segal and Martin Sheen, on September 19.

The innovative, filmed-on-location series *Route 66* ran on CBS for four seasons (1960-1964). Glenda appears as a Chicago amusement park employee in a single brief-but-poignant scene of the third-season episode "Man Out of Time," which aired on October 5, 1962. None other than Frank McHugh as a

214

Glenda and Salome Jens in *The Defender's* "The Naked Heiress"

Glenda worked on a documentary called *Special for Women: The Glamour Trap.* Unfortunately, very little information is available on this title.

"The Glamour Trap" a study of the American fetish of beauty and youth, will be presented Thursday, Nov. 16 as a "Special for Women" on Channel 2 at 1 p. m.

The program will be built around the belief that beauty is the prerequisite to fulfillment in happiness, love and marriage. The pursuit of physical beauty will be discussed with reporter Pauline Frederick by psychoanalyst Dr. Sarah Shelner and by an expert from the field of glamour.

215

retired newspaperman, Bruce Gordon as a wealthy former bootlegger and Luther Adler as a "payoff man" fresh out of prison following a 32-year sentence joined regulars Martin Milner and George Maharis.

After being rescued from a potentially fatal accident by Todd Stiles (Martin Milner), Harry Wender (Luther Adler) seeks out his old 1930 haunts, becoming increasingly paranoid as he believes someone is trying to kill him. In the end, his delusions about hearing threatening phone calls prove that the "hit" is a product of his troubled mind.

Adler is superb, particularly in his scene with Glenda, whose Laverne reveals that she and Harry had been parents to a child who died. Admitting that he "killed" the boy, Wender breaks down, but is forgiven by Laverne, who has stored an old steamer trunk full of his Prohibition-era clothing. Fearing that it was she who "wanted him dead," Harry is assured by her revelation, "I stopped hating you the day I stopped loving you."

Glenda looks suitably faded, wearing aging makeup applied by Abe Haberman. Interestingly, McHugh plays an older version of his character in *Mystery of the Wax Museum*, in which he shares many scenes with Glenda. The 1930 reference also calls to mind her participation in *Little Caesar*.

Shot by Bing Crosby Productions at Desilu Studios, the groundbreaking medical drama *Ben Casey* made its ABC debut on October 2, 1961 and ran for

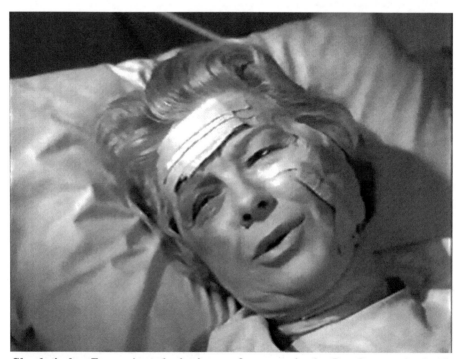

Glenda in her Emmy Award-winning performance in the *Ben Casey* episode "A Cardinal Act of Mercy."

five seasons. Broadcast on January 14 and 21, 1963, the two-part episode "A Cardinal Act of Mercy" features Glenda in a strong supporting role as Martha Morrison, a mother whose smothering attention prompts her son, Willie (Timmy Everett), to commit parental abuse that sends her to the hospital.

Kim Stanley stars as Faith Parsons, a successful but cynical and egomaniacal attorney, who challenges both Casey (Vince Edwards) and the hospital administration (represented by Sam Jaffe's intense Dr. Zorba) with outrageous behavior resulting from an addiction to morphine. Interspersed throughout the two episodes, Glenda gives an honest and moving performance as the lonely, disabled woman whose years of controlling her child has led them to the brink of tragedy.

Though their characters never really interact in the show, both Glenda and Kim Stanley won Emmy Awards for their work. Director Sydney Pollack and writer Norman Katkov also received nominations.

Glenda's swansong on *The U.S. Steel Hour* came on March 6, 1963, in "Moment of Rage," costarring another busy small-screen presence, Charles Aidman. She followed this performance with a much-needed rest.

Emmy winners Glenda Farrell and E.G. Marshall hold their awards.

U.S. Steel Hour: "Moment of Rage" (CBS, March 6, 1963). This publicity portrait was used to promote Glenda's guest-starring role on the highly acclaimed live television series.

> The prizes to Kim Stanley and Glenda Farrell for their roles in the "Ben Casey" installment entitled "A Cardinal Act of Mercy" were appropriate but also a reminder of those happier days when they were seen in live plays originating in New York. Trevor Howard's award for the lead in "The Invincible Mr. Disraeli" recognized the most rewarding aspect of an otherwise disappointing production.
>
> *New York Times*, June 2, 1963

She made her television comeback with gusto, guest starring in two television programs broadcast on October 31, 1963. More interesting is the fact that her son Tommy also appeared in both. NBC's *Dr. Kildare*: "The Exploiters" featured them alongside series regulars Richard Chamberlain and Raymond Massey.

Rawhide: "Incident at Farragut Pass" costars Glenda in the episode's "bookends," as Elizabeth Farragut, the matriarch of a ranching dynasty who refuses to allow Gil Favor (Eric Fleming) and Rowdy Yates (Clint Eastwood) to drive their herd across her land without paying a hefty price. Her rebellious, sadistic grandson Billy (Frankie Avalon, in a surprisingly effective turn) needs to be cut down a peg or two, and Elizabeth selects Favor to do just that, by signing him on as a cattle drover.

Billy's reckless, selfish shenanigans eventually lead to his death in a stampede, and Elizabeth realizes the irredeemable nature of the boy. Glenda is a tough, no-nonsense Western woman who displays a rational, accepting side in this episode of the 1959-1965 CBS series.

Glenda as Elizabeth Farragut in *Rawhide*

Tommy Farrell recalled a humorous incident that occurred while shooting the closing scene:

> Clint Eastwood broke up one day when we were working on it. At the end of the episode, I drive in, in a buggy, and Mom's in the back. She played a big ranch owner, and I was her secretary-assistant … At the end of it, she says, "Okay, you can take your cattle through my land. No charge."

219

Glenda as a ranch owner in *Rawhide* "Incident at Farragut Pass." Glenda's son Tommy Farrell (below left) said Glenda" broke up" Clint Eastwood when she told her son not to drive too fast.

So then we drive off. The soundman fell into hysterics because as we were driving away, my mother is telling me, "Not too fast now, honey. Don't go too fast. Slow down now, we're not in a big rush." Eastwood was hysterical. He said, "Keep that in!"[1]

The Golden Globe and Emmy Award–winning series *The Fugitive* ran on CBS for four seasons (1963-1967). Ida Lupino directed Glenda in her "special guest star" role in the first-season episode "Fatso," aired November 19, 1963. As on-the-lam Dr. Richard Kimball, sentenced to death for a murder he didn't commit, David Janssen is supported by Jack Weston as Davey Lambert, a wrongfully accused (of arson) young man abusively referred to as "Fatso" by his brother, Frank (Burt Brinckerhoff).

Lambert's father, David, Sr. (King Calder), believes that Davey is guilty of burning down the ranch barn and killing the horses, but his mother Maggie (Glenda) does not hold the past against him. In an interesting turn, Glenda reverses the actions of her venal Marie in *I Am a Fugitive from a Chain Gang* when Maggie, learning from Kimball that Davey is innocent, helps "The Fugitive" escape from the local sheriff (Vaughn Taylor) and Lieutenant Philip Gerard (Barry Morse), who has flown to Kentucky in an attempt to recapture his quarry.

Maggie stands up to Frank when he tries to hold Kimball at bay with a rifle. When she orders him to say nothing about their guest to the authorities, he obeys. Revealed, not only as an arsonist, but also having received a court-martial from the army eight years earlier, Frank is replaced by Davey as heir to the ranch. Moreover, the elder son is no longer called (the now politically incorrect terms) "fatso" or "big, fat, stupid slob."

The great Dan Blocker naturally dominates every episode of *Bonanza* (1959-1973) in which he is featured. Part of an ensemble cast of one of the most popular and influential series in television history, Blocker created a brilliant gentle giant in Eric "Hoss" Cartwright, a man of formidable size and power imbued with a kind heart and a fair mind in the very image

David Janssen, Glenda Farrell and Jack Weston pose together while working on *The Fugitive*.

Glenda as Looney Watkins, who saves Hoss (Dan Blocker) from the sheriff as well as cures his spring fever in *Bonanza* "The Plain Truth," which became the series' highest rated episode.

of his father, Ben (Lorne Greene). Backing him up are his two brothers, the educated, rational Adam (Pernell Roberts) and impulsive, hot-headed "Little" Joe (Michael Landon).

The list of directors, writers and performers who worked on *Bonanza* is as impressive as any television series has ever accumulated. Along with Glenda, actors from the great Warner Bros. studio era who guest-starred or played a supporting role on the show include Addison Richards, Philip Ahn, Sidney Blackmer, Henry Hull, Paul Fix, Stuart Erwin, Victor Jory, Dick Foran, Ida Lupino, Ricardo Cortez, Bruce Cabot, J. Carrol Naish, Jerome Cowan, Bobs Watson, Josephine Hutchinson, John Eldredge, Lyle Talbot and Joan Blondell. But Glenda topped them all by helping to achieve a milestone in the history of the series.

"Did you ever notice how little people pay attention to the truth?" prospector Lulabelle "Looney" Watkins (Glenda) asks Hoss as he runs from a posse intent on lynching him for a crime he didn't commit. In her efforts to help Hoss prove that the institution's owner (Lloyd Corrigan) masterminded the bank robbery, she instinctively tells the truth, yet hardly anyone ever listens.

Glenda gives a terrific, endearing comic performance in "The Pure Truth," a well-paced (by director Don McDougall) episode craftily written by a female, Lois Hire (who penned four scripts for the show during its fifth season). There are plenty of humorous moments, including Hoss' accidental detonating (with blasting powder) of Looney's camp. "For a body with a head as big as yours," she tells him, "you make little use of it!"

Dwarfed by the 6'4", 300-pound Blocker, 5'3", 115-pound Glenda adds a delightful physical component to her characterization, shoving Hoss into her tent and out of a jail cell and clobbering a criminal (Jay Lanin) in the noggin with a well-pitched rock. During the climactic fight with the bank burglars, she swiftly punches out Corrigan.

All ends well for the spring fever-wracked Hoss, who benefits from Looney's special "tonic" (a welcome replacement for the sulfur and molasses concoction force-fed him by Ben). Broadcast March 8, 1964, "The Pure Truth," thanks to an impeccable ensemble of artists, including Glenda, went on to become the highest-rated episode in the show's 14-year run.

In real life, Elvis Presley drove and gave away Cadillacs as gifts but, from 1962 through 1968, his cinematic vehicles were more the equivalent of a Rambler Cross Country station wagon. Glenda plays Ma Tatum, aunt to a 29-year-old Elvis, in *Kissin' Cousins* (1964), one of Colonel Tom Parker's formula musical-comedy pictures that padded his bank account while taking

Elvis, the soldier, poses with his mountain kinfolk, the moonshining Tatum family and their hound-dog "Hezekiah."

Metro-Goldwyn-Mayer presents **"KISSIN' COUSINS"** in Panavision® and Metrocolor

Copyright © 1964 Metro-Goldwyn-Mayer Inc.   Printed in U.S.A.   64/75

Kissin' Cousins (**Metro-Goldwyn-Mayer, 1964; directed by Gene Nelson**). **Glenda tangles with two Elvis Presleys and a hound dog in arguably her most absurd feature film.**

Above: Elvis as twins, one blond, in *Kissin' Cousins*. Glenda played Ma Tatum in one of the more ridiculous Elvis films.
Below: Jack Albertson, Glenda Farrell, Pam Austin, Yvonne Craig and Elvis.

"The King" further away from the "dramatic films" he wanted to make. The Colonel's reasoning was perfectly simple and commercially sound. Why waste precious moneymaking time attempting to design a potential luxury product, when a practical, economy one would outsell it manifold?

For a solid seven years, the Presley-Parker duo cranked out *18* variations on the same model, with just a few trimmings altered here and there. To achieve the proper "hillbilly" flavor for Gerald Drayson Adams and Gene Nelson's *Kissin' Cousins* script, producer Sam Katzman shot much of the film on location at Big Bear in the San Bernardino Mountains during October 1963.

According to Katzman, former dancer-actor Nelson, who also directed:

> … knew how to make pictures. The fact that he had lousy taste
> has nothing to do with it. He knew every angle, every possible
> way to "cheat"; he could have done a good picture the same
> way and he would have been even more of a hero. He just had

lousy taste in writers, and he wouldn't know a story if it hit him in the face.[2]

In a ridiculous premise, Elvis plays two characters: Josh Morgan, a U.S. Air Force recruit sent to Tennessee's Big Smoky Mountain to obtain permission to build an ICBM base, and his doppelganger, Jodie Tatum, the nephew of the land owners Ma and Pappy Tatum (Arthur O'Connell). The blonde wig Elvis was forced to wear while he played Jodie drove him to distraction, a fact that made the Colonel happy as he roamed around the set, grabbing the hairpiece whenever his star took a break.

Glenda got on famously with Elvis, who was generally very respectful, especially around older women. Tommy Farrell, who plays a supporting role in the film, recalled that "he treated her like his mom! She loved him!"[3] Nelson finished shooting the picture in 17 days, and post-production was completed two weeks later. Considering the haste and the shoddy craftsmanship with which the film was made, Elvis found the whole project to be "an embarrassment."[4]

Much of the film is devoted to Elvis doing three things: (1) singing to scantily clad young ladies, (2) being chased by scantily clad young ladies, and (3) kissing scantily clad young ladies. But Glenda also gets her screen time with him. While Ma hugs the Josh Morgan version, she applies a wrestling hold and flips the Jodie Tatum version flat on his back! Glenda wisely didn't use a "hick" accent while playing the character, whose hairstyle and wardrobe are contenders for the worst she ever wore on film. Following this fiasco, she dove right into another feature comedy, with far better results.

Early in his "solo" career, Jerry Lewis made some of his best films with comedy specialist Frank Tashlin, who had directed two of the final three Martin

Glenda as Dr. Jean Howard in *The Disorderly Orderly*.

The Disorderly Orderly (**Paramount, 1964; directed by Frank Tashlin**). **Mayhem abounds as Dr. Jean Howard (Glenda) wrestles with Nurse Maggie Higgins (Kathleen Freeman), Julie Blair (Karen Sharpe), and walking catastrophe Jerome Littlefield (Jerry Lewis).**

and Lewis efforts, *Artists and Models* (1955) and *Hollywood or Bust* (1956). Working from his own screenplay, Tashlin directed Lewis for the eighth and final time in Paramount's *The Disorderly Orderly* (1964), which was shot primarily on location at the Greystone Park and Mansion on Loma Vista Drive in Beverly Hills.

Also serving as executive producer, Lewis plays Jerome Littlefield, a sanitarium orderly whose dream of following in his physician father's footsteps has been derailed by a "neurotic identification empathy" complex that causes him to feel intensely the pain of others. His greatly variable workload, coupled with two romantic attachments—one to Julie Blair (Karen Sharpe), a nurse and the other to Susan Andrews (Susan Oliver), a suicidal patient—adds up to a continual reign of mayhem.

Fortunately for Jerome, all the insanity is tolerated by hospital supervisor Dr. Jean Howard (Glenda), who maintains her cool head and fondness for the walking disaster, due in part to her past feelings for his late father. A charming moment occurs when Dr. Howard shows Julie a black-and-white photograph of herself, sitting with Dr. Littlefield (actually an image of the lovely 1930s Glenda combined with the 1964 Jerry).

A complete turnabout from her wisecracking characters of the 1930s, Dr. Howard allowed Glenda to play the perfect unflappable "straight man" to Lewis' maniacally rampant comic tornado. Amidst all the anarchy, including an Olympian ambulance chase concluding the film in classic slapstick style, both Glenda and Jerry imbue the story with its heart, a subplot dealing with a patient's inability to afford healthcare (decades before Presidents Bill Clinton and Barack Obama made actual attempts to deal with the national albatross). While Jerome, despite his physical ineptitude, genuinely cares for people at the individual level, Dr. Howard walks out of a meeting chaired by the rabidly capitalist Chairman of the Board, Mr. Tuffington (Everett Sloane), who receives his comeuppance during a wild ride on a hospital gurney, terminating with a plunge into the Pacific Ocean (over which "The End" appears).

Discovering (through a prolonged comic kissing sequence) that his longtime feelings for Susan were only an infatuation, Jerome overcomes his complex and proposes to Julie. Fired, then re-hired, Dr. Howard is determined to continue running the sanitarium *her* way.

Billed second, immediately after Lewis, Glenda, ever the professional, created one of her strongest feature-film characters, a serious anchor in a wildly out-of-control cinematic cataclysm. The supporting cast is excellent, particularly Del Moore as Dr. Davenport, the self-administering therapist, and Kathleen Freeman as head nurse Maggie Higgins, whose stress level has been pushed to the breaking point by Jerome's maddeningly sincere incompetence. Interestingly, ubiquitous character actor Murray Alper plays one of Dr. Howard's patients, and Alper worked with Glenda in *High Tension* at 20th Century-Fox 28 years earlier.

Notes:
[1]Tommy Farrell, in Dan Van Neste, "Glenda Farrell: Diamond in the Rough," *Classic Images*, Vol. 275, May 1998.
[2]Peter Guralnick, *Careless Love: The Unmaking of Elvis Presley* (New York: Little, Brown and Company, 1999), pp. 155-156.
[3]Tommy Farrell, in *Classic Images*.
[4]Alanna Nash, *The Colonel: The Extraordinary Story of Colonel Tom Parker and Elvis Presley* (Chicago: Chicago Review Press, Inc., 2003)

PREMIERE PERFORMANCE, DECEMBER 26, 1968

THE
MOROSCO THEATRE

DAVID MERRICK

presents

JULIE HARRIS

in

FORTY CARATS

A New Comedy

Adapted by **JAY ALLEN**

From a play by **BARILLET and GREDY**

Also Starring

GLENDA FARRELL

with

MARCO ST. JOHN   **POLLY ROWLES**   **FRANKLIN COVER**

NANCY   GRETCHEN   IVA   JOHN CECIL   MICHAEL
MARCHAND   CORBETT   WITHERS   HOLM   NOURI

and

MURRAY HAMILTON

Scenery Designed by   *Lighting by*   *Costumes by*
WILL STEVEN ARMSTRONG   MARTIN ARONSTEIN   WILLIAM McHONE

Hairstyles by Ernest Adler

Associate Producer SAMUEL LIFF

Directed by **ABE BURROWS**

Forty Carats (Broadway, Morosco Theatre, 1968; directed by Abe Burrows). Opening night *Playbill*, signed by Glenda and her colleagues, including Julie Harris, Polly Rowles, Iva Withers and Murray Hamilton.

Chapter 15
Something Very Glenda

Now that the show's a hit, wouldn't you think they could afford to buy me a decent wig?
—Glenda, on the production of *Forty Carats* (1969)[1]

By the late 1960s, Glenda was slowing down. She ended her four-year absence from television with "The Deadly Innocents," the October 3, 1968, episode of ABC's *Felony Squad*. Pairing her once more with Warners colleague Donald Woods, the show also featured Howard Duff, Dennis Cole, Brooke Bundy and Jeff Donnell.

After a decade's absence from the stage, Glenda signed on to play Julie Harris' mother, Maud Hayes, in the Jay Allen comedy *Forty Carats* at the Morosco Theatre. The David Merrick production, set in Greece and New York, featured a superb supporting cast, including Murray Hamilton, Marco St. John, Polly Rowles and Nancy Marchand. Director Abe Burrows premiered the play on December 26, 1968.

Playbill included a lengthy biography of Glenda, focusing on her stage career but also listing *Little Caesar*, *Life Begins*, the *Gold Diggers* musicals and the Torchy Blane series, noting that she had appeared in a total of 122 feature films. Reporting that she "is seen constantly on television," the magazine also mentioned her Emmy Award–winning performance on *Ben Casey*.[2]

Though they may have used different "motivations," Glenda and Julie Harris agreed that every actor has a "method," regardless of his background and training. In 1996, Harris said, "It doesn't matter *how* you get there, as long as you get there."[3]

The popular sitcom *Bewitched* (1964-1972) occasionally touched upon social issues of the era. On March 13, 1969, Glenda made her small-screen swansong in the fifth-season episode "The Battle of Burning Oak," in which Samantha (Elizabeth Montgomery) and Darrin (Dick York) find distasteful the requirement of joining an exclusive country club to close a business deal for Larry Tate (David White).

During a second meeting with the club's board of directors (including June Vincent and that supreme purveyor of snobbery, Edward Andrews), Samantha addresses the policy of courting "pure bred Americans," pointing out that the only such individuals are "American Indians," who wouldn't possibly be accepted as members. As Andrews' wife Hortense Rockford, Glenda, unfortunately, has very little to do.

Glenda's final feature film, *Tiger by the Tail* (1970), is a low-budget crime drama directed by R.G. Springsteen and released through American Interna-

tional Pictures. The incredibly diverse cast (in which Glenda receives seventh billing) includes Christopher George, Tippi Hedren, Dean Jagger, John Dehner, Charo, Lloyd Bochner, Alan Hale, Jr., Skip Homeier, R.G. Armstrong and Dennis Patrick.

When Vietnam veteran Steve Michaelis (Christopher George) returns to California to find that his brother Frank (Dennis Patrick) has been murdered, he sets out to disprove the theory that "two Mexican burglars" were responsible for the crime. In the process, he and his girlfriend, Rita Armstrong (Tippi Hedren) identify the real killers, led by Sheriff Chancey Jones (John Dehner). Also making appearances in the film are the Mescalero Apache Horn Dancers and Meredith Neal and the Boot Heal Boys. (Glenda topped off her film career in grand style.)

During the autumn of 1970, Glenda, who smoked only rarely on screen, was diagnosed with lung cancer. Too ill to continue in *Forty Carats*, she was succeeded in the role of Maud Hayes by Violet Dunn. (The play closed its lengthy run on November 7, 1970.)

After attempting to recuperate in Florida, Glenda returned to New York, where she passed away in the 480 Park Avenue apartment on May 1, 1971. She was 69 years old.

On May 2, a Catholic Requiem Mass, attended by her husband, "Hank," Tommy and her four grandchildren, was held at the Faith, Hope and Charity Chapel at 487 Park Avenue. That afternoon, she became the only actress to be interred at the West Point Military Academy.

The following day, the *New York Times* ran a splendid tribute to Glenda by writer-director Garson Kanin. He wrote, in part:

This morning, under a still-soft mound of earth overlooking the stately Hudson at West Point, there rests the body of Glenda Farrell, American actress. She ... specifically chose the site during the last of her gallant days. Her grave is marked by the cross symbolizing her devout Catholicism. When, in time to come, her husband joins her there, the cross will be matched by a graven Star of David. There is something very Glenda about all this.

Donated by Glenda's late husband, the Glenda Farrell–Henry Ross Preserve is a public-accessible area located in Putnam County, New York. For more information, go to the Putnam County Land Trust website at www.pclt.net.

She was one of the few real Americans I have known. Most of us are welcome assimilates. Not Glenda. She began in Enid, Oklahoma; was educated in Kansas, and made her way to Broadway via California ...

There are players who create characters; some of the great ones, a single character. ... Most rare are those who, like Glenda, created a *type*.

She invented and developed that made-tough, uncompromising, knowing, wisecracking, undefeatable blonde ... She was, in the noblest sense of the word, a professional—which means, among other things, that she loved to work ...

We shall remember her: a look, a scene; a line, a stance; that strong presence, or her marvelously wry, understanding, sudden American smile.[4]

In 1977, Dr. Ross donated 38 acres of the Brewster estate in Glenda's honor to the Putnam County Land Trust. The parcel was named the Glenda Farrell–Henry Ross Preserve. Visitors may explore the preserve via two

Glenda Farrell, Film Star, Dies at 66

Glenda Farrell, who appeared in 122 movies, as well as in many plays on stage and television, died yesterday in her home at 480 Park Avenue. She was 66 years old and was the wife of Dr. Henry Ross, a physician.

Miss Farrell was the dizzy, fun-loving, gum-chewing blonde who wisecracked her way through numerous rough-and-tumble movies of the nineteen-thirties.

She also scored largely in hard-boiled parts, but if the authors made her appear too tough, she would often blue-pencil some of the lines.

Miss Farrell last appeared on Broadway two years ago as the mother of Julie Harris, in the hit play "Forty Carats." She became ill during the run of the show, and never fully recovered.

In an interview two years ago, Miss Farrell recalled effervescently her good old days in Hollywood.

"When I went out there to do 'Little Caesar' in 1930," she said, "the talkies were still new. Not many actors could talk, so they shoved the ones who came from Broadway into everything. It all went so fast."

She was born in Enid, Okla., and studied at Mount Carmel Academy in Wichita, Kan. Her earliest ambition was to go on the stage. At the age of 7 she made her debut as Little Eva in "Uncle Tom's Cabin."

After leaving school, Miss Farrell joined a stock company. Early in her career she was a member of the Brissac Stock

Avery Willard

Glenda Farrell in 1959

Company in San Diego, the Morosco in Los Angeles and the Alcazar in San Francisco.

She worked her way to Broadway and two weeks after arriving replaced the leading lady in a play called "Skidding," which later became Hollywood's Andy Hardy series.

Her next play, in 1929, was the short-lived "Divided Honors," but enthusiastic personal notices won her the ingénue role in "Love, Honor and Betray," in which she shared the spotlight with Clark Gable and George Brent.

Miss Farrell appeared in "Recaptured," with Melvyn Douglas, and then in a hit, "On the Spot," in which she played a gangster's moll, a role that propelled her into that of Olga in the movie "Little Caesar," with Edward G. Robinson. She appeared both on stage and screen in "Life Begins."

Miss Farrell teamed with Joan Blondell in the "Gold Diggers" series and also made a hit in the "Torchy Blane" series. Other of her movies were "I Am a Fugitive from a Chain Gang," with Paul Muni, "Hi, Nellie," "Talk of the Town," and "Middle of the Night."

Won Emmy in 1963

She won an Emmy as best supporting actress in 1963 for her role in "A Cardinal Act of Mercy" on the Ben Casey television show. She was also seen in "Wagon Train," "Bonanza," "The Fugitive," The Defenders" and "Dr. Kildare," among other shows.

She commuted regularly to Broadway to appear in such plays as "Separate Rooms," "The Overtons" and "Home Is the Hero."

Surviving, besides her husband, are a son, by a former marriage, Tommy Farrell of Los Angeles, an actor, and four grandchildren.

A funeral service will be held tomorrow at 9:30 A.M. at SS. Faith, Hope and Charity Chapel, 487 Park Avenue. As the wife of a West Point graduate, she will be buried privately at the United States Military Academy at West Point.

Above left: Glenda Farrell tribute in *Theatre World*, volume 27: 1970-1971. Above right: Glenda's star on the Hollywood Walk of Fame was awarded 2/8/1960..

Tommy Farrell

trails through heavily wooded areas, across streams and around wetlands and rocky outcroppings. Many flora and fauna thrive there. Across the continent, in the nation's movie capital, Glenda's star on the Hollywood Walk of Fame is located at 6524 Hollywood Boulevard.

Glenda's legacy also lives on in the prolific life and career of her son, Tommy, who passed away, aged 82, in 2004. At the time of his death, he had been married to his third wife, Bobbi, since 1961. Their four children are Mark, Erin, Ellen and Kathy.

Tommy's impressive resume includes several classic feature films, including *Strangers on a Train* (1951), *Singin' in the Rain* (1952), *North by Northwest* (1959) and *Breakfast at Tiffany's* (1961). His final feature was *A Guide for the Married Man* (1967), directed by Gene Kelly and starring Walter Matthau.

Perhaps even more remarkable is Tommy's eclectic list of television performances. Like his mother, he greatly enjoyed the medium. For two decades, he truly was a ubiquitous presence on the small screen. His credits include appearances on *The Abbott and Costello Show* (1953), *Maverick* (1957), *Cheyenne* (1958-1961), *Dragnet* (1958), *Gunsmoke* (1958), *Wanted: Dead or Alive* (1959), *The Donna Reed Show* (1960), *Thriller* (1961), *Perry Mason* (1962-1965), *77 Sunset Strip* (1963), *Rawhide* (1963), *The Fugitive* (1964), *The Munsters* (1965), *The Addams Family* (1965), *The Lucy Show* (1965), *The Man from U.N.C.L.E.* (1966), *Gomer Pyle, USMC* (1966-1968), *Lost in Space* (1967), *Julia* (1968), *The Red Skelton Hour* (1969) and *Get Smart* (1970). His last television appearance occurred on the series *Hart to Hart* (1983), in which he played a character called "Roaring Tommy."

On five occasions, Tommy appeared in productions with his famous mother: *Girls in the Night*, *Dr. Kildare*, *Rawhide*, *Kissin' Cousins* and *The Disorderly Orderly*. In 2003, he received a Golden Boot Award for his contributions to the Western genre.

Notes:

[1] *New York Times*, 9 February 1969.
[2] *Forty Carats* Playbill, Morosco Theatre, Volume 5, Issue 12, December 1968, p. 40.
[3] Julie Harris, interview with Scott Allen Nollen, May 1996.
[4] *New York Times*, 3 May 1971.

Appendix A
Feature Films

This complete listing of Glenda Farrell's feature films includes primary cast and crew members for each title. Glenda's character names are also included.

Lucky Boy (February 2, 1929) Tiffany-Stahl Productions
Credits: Directors: Norman Taurog, Charles C. Wilson, Rudolph Flothow; Producer: John M. Stahl; Screenplay: Isadore Bernstein, George Jessel; Story: Viola Brothers Shore; Directors of Photography: Harry Jackson, Frank Zucker; Editors: Desmond O'Brien, Russell G. Shields; Art Director: Hervey Libbert; Musical Score: Hugo Riesenfeld; Production Dates: late May-late June 1928; Running Time: 100 minutes
Cast: George Jessel, Gwen Lee, Richard Tucker, Gayne Whitman, Margaret Quimby, Rosa Rosanova, William H. Strauss, Mary Doran, Patty and Fields, Joe Sevely, William Gargan, Sig Ruman, Charles C. Wilson, Glenda Farrell (bit)

Little Caesar (January 25, 1931) Warner Bros.-First National Pictures
Credits: Director: Mervyn LeRoy; Producers: Hal B. Wallis, Darryl F. Zanuck; Screenplay: Francis Edwards Faragoh, Robert N. Lee, Robert Lord, Darryl F. Zanuck; Based on the novel by W.R. Burnett; Director of Photography: Tony Gaudio; Editor: Ray Curtiss; Art Director: Anton Grot; Musical Director: Erno Rapee; Running Time: 79 minutes
Cast: Edward G. Robinson, Douglas Fairbanks, Jr., Glenda Farrell (Olga Stassoff), William Collier, Jr., Sidney Blackmer, Ralph Ince, Thomas E. Jackson, Stanley Fields, Maurice Black, George E. Stone, Armand Kaliz, Nicholas Bela, Lucille La Verne, Landers Stevens

Scandal for Sale (April 17, 1932) Universal Pictures
Credits: Director: Russell Mack; Producer: Carl Laemmle, Jr.; Associate Producer: E.M. Asher; Screenplay: Ralph Graves, Robert Keith; Story: Emile Gauvreau; Director of Photography: Karl Freund; Editor: Robert Carlisle; Art Director: Charles D. Hall; Special Effects: John P. Fulton; Running Time: 75 minutes
Cast: Charles Bickford, Rose Hobart, Pat O'Brien, Claudia Dell, J. Farrell MacDonald, Harry Beresford, Berton Churchill, Glenda Farrell (Stella), Betty Jane Graham, Buster Phelps, Paul Nicholson, James Farley, Mitchell Harris, Hans Heinrich von Twardowski, Tully Marshall, Lew Kelly, Jack Richardson, Angie Norton

Life Begins (September 10, 1932) Warner Bros.-First National Pictures
Credits: Directors: James Flood, Elliott Nugent; Executive Producer: Darryl F. Zanuck; Screenplay: Earl Baldwin; Based on the play by Mary M. Axelson; Director of Photography: James Van Trees; Editor: George Marks; Art Director: Esdras Hartley; Musical Conductor: Leo F. Forbstein; Running Time: 71 minutes
Cast: Loretta Young, Eric Linden, Aline MacMahon, Glenda Farrell (Florette Darian), Clara Blandick, Preston Foster, Frank McHugh, Walter Walker, Hale Hamilton, Vivienne Osborne, Dorothy Peterson, Gilbert Roland, Herbert Mundin, Gloria Shea, Elizabeth Patterson, Helena Phillips, Reginald Mason, Ruthelma Stevens, Dorothy Tree, Terrance Ray, Mary Phillips

Three on a Match (October 29, 1932) Warner Bros.-First National Pictures
Credits: Director: Mervyn LeRoy; Producers: Samuel Bischoff, Darryl F. Zanuck; Screenplay: Lucien Hubbard; Story: Kubec Glasmon, John Bright; Director of Photography: Sol Polito; Editor: Ray Curtiss; Art Director: Robert M. Haas; Musical Arranger: Ray Heindorf; Running Time: 63 minutes
Cast: Virginia Davis, Joan Blondell, Anne Shirley [aka Dawn O'Day], Ann Dvorak, Betty Carse, Bette Davis, Warren William, Lyle Talbot, Humphrey Bogart, Allen Jenkins, Edward Arnold, Frankie Darro, Glenda Farrell (Mrs. Black), Buster Phelps, Grant Mitchell, Sheila Terry, Clara Blandick, John Marston, Patricia Ellis, Hale Hamilton, Dick Brandon, Junior Johnson, Sidney Miller, Blanche Frederici, Hardie Albright, Spencer Charters, Ann Brody, Jack La Rue, Stanley Price, Harry Seymour, Mary Doran, Herman Bing, Selmer Jackson

I Am a Fugitive from a Chain Gang (November 19, 1932) Warner Bros. Pictures
Credits: Director: Mervyn LeRoy; Executive Producer: Hal B. Wallis; Screenplay: Howard J. Green, Brown Holmes, Sheridan Gibney; Based on the book by Robert E. Burns; Director of Photography: Sol Polito; Editor: William Holmes; Art Director: Jack Okey; Musical Score: Bernhard Kaun; Production Dates: July 29-September 7, 1932; Running Time: 92 minutes
Cast: Paul Muni, Glenda Farrell (Marie Woods), Helen Vinson, Preston Foster, Allen Jenkins, Berton Churchill, Edward Ellis, David Landau, Hale Hamilton, Sally Blane, Louise Carter, Willard Robertson, Robert McWade, Robert Warwick, William LeMaire, Edward J. McNamara, Sheila Terry, James Bell, John Wray, Everett Brown, Edward Arnold, Oscar Apfel, Erville Alderson, William Janney, C. Henry Gordon, Spencer Charters, Roscoe Karns, Charles Middleton, Harry Holman, John Marston, Jack La Rue, Reginald Barlow, Charles Sellon, G. Pat Collins, William Pawley, Lew Kelly, Dewey Robinson, Sam Baker, Morgan Wallace, Russell Simpson

The Match King (December 31, 1932) Warner Bros.-First National Pictures
Credits: Directors: Howard Bretherton, William Keighley; Producer: Hal B. Wallis; Screenplay: Houston Branch, Sidney Sutherland; Based on the novel by Einer Thorvalson; Director of Photography: Robert Kurle; Editor: Jack Killifer; Art Director: Anton Grot; Musical Score: Bernhard Kaun; Production Dates: August 29-early October 1932; Running Time: 79 minutes
Cast: Warren William, Lili Damita, Glenda Farrell (Babe), Juliette Compton, Claire Dodd, Harold Huber, John Wray, Spencer Charters, Murray Kinnell, Hardie Albright, Alan Hale, Edmund Breese, Robert McWade, Greta Meyer, Oscar Apfel, Irving Bacon, Harry Beresford, George Meeker, De Witt Jennings, Alphonse Ethier, Bodil Rosing, Wallis Clark

Mystery of the Wax Museum (February 18, 1933) Warner Bros. Pictures
Credits: Director: Michael Curtiz; Producers: Henry Blanke, Hal B. Wallis; Screenplay: Don Mullaly, Carl Erickson; Story: Charles Belden; Director of Photography: Ray Rennahan; Editor: George Amy; Art Director: Anton Grot; Musical Score: Bernhard Kaun; Production Dates: began October 8, 1932; Running Time: 77 minutes
Cast: Lionel Atwill, Fay Wray, Glenda Farrell (Florence), Frank McHugh, Allen Vincent, Gavin Gordon, Edwin Maxwell, Holmes Herbert, Claude King, Arthur Edmund Carewe, Thomas E. Jackson, De Witt Jennings, Matthew Betz, Monica Bannister, Pat O'Malley, Bull Anderson

Grand Slam (March 18, 1933) Warner Bros.-First National Pictures
Credits: Director: William Dieterle; Producer: Hal B. Wallis; Screenplay: Erwin Gelsey, David Boehm; Based on the novel by B. Russell Herts; Director of Photography: Sid Hickox; Editor: Jack Killifer; Art Director: Jack Okey; Musical Score: Bernhard Kaun; Running Time: 67 minutes
Cast: Paul Lukas, Loretta Young, Frank McHugh, Glenda Farrell (Blondie), Helen Vinson, Roscoe Karns, Ferdinand Gottschalk, Walter Byron, Joseph Cawthorn, Milton Kibbee, Charles Lane, Dennis O'Keefe, Paul Porcasi, Mary Doran, Lucien Prival, Tom Dugan, Maurice Black, Lee Moran, Ruthelma Stevens, Emma Dunn, Reginald Barlow, Harry C. Bradley, Charles Levinson, De Witt Jennings, George Cooper, John Sheehan, Esther Howard

Girl Missing (March 4, 1933) Warner Bros. Pictures
Credits: Director: Robert Florey; Screenplay: Carl Erickson, Don Mullaly, Ben Markson; Story: Carl Erickson, Don Mullaly; Director of Photography: Arthur L. Todd; Editor: Ralph Dawson; Art Director: Esdras Hartley; Musical Score: Bernhard Kaun; Running Time: 69 minutes
Cast: Glenda Farrell (Kay Curtis), Ben Lyon, Mary Brian, Lyle Talbot, Guy Kibbee, Harold Huber, Edward Ellis, Peggy Shannon, Helen Ware, Ferdinand

Gottschalk, George Pat Collins, Louise Beavers, Walter Brennan, Mike Marita, Fred Kelsey

Pre-code publicity photo for *The Keyhole*

The Keyhole (March 25, 1933) Warner Bros. Pictures
Credits: Director: Michael Curtiz; Screenplay: Robert Presnell; Story: Alice D.G. Miller; Director of Photography: Barney McGill; Editor: Ray Curtiss; Art Director: Anton Grot; Musical Score: W. Franke Harling, Ray Heindorf; Running Time: 69 minutes

Cast: Kay Francis, George Brent, Glenda Farrell (Dot), Monroe Owsley, Allen Jenkins, Helen Ware, Henry Kolker, Ferdinand Gottschalk, Irving Bacon, George Chandler, Heinie Conklin, George Humbert, Gino Corrado, Clarence Wilson

Central Airport (April 13, 1933) Warner Bros.-First National Pictures [Glenda's scenes cut]
Credits: Director: William A. Wellman; Screenplay: Rian James, James Seymour; Story: Jack Moffit; Director of Photography: Sid Hickox, Elmer Dyer (aerial sequences); Editor: James Morley; Art Director: Jack Okey; Musical Score: Leo F. Forbstein; Running Time: 76 minutes
Cast: Richard Barthelmess, Sally Eilers, Tom Brown, Grant Mitchell, James Murray, Claire McDowell, Willard Robertson, Arthur Vinton, John Vosper, Lucille Ward, Russ Powell, Bradley Page, Harry Semels, Walter Miller, Betty Jane Gordon, Theodore Newton, Charles Lane, John Wayne, Dick Elliott, George Regas, Irving Bacon, James Ellison, James Bush, Sam McDaniel, Louise Beavers, Jed Prouty, Lester Dorr, Fred "Snowflake" Toones, Charles Williams, Phil Tead, J. Carrol Naish, Harry C. Bradley, Toby Wing, Milton Kibbee

Gambling Ship (June 23, 1933) Paramount Pictures
Credits: Directors: Louis J. Gasnier, Max Marcin; Screenplay: Claude Binyon, Max Marcin, Seton I. Miller; Story: Peter Ruric; Director of Photography: Charles Lang; Musical Score: Werner R. Heymann, Oscar Levant; Running Time: 72 minutes
Cast: Cary Grant, Benita Hume, Jack La Rue, Glenda Farrell (Jeanne Sands), Roscoe Karns, Arthur Vinton, Charles Williams, Edwin Maxwell, Spencer Charters, Kate Campbell, Edward

Glenda Farrell and Benita Hume in *Gambling Ship*

Gargan, Sid Saylor, Harry Shutan, Frank Moran, Otho Wright, Evelyn Selbie, Jack Grey, William Welsh, Hooper Atchley, Larry Alexander, Louis Natheaux, Gum Chang, Sam Bricker

Mary Stevens, M.D. (July 22, 1933) Warner Bros. Pictures
Credits: Director: Lloyd Bacon; Executive Producer: Hal B. Wallis; Screenplay: Rian James, Robert Lord; Story: Virginia Kellogg; Director of Photog-

Mary Stevens, M.D.

raphy: Sid Hickox; Editor: Ray Curtiss; Art Director: Esdras Hartley; Musical Score: Bernhard Kaun; Running Time: 72 minutes
Cast: Kay Francis, Lyle Talbot, Glenda Farrell (Glenda Carroll), Thelma Todd, Harold Huber, Una O'Connor, Charles C. Wilson, Hobart Cavanaugh, George Cooper, John Marston, Christian Rub, Walter Walker, Reginald Mason, Ann Hovey

Lady for a Day (September 13, 1933) Columbia Pictures
Credits: Director: Frank Capra; Executive Producer: Harry Cohn; Screenplay: Robert Riskin; Based on the story by Damon Runyon; Director of Photography: Joseph Walker; Editor: Gene Havlick; Art Director: Stephen Goosson; Musical Score: Howard Jackson; Production Dates: May 9-June 6, 1933; Running Time: 96 minutes

Cast: Warren William, May Robson, Guy Kibbee, Glenda Farrell (Missouri Martin), Ned Sparks, Walter Connolly, Jean Parker, Nat Pendleton, Barry Norton, Halliwell Hobbes, Hobart Bosworth, Robert Emmett O'Connor, Wallis Clark, Samuel S. Hinds, Irving Bacon, Ward Bond

Bureau of Missing Persons (September 16, 1933) Warner Bros.-First National Pictures
Credits: Director: Roy Del Ruth; Supervising Producer: Henry Blanke; Screenplay: Robert Presnell; Story: John H. Ayers, Carol Bird; Director of Photography: Barney McGill; Editor: James Gibbon; Art Director: Robert M. Haas; Musical Score: Bernhard Kaun; Running Time: 73 minutes
Cast: Lewis Stone, Pat O'Brien, Glenda Farrell (Belle Howard Saunders), Bette Davis, Allen Jenkins, Ruth Donnelly, Hugh Herbert, Alan Dinehart, Marjorie Gateson, Tad Alexander, Noel Francis, Wallis Clark, Adrian Morris, Clay Clement, Henry Kolker, Harry Beresford, George Chandler

Bureau of Missing Persons

Man's Castle (October 27, 1933) Columbia Pictures
Credits: Director and Producer: Frank Borzage; Screenplay: Jo Swerling; Based on the play by Lawrence Hazard; Director of Photography: Joseph H. August; Editor: Viola Lawrence; Art Director: Stephen Goosson; Musical Score: W. Frank Harling; Production Dates: July 28-September 6, 1933; Running Time: 75 minutes

Cast: Spencer Tracy, Loretta Young, Marjorie Rambeau, Glenda Farrell (Fay La Rue), Walter Connolly, Arthur Hohl, Dickie Moore, Harvey Clark, Helen Jerome Eddy

Havana Widows (November 18, 1933) Warner Bros.-First National Pictures
Credits: Director: Ray Enright; Screenplay: Earl Baldwin; Director of Photography: George Barnes; Editor: Clarence Kolster; Art Director: Esdras Hartley; Musical Conductor: Leo F. Forbstein; Running Time: 62 minutes
Cast: Joan Blondell, Glenda Farrell (Sadie Appleby), Guy Kibbee, Allen Jenkins, Lyle Talbot, Frank McHugh, Ruth Donnelly, Hobart Cavanaugh, Ralph Ince, Maude Eburne, George Cooper, Charles C. Wilson, Joseph Crehan, Noel Francis, J. Carrol Naish

The Big Shakedown (January 6, 1934) Warner Bros.-First National Pictures
Credits: Director: John Francis Dillon; Producer: Samuel Bischoff; Screenplay: Niven Busch, Rian James; Story: Samuel G. Engel, Niven Busch; Director of Photography: Sid Hickox; Editors: Thomas Richards, James Gibbon; Art Director: John Hughes; Musical Director: Leo F. Forbstein; Running Time: 64 minutes
Cast: Charles Farrell, Bette Davis, Ricardo Cortez, Glenda Farrell (Lily "Lil" Duran), Allen Jenkins, Henry O'Neill, Dewey Robinson, John Wray, Phillip Faversham, Robert Emmett O'Connor, Renee Whitney, George Pat Collins, Adrian Morris, Ben Hendricks, Jr., George Cooper, Earl Foxe, Samuel S. Hinds, Sidney Miller, James C. Eagles, Charles Williams, Matt Briggs, Ben Taggert, Sam Godfrey, Francis Sayles, Harry C. Bradley, Katherine Clare Ward, Robert Wayne, James Spottswood, Philip Morris, Wallis Clark, Frederick Burton, William B. Davidson, Lee Shumway, Jack Kenny, Oscar Apfel, Charles Hills Mailes, Landers Stevens, Larry Steers, Alphonz Ethier, Antrim Short, Frank Layton, Ed Stanley, Edward Le Saint, John Hyams, Eleanor Jackson, May Foster

Hi, Nellie! (January 20, 1934) Warner Bros. Pictures
Credits: Director: Mervyn LeRoy; Producer: Robert Presnell; Executive Producers: Hal B. Wallis, Jack L. Warner; Screenplay: Abem Finkel, Sidney Sutherland; Story: Roy Chanslor; Director of Photography: Sol Polito; Editor: William Holmes; Art Director: Robert M. Haas; Musical Score: Bernhard Kaun; Running Time: 75 minutes
Cast: Paul Muni, Glenda Farrell (Gerry Krale), Ned Sparks, Robert Barrat, Berton Churchill, Kathryn Sergava, Hobart Cavanaugh, Douglass Dumbrille, Edward Ellis, Paul Kaye, Donald Meek, Dorothy La Baire, Marjorie Gateson, George Meeker, Harold Huber, Allen Vincent, Pat Wing, Frank Reicher, George Chandler, George Humbert, Sidney Miller, James Donlan, Milton

Kibbee, Harry Seymour, Ralph McCullough, Gus Reed, Harold Miller, Nina Campana, John Qualen, Antonio Filauri, Howard Hickman, Sidney Skolsky

Dark Hazard (February 3, 1934) Warner Bros.-First National Pictures
Credits: Director: Alfred E. Green; Executive Producers: Hal B. Wallis, Jack L. Warner; Screenplay: Ralph Block, Brown Holmes; Based on the novel by W.R. Burnett; Director of Photography: Sol Polito; Editor: Herbert Levy; Art Director: Robert M. Haas; Musical Score: Bernhard Kaun; Running Time: 72 minutes
Cast: Edward G. Robinson, Genevieve Tobin, Glenda Farrell (Valerie "Val" Wilson), Robert Barrat, Hobart Cavanaugh, Gordon Westcott, Sidney Toler, War Cry (dog), Henry B. Walthall, George Meeker, Emma Dunn, Willard Robertson, William V. Mong, Barbara Rogers

I've Got Your Number (February 24, 1934) Warner Bros. Pictures
Credits: Director: Ray Enright; Screenplay: Warren Duff, Sidney Sutherland; Story: William Rankin; Director of Photography: Arthur L. Todd; Editor: Clarence Kolster; Art Director: Esdras Hartley; Musical Score: Bernhard Kaun; Production Dates: began early November 1933; Running Time: 69 minutes
Cast: Joan Blondell, Pat O'Brien, Allen Jenkins, Glenda Farrell (Bonnie), Eugene Pallette, Gordon Westcott, Henry O'Neill, Hobart Cavanaugh, Renee Whitney, Wallis Clark, Robert Ellis, Douglas Cosgrove, Selmer Jackson, Louise Beavers, Henry Kolker, Charles Wilson, Tom Costello, Clay Clement

Heat Lightning (March 3, 1934) Warner Bros. Pictures
Credits: Director: Mervyn LeRoy; Producer: Samuel Bischoff; Screenplay: Brown Holmes, Warren Duff; Director of Photography: Sid Hickox; Editor: Howard Bretherton; Art Director: Jack Okey; Musical Score: Bernhard Kaun; Production Dates: began November 20, 1933; Running Time: 63 minutes
Cast: Aline MacMahon, Ann Dvorak, Preston Foster, Lyle Talbot, Glenda Farrell (Mrs. "Feathers" Tilton), Frank McHugh, Ruth Donnelly, Theodore Newton, Willard Robertson, Harry C. Bradley, James Durkin, Jane Darwell, Edgar Kennedy, Muriel Evans

Merry Wives of Reno (May 12, 1934) Warner Bros. Pictures
Credits: Director: H. Bruce Humberstone; Screenplay: Robert Lord, Joe Traub, Wilson Mizner; Story: Robert Lord; Director of Photography: Ernest Haller; Editor: Thomas Pratt; Art Director: Jack Okey; Musical Score: Heinz Roemheld; Running Time: 64 minutes
Cast: Guy Kibbee, Glenda Farrell (Bunny Fitch), Donald Woods, Margaret Lindsay, Hugh Herbert, Frank McHugh, Ruth Donnelly, Roscoe Ates, Hobart Cavanaugh, Renee Whitney, Hattie McDaniel, Lorena Layson, Richard Pow-

ell, Irving Bacon, Edna Bennett, Ruth Warren, Joseph Crehan, Ray Brown, Helena Phillips, Vivienne Oakland, Betty Farrington, Inez Palange, Geneva Mitchell, Louise Beavers, Addie McPhail

The Personality Kid (July 7, 1934) Warner Bros. Pictures
Credits: Director: Alan Crosland; Screenplay: F. Hugh Herbert, Erwin Gelsey, David Boehm; Story: Gene Towne, C. Graham Baker; Director of Photography: William Rees; Editor: Terry Morse; Art Director: John Hughes; Musical Score: Bernhard Kaun; Production Dates: February 12-March 5, 1934; Running Time: 68 minutes
Cast: Pat O'Brien, Glenda Farrell (Joan McCarty), Claire Dodd, Robert Gleckler, Henry O'Neill, Thomas E. Jackson, Arthur Vinton, Clarence Muse, Clay Clement, George Cooper, George Pat Collins, Al Hill, Mushy Callahan, Myron Shlechter, Jack Perry, Harry Seymour, Mary Russell, Paul Power, Phil Regan, Billy Arnold, Howard Russell, Howard Hickman, Margaret Morris, Landers Stevens, Harry Holman, Jack Kennedy, Sailor Vincent, Max Wagner, Huey White, Pauline True, Bess Flowers, Dan Toby, Morrie Cohan, John Sheehan

Kansas City Princess (October 13, 1934) Warner Bros. Pictures
Credits: Director: William Keighley; Screenplay: Sy Bartlett, Manuel Seff; Story: Sy Bartlett; Director of Photography: George Barnes; Editor: William Clemens; Art Director: John Hughes; Musical Conductor: Leo F. Forbstein; Production Dates: began May 9, 1934; Running Time: 64 minutes
Cast: Joan Blondell, Glenda Farrell (Marie Callahan), Robert Armstrong, Hugh Herbert, Osgood Perkins, T. Roy Barnes, Hobart Cavanaugh, Gordon Westcott, Vince Barnett, Ivan Lebedeff, Renee Whitney, Arthur Hoyt

The Secret Bride (December 22, 1934) Warner Bros. Pictures
Credits: Director: William Dieterle; Associate Producer: Henry Blanke; Screenplay: Tom Buckingham, F. Hugh Herbert, Mary McCall, Jr.; Based on the play by Leonard Idle; Director of Photography: Ernest Haller; Editor: Owen Marks; Art Director: Anton Grot; Musical Score: M.K. Jerome, Bernhard Kaun; Production Dates: ended October 3, 1934; Running Time: 64 minutes
Cast: Barbara Stanwyck, Warren William, Glenda Farrell (Hazel Normandie), Grant Mitchell, Arthur Byron, Henry O'Neill, Douglass Dumbrille, Arthur Aylesworth, Willard Robertson, William B. Davidson, Russell Hicks, Vince Barnett, Frank Darien, John Larkin, Emmett Vogan, Frank Dawson, Gordon Elliott, Bill Ray, James P. Burtis, Spencer Charters, James Burke, Wade Boteler, Cliff Saum, Thomas E. Jackson, Charles C. Wilson, Katherine Clare Ward, Florence Fair, Walter Walker, Rosalie Roy, Purnell Pratt, Wallis Clark, Wilfred

Lucas, Eddy Chandler, Samuel T. Godfrey, Milton Kibbee, Frederick Burton, Monte Vandergrift, Davison Clark, Howard Hickman, Selmer Jackson, Niles Welch, Joseph Crehan, Mary Russell, Mick Copeland

Gold Diggers of 1935 (March 16, 1935) Warner Bros.-First National Pictures
Credits: Director: Busby Berkeley; Screenplay: Manuel Seff, Peter Milne; Story: Robert Lord, Peter Milne; Director of Photography: George Barnes; Editor: George Amy; Art Director: Anton Grot; Songs: Al Dubin; Musical Score: Bernhard Kaun, Heinz Roemheld; Choreographer: Busby Berkeley; Production Dates: ended January 14, 1935; Running Time: 95 minutes
Cast: Dick Powell, Adolphe Menjou, Gloria Stuart, Alice Brady, Hugh Herbert, Glenda Farrell (Betty Hawes), Frank McHugh, Joseph Cawthorn, Grant Mitchell, Dorothy Dare, Winifred Shaw, Arthur Aylesworth, Walter Brennan, Thomas Jackson, Ramon and Rosita, Phil Tead, Eddie Kane, Nora Cecil, Harry Holman, Jan Buckingham, Olive Jones, Rosalie Roy, Mary Russell, Gordon Elliott, Marjorie Nichols, Grace Hayle, Amos Ingraham, Don Brodie, Eddie Fetherston, Billy Newell, George Riley, Harry Seymour, Ray Cooke, John Quillan, Florence Fair

Traveling Saleslady (April 8, 1935) Warner Bros.-First National Pictures
Credits: Director: Ray Enright; Producer: Samuel Bischoff; Screenplay: F. Hugh Herbert, Manuel Seff, Benny Rubin; Based on the play by Frank Howard Clark; Director of Photography: George Barnes; Editor: Owen Marks; Art Director: Anton Grot; Musical Score: Bernhard Kaun; Running Time: 65 minutes
Cast: Joan Blondell, Glenda Farrell (Claudette Ruggles), William Gargan, Hugh Herbert, Grant Mitchell, Al Shean, Ruth Donnelly, Johnny Arthur, Bert Roach, Joseph Crehan, Mary Treen, James Donlan, Gordon Elliott, Carroll Nye, Harry Holman, Hattie McDaniel, Selmer Jackson, Milton Kibbee, Bill Ray, Frances Lee, Gertrude Sutton, Glen Cavender, Leo White, Ferdinand Schumann-Heink, Olaf Hytten, Eddie Shubert, Olive Jones, Nick Copeland, Charlotte Sullivan, Harvey Clark, Harry Seymour

Go Into Your Dance (April 20, 1935) Warner Bros.-First National Pictures
Credits: Directors: Archie Mayo, Michael Curtiz, Robert Florey; Producer: Samuel Bischoff; Screenplay: Earl Baldwin; Based on the novel by Bradford Ropes; Directors of Photography: Tony Gaudio, Sol Polito; Editor: Harold McLernon; Art Director: John Hughes; Musical Director: Leo F. Forbstein; Running Time: 89 minutes
Cast: Al Jolson, Ruby Keeler, Glenda Farrell (Molly Howard), Barton MacLane, Patsy Kelly, Akim Tamiroff, Helen Morgan, Sharon Lynne, Benny Rubin, Phil Regan, Gordon Westcott, William B. Davidson, Joyce Compton,

Joseph Crehan, Harry Warren, Al Dubin, James Donlan, Robert Gleckler, Bobby Connolly, Mary Carr, John Hyams, Edward Keane, Gordon Elliott, Arthur Treacher, Joyzelle, James P. Burtis, Harold Daniels, Freeman Wood, Milton Kibbee, Ward Bond, Sam Rice, Harry Seymour, Marc Lawrence, Huey White, Sam Hayes, Nick Copeland, Frances Morris, Rosalie Roy, Treva Lawler, Florence Dudley, Theresa Harris, Fred "Snowflake" Toones, Henry Kolker, Lita Chevret, Martha Merrill

In Caliente (May 25, 1935) Warner Bros.-First National Pictures
Credits: Director: Lloyd Bacon; Producer: Edward Chodorov; Screenplay: Jerry Wald, Julius J. Epstein, Ralph Block, Warren Duff; Story: Ralph Block, Warren Duff; Directors of Photography: George Barnes, Sol Polito; Editor: James Gibbon; Art Director: Robert M. Haas; Musical Score: Bernhard Kaun; Production Dates: December 27, 1934-March 30, 1935; Running Time: 84 minutes
Cast: Dolores del Rio, Pat O'Brien, Leo Carrillo, Edward Everett Horton, Glenda Farrell (Miss Clara Thorne), Phil Regan, Winifred Shaw, Luis Alberni, George Humbert, Soledad Jimenez, Herman Bing, Florence Fair, Judy Canova, Sally De Marco, Tony De Marco, Dorothy Dare, Olive Jones, John Hyams, Martin Garralaga, Henry De Silva, Milton Kibbee, Sam Appel, George Regas, Alfonso Pedroza, Agostino Borgato, Chris Pin Martin, C. I. Dafau, Carlos Salazar, L. R. Felix, Florence Fair, James Donlan, Clayton E. Kirby, George Mendoza, Juan Duval, Selmer Jackson, William Davidson

We're in the Money (August 17, 1935) Warner Bros. Pictures
Credits: Director: Ray Enright; Screenplay: F. Hugh Herbert, Brown Holmes, Erwin Gelsey; Story: George R. Bilson; Director of Photography: Arthur L. Todd; Editor: Owen Marks; Art Director: Carl Jules Weyl; Songs: Mort Dixon, Allie Wrubel; Musical Score: Bernhard Kaun, Heinz Roemheld; Production Dates: May 8-June 12, 1935; Running Time: 66 minutes
Cast: Joan Blondell, Glenda Farrell (Dixie Tilton), Hugh Herbert, Ross Alexander, Hobart Cavanaugh, Phil Regan, Anita Kerry, Henry O'Neill, Joseph King, E.E. Clive, Edward Gargan, Lionel Stander, Man Mountain Dean, Chief Little Wolf, Walter Brennan, Myron Cox, Gene Morgan, Dewey Robinson, Bob Perry, Frank O'Connor, Eddie Shubert, Charles McNaughton, Harvey Clark, Edwin Mordant, Harlan Briggs, Virginia Sale, Sam McDaniel, Frank Moran, John Kelly, Ethel Wales

Little Big Shot (September 7, 1935) Warner Bros. Pictures
Credits: Director: Michael Curtiz; Producer: Samuel Bischoff; Screenplay: Jerry Wald, Julius J. Epstein, Robert Andrews; Story: Harrison Jacobs; Directors of Photography: Tony Gaudio, Byron Haskin; Editor: Jack Killifer; Art

Director: Hugh Reticker; Songs: Mort Dixon, Allie Wrubel; Musical Score: Heinz Roemheld; Running Time: 78 minutes

Cast: Sybil Jason, Glenda Farrell (Jean), Robert Armstrong, Edward Everett Horton, Jack La Rue, Arthur Vinton, J. Carrol Naish, Edgar Kennedy, Addison Richards, Joe Sawyer, Emma Dunn, Ward Bond, Tammany Young, Murray Alper, Marc Lawrence, Guy Usher, Mary Foy, Jackie Saunders, George Humbert, Gene Morgan, Ernest Wood, Don Downen, Jesse Scott, Arvert Pott, Stuart Holmes, Burr Caruth, Gloria Fisher, Joseph Crehan, Kernan Cripps, Lee Prather, Lee Shumway, Dell Henderson, Howard C. Hickman, Milton Kibbee, Richard Powell, Georgia O'Dell, Claudia Coleman, Dorothy Gray

Miss Pacific Fleet (December 14, 1935) Warner Bros. Pictures
Credits: Director: Ray Enright; Executive Producers: Hal B. Wallis, Jack L. Warner; Screenplay: Peter Milne, Lucille Newmark, Patsy Flick, Delmer Daves; Story: Frederick Hazlitt Brennan; Director of Photography: Arthur L. Todd; Editor: Clarence Kolster; Art Director: Esdras Hartley; Musical Score: M. K. Jerome, Paul Marquardt; Production Dates: September 9-October 5, 1935; Running Time: 66 minutes

Cast: Joan Blondell, Glenda Farrell (Mae O'Brien), Hugh Herbert, Allen Jenkins, Warren Hull, Eddie Acuff, Marie Wilson, Minna Gombell, Guinn "Big Boy" Williams, Eddy Chandler, Edward Gargan, Anita Kerry, Mary Doran, Mabel Colcord, Harry Harvey, Connie Bergen, Paul Fix, Mary Treen

Snowed Under (April 4, 1936) Warner Bros.-First National Pictures
Credits: Director: Ray Enright; Producer: Harry Joe Brown; Executive Producers: Hal B. Wallis, Jack L. Warner; Screenplay: F. Hugh Herbert, Brown Holmes, Edward Chodorov, Mary C. McCall, Jr.; Story: Lawrence Saunders; Director of Photography: Arthur L. Todd; Editor: Harold McLernon; Art Director: Robert M. Haas; Musical Score: Heinz Roemheld; Production Dates: began November 20, 1935; Running Time: 64 minutes

Cast: George Brent, Genevieve Tobin, Glenda Farrell (Daisy Lowell), Patricia Ellis, Frank McHugh, John Eldredge, Porter Hall, Helen Lowell, Dick Purcell, Olin Howard, Joseph King, Alma Lloyd, Mary Treen, John Elliott, Stuart Holmes, John T. Murray, Andre Beranger, John Graham, Lester Dorr, Edward Piel, Sr., George Sorrell, Kay Hughes, Jack Herrick, Shirley Lloyd, Milton Kibbee, Eddie Shubert, Iris March, Naomi Judge

The Law in Her Hands (May 16, 1936) Warner Bros.-First National Pictures
Credits: Director: William Clemens; Producer: Bryan Foy; Screenplay: George Bricker, Luci Ward; Story: George Bricker; Director of Photography: Sid Hickox; Editor: Clarence Kolster; Art Director: Esdras Hartley; Musical Score: Heinz Roemheld; Production Dates: began early February 1936; Running Time: 58 minutes

Cast: Margaret Lindsay, Glenda Farrell (Dorothy "Dot" Davis), Warren Hull, Lyle Talbot, Eddie Acuff, Dick Purcell, Al Shean, Addison Richards, Joseph Crehan, Matty Fain, Milton Kibbee, Eddie Shubert, Mabel Colcord, Billy Wayne

Nobody's Fool (May 31, 1936) Universal Pictures
Credits: Directors: Arthur Greville Collins, Irving Cummings; Producer: Irving Starr; Screenplay: Ralph Block, Ben Markson, Jerry Sackheim; Story: Frank Mitchell Dazey, Agnes Christine Johnston; Director of Photography: Norbert Brodine; Editor: Morris Wright; Art Director: Charles D. Hall; Running Time: 75 minutes
Cast: Edward Everett Horton, Glenda Farrell (Ruby Miller), Cesar Romero, Frank Conroy, Warren Hymer, Clay Clement, Henry Hunter, Florence Roberts, Edward Gargan, Pierre Watkin, Ivan Miller, Robert Middlemass, Diana Gibson, George Irving, Marla Shelton, John King, Alyce King, Frank Reicher, Leonard Sues, John Marston, Bobby Gordon, Milburn Stone, Jane Buckingham, John Roche, Roy Brent, Frank Rhodes, Lee Phelps, William Royle, Stanley Price, Vance Carroll, Tom Steele, Larry Stanton, Louise Lorimer, Alphonse Martell, Adrian Rosley, Jack Chefe, John Ardell, Jacques Vanaire, Nan Grey, Bud Flannigan, Fifi Hall, Alphonse De Cruz, Albert Morin, Shirley Louie, Irving Bacon, Wade Boteler, Monte Vandegrift, Allan Cavan, Hal Craig, David Thursby, Ann Merrill

High Tension (July 17, 1936) 20th Century-Fox Pictures
Credits: Director: Allan Dwan; Producer: Sol M. Wurtzel; Screenplay: Lou Breslow, Edward Eliscu, John Patrick; Story: J. Robert Bren, Norman Houston; Director of Photography: Barney McGill; Editor: Louis R. Loeffler; Art Director: Duncan Cramer; Musical Director: Samuel Kaylin; Production Dates: April 27-late May 1936; Running Time: 63 minutes
Cast: Brian Donlevy, Glenda Farrell (Edith McNeil), Norman Foster, Helen Wood, Robert McWade, Theodore von Eltz, Romaine Callender, Joseph Sawyer, Hattie McDaniel, Murray Alper, Ward Bond, Beulah Hutton, Margaret Brayton, Dewey Bender, Marvin Stephens, June Gittleson, Sherry Hall, Louis Natheaux, Anita Thompson, Lucille Miller, Virginia Paxton, Ruth Peterson, Christine Gossett, Julie Carter, Dorothy Jones, Sonya Mitchell, Florence Wright, Gloria Roy, Landers Stevens, Wilfred Lucas, Eddie Hearn, John Rogers, Joe Brown, Harry Tenbrook, Harvey Perry, Sam Benson, Gordon Carveth, Duke Green, James Dundee, John Collins, Bob Rose, Matt Gillman, Charles Dorety, Philo McCullough, Dale Van Sickel, Eric Alden, Fred Kelsey, Bruce Mitchell, Ernest Wood, Mabel Kialoha, Mia Schiska, Sol Hoopii, Al Kikume, Iris Yamaoka, Dick Elliott, Ben F. Hendricks, Wade Boteler, Russ Clark, Earl Eby, J. Anthony Hughes, Walter Lawrence, Pat O'Malley, Pat Hartigan. Ethan Laidlaw, Fred N. Brown, A.H. Bogard, Wayne Rivers, George Chandler

Here Comes Carter (October 24, 1936) Warner Bros.-First National Pictures
Credits: Director: William Clemens; Producer: Brian Foy; Executive Producers: Hal B. Wallis, Jack L. Warner; Screenplay: Roy Chanslor; Story: Michael Jacoby; Director of Photography: Arthur L. Todd; Editor: Louis Hesse; Art Director: Ted Smith; Musical Score: Harold Arlen, Howard Jackson; Production Dates: began mid-June 1936; Running Time: 58 minutes
Cast: Ross Alexander, Glenda Farrell (Verna Kennedy), Anne Nagel, Craig Reynolds, Hobart Cavanaugh, George E. Stone, John Sheehan, Joseph Crehan, Dennis Moore, Norman Willis, John T. Murray, Charley Foy, Eddy Chandler, Davison Clark, Wayne Morris, Jane Wyman, Effie Afton, Billy Wayne, John Butler, Marjorie Weaver, Jack Wise, Al Herman, Billy Hampton

Gold Diggers of 1937 (December 28, 1936) Warner Bros.-First National Pictures
Credits: Director: Lloyd Bacon; Associate Producer: Earl Baldwin; Executive Producers: Hal B. Wallis, Jack L. Warner; Screenplay: Warren Duff; Based on the play by Richard Maibaum, Michael Wallace and George Haight; Director of Photography: Arthur Edeson; Editor: Thomas Richards; Art Director: Max Parker; Choreographer: Busby Berkeley; Musical Score: Heinz Roemheld; Production Dates: began mid-July 1936; Running Time: 101 minutes
Cast: Dick Powell, Joan Blondell, Glenda Farrell (Genevieve "Gen" Larkin), Victor Moore, Lee Dixon, Osgood Perkins, Charles D. Brown, Rosalind Marquis, Irene Ware, William B. Davidson, Olin Howland, Charles Halton, Paul Irving, Harry C. Bradley, Joseph Crehan, Susan Fleming, Fred "Snowflake" Toones, Pat West, Iris Adrian, Cliff Saum, Tom Wilson, Joseph Cunningham, Billy Wayne, Eddie Fetherston, Billy Arnold, Max Hoffman, Jr., Louis Natheaux, Bobby Watson, Harry Harvey, Dudley Dickerson, Frank Faylen, John Lester Johnson, Jack Mower, Antonio Filauri, Eric Wilton, Jack Norton, Charles Sylber, Gordon Hart, George Sorel, Harrison Green, Myrtle Stedman, Jacqueline Saunders, Tom Ricketts, Wedgwood Nowell, Rebecca Wassem, Arthur Stuart Hull, George Andre Beranger, Frances Morris, Louise Stanley, Milton Kibbee, Bobby Jarvis, Carl McBride, Selmer Jackson, Irene Coleman, Shirley Lloyd, Betty Mauk, Naomi Judge, Betty Melvor, Sheila Bromley, Lois Lindsay, Marjorie Weaver, Lucille Keeling, Virginia Dabney, Jane Marshall, Victoria Vinton

Smart Blonde (January 2, 1937) Warner Bros. Pictures
Credits: Director: Frank McDonald; Producer: Bryan Foy; Executive Producers: Hal B. Wallis, Jack L. Warner; Screenplay: Kenneth Gamet, Don Ryan, Harold Buckley, William Jacobs, Ben Grauman Kohn, Barry Starr; Based on a story by Frederick Nebel; Director of Photography: Warren Lynch; Editor: Frank Magee; Art Director: Carl Jules Weyl; Musical Score: Howard Jackson, Heinz Roemheld; Running Time: 59 minutes

Cast: Glenda Farrell (Torchy Blane), Barton MacLane, Winifred Shaw, Addison Richards, Robert Paige, Craig Reynolds, Charlotte Wynters, Jane Wyman, Joseph Crehan, Tom Kennedy, John Sheehan, Max Wagner, George Lloyd, Cliff Saum, Paul Panzer, Al Hill, Allen Pomeroy, Joseph Cunningham, Jack Richardson, Robert E. Homans, Jack Mower, Chic Bruno, Al Herman, Lyle Moraine, Jack Wise, Ferdinand Schumann-Heink, George Andre Beranger, Saul Gorss, George Guhl, Glen Cavender, Harry Jacobson, Carlyle Moore, Jr., Eddy Chandler, Alexander Cross, Harry Fox, Frank Faylen, Dennis Moore, Stuart Holmes, Tom Wilson, Wayne Morris, Martin Turner, Fred "Snowflake" Toones, Milton Kibbee

Fly Away Baby (June 17, 1937) Warner Bros. Pictures
Credits: Director: Frank McDonald; Producer: Brian Foy; Executive Producers: Hal B. Wallis, Jack L. Warner, Screenplay: Kenneth Gamet, Don Ryan; Story Idea: Dorothy Kilgallen; Director of Photography: Warren Lynch; Editor: Doug Gould; Art Director: Esdras Hartley; Musical Score: Howard Jackson; Running Time: 60 minutes
Cast: Glenda Farrell (Torchy Blane), Barton MacLane, Gordon Oliver, Hugh O'Connell, Marcia Ralston, Tom Kennedy, Joe King, Raymond Hatton, Gordon Hart, Anderson Lawler, Harry Davenport, Emmett Vogan, George Guhl, Lane Chandler, Carole Landis

Dance Charlie Dance (August 14, 1937) Warner Bros.-First National Pictures
Credits: Director: Frank McDonald; Producer: Bryan Foy; Executive Producers: Hal B. Wallis, Jack L. Warner; Screenplay: Crane Wilbur, William Jacobs; Based on a play by George S. Kaufman; Director of Photography: Warren Lynch; Editor: Frank Magee; Art Director: Carl Jules Weyl; Song: M. K. Jerome, Jack Scholl; Musical Score: Howard Jackson; Production Dates: mid-January 1937; Running Time: 64 minutes
Cast: Stuart Erwin, Jean Muir, Glenda Farrell (Fanny Morgan), Allen Jenkins, Addison Richards, Mary Treen, Charley Foy, Chester Clute, Collette Lyons, Tommy Wonder, Frank Faylen, Robert Homans, Harvey Clark, Olive Olson, Bernice Pilot, Glen Cavender, Tom Wilson, Al Herman, Jack Mower, Jack Wilsey, Edward Price, Fern Barry, Frances Morris, Mary Doyle, Don Downen, George Lloyd, Bob Cautiero, Edward Harkey, George Sorel, Loia Cheaney, Stuart Holmes, Ferdinand Schumann-Heink, John Harron, Sam Rice

You Live and Learn (September 1937) Warner Bros.-First National Pictures
Credits: Director: Arthur B. Woods; Producer: Irving Asher; Screenplay: Tom Phipps, Brock Williams; Story: Norma Patterson; Director of Photography: Basil Emmott; Running Time: 81 minutes

Cast: Glenda Farrell (Mamie Wallis), Claude Hulbert, Glen Elyn, John Carol, James Stephenson, Arthur Finn, George Galleon, Wallace Evennett, Margaret Yarde, Charlotte Leigh, Pat Fitzpatrick, Anna Murrell, Gibb McLaughlin, Muriel Blatcher

Breakfast for Two (October 22, 1937) RKO-Radio Pictures
Credits: Director: Alfred Santell; Producer: Edward Kaufman; Executive Producer: Samuel J. Briskin; Screenplay: Charles Kaufman, Paul Yawitz, Viola Brothers Shore, Horace Jackson, Jack Mintz, Lawrence Pohle, Harry Segall; Story: David Garth; Director of Photography: J. Roy Hunt; Editor: George Hively; Art Director: Van Nest Polglase; Musical Score: Nathaniel Shilkret, Max Steiner, Roy Webb; Production Dates: mid-July-August 16, 1937; Running Time: 67 minutes
Cast: Barbara Stanwyck, Herbert Marshall, Glenda Farrell (Carol Wallace), Eric Blore, Donald Meek, Etienne Girardot, Frank M. Thomas, Pierre Watkin

Torchy Blane, the Adventurous Blonde (November 13, 1937) Warner Bros.-First National Pictures
Credits: Director: Frank McDonald; Producer: Bryan Foy; Executive Producers: Hal B. Wallis, Jack L. Warner; Screenplay: Robertson White, David Diamond; Based on characters created by Frederick Nebel; Director of Photography: Arthur L. Todd; Editor: Frank Magee; Art Director: Max Parker; Musical Score: Howard Jackson, Heinz Roemheld; Production Dates: began late June 1937; Running Time: 61 minutes
Cast: Glenda Farrell (Torchy Blane), Barton MacLane, Anne Nagel, Tom Kennedy, George E. Stone, Natalie Moorhead, William Hopper, Charley Foy, Anderson Lawlor, Bobby Watson, Charles Wilson, Virginia Brissac, Leland Hodgson, Raymond Hatton, Frank Shannon, James Corilon, Granville Owen, Walter Young, George Guhl, Al Herman, Melbourne Ford, Dudley Dickerson, James Adamson, John Harron, Eddie Graham, Jack Mower, Robert Darrell, Willard Parker, Jerry Fletcher, Daisy Bufford, Houseley Stevenson, Sr., Howard Mitchell, Henry Otho, Rosella Towne, Robert Barrat, Hugh O'Connell

Hollywood Hotel (January 15, 1938) Warner Bros.-First National Pictures
Credits: Director: Busby Berkeley; Associate Producers: Samuel Bischoff, Bryan Foy; Executive Producers: Hal B. Wallis, Jack L. Warner; Screenplay: Jerry Wald, Maurice Leo, Richard Macauley; Story: Jerry Wald, Maurice Leo; Directors of Photography: George Barnes, Charles Rosher; Editor: George Amy; Art Director: Robert M. Haas; Choreography: Busby Berkeley; Musical Score: Ray Heindorf, Heinz Roemheld; Production Dates: early August-early November 1937; Running Time: 109 minutes

Hollywood Hotel

Cast: Dick Powell, Rosemary Lane, Lola Lane, Hugh Herbert, Ted Healy, Glenda Farrell (Miss Jones, aka "Jonesy"), Johnnie Davis, Louella Parsons, Alan Mowbray, Mabel Todd, Frances Langford, Jerry Cooper, Ken Niles, Duane Thompson, Allyn Joslyn, Grant Mitchell, Edgar Kennedy, Fritz Feld, Curt Bois, Perc Westmore, Eddie Acuff, Clinton Rosemond, William B. Davidson, Wally Maher, Georgie Cooper, Libby Taylor, Joseph Romantini, Paul Irving, Raymond Paige and His Orchestra, Benny Goodman and His Orchestra, Ziggy Elman, Ronald Reagan, Jeffrey Sayre, Jack Mower, Marianne Edwards, Sunny Bupp, David Leo Tillotson, John Ridgely, Jackie Morrow, William Worthington, Billy Wayne, Harry Fox, John Harron, Georgie Cooper, David Newell, Patsy Kane, Frances Morris, Sidney Perlman, Bobby Watson, Lester Dorr, Allen Fox, Allan Conrad, Edward Earl Ray, Owen King, George O'Hanlon, Jean Maddox, George Offerman, Jr., Betty Farrington, Helen Dickson, George Guhl, Jerry Mandy, Demetris Emanuel, Carole Landis, John Sheehan, William Mansell, Rosella Towne, Dina Smirnova, Jean Perry, Robert Homans, Alan Davis, Al Herman, Al Shean, Milton Kibbee, Harrison Greene, Clinton Rosemond, Pearl Adams, Helen Valkis, Ellen Clancy, Don Barclay, Leonard Carey, Dan Wolheim

Blondes at Work (February 5, 1938) Warner Bros. Pictures
Credits: Director: Frank McDonald; Producer: Bryan Foy; Executive Producers: Hal B. Wallis, Jack L. Warner; Screenplay: Albert DeMond; Director of Photography: Warren Lynch; Editor: Everett Dodd; Art Director: Charles Novi; Production Dates: early October-early November 1937; Running Time: 63 minutes
Cast: Glenda Farrell (Torchy Blane), Barton MacLane, Tom Kennedy, Rosella Towne, Donald Briggs, John Ridgely, Betty Compson, Thomas E. Jackson, Frank Shannon, Jean Benedict, Carole Landis, Suzanne Kaaren, Theodore von Eltz, Charles Richman, Robert Middlemass, Kenneth Harlan, George Guhl, Joe Cunningham, Ralph Sanford, Milton Owen, David Newell, Minerva Urecal, John Harron, Egon Brecher, Richard Loo, Cliff Saum, Spec O'Donnell, Jimmy Conlin, Jack Mower, Loia Cheaney, Bobby Jarvis, Glen Cavender, William Marceau, Roy Bancroft, Eddie Foster, Jack Goodrich, J.G. McMahon, Stuart Holmes, Gordon Hart, George O'Hanlon, Julius Molnar, Jr

Stolen Heaven (May 11, 1938) Paramount Pictures
Credits: Director: Andrew L. Stone; Screenplay: Eva Greene, Frederick J. Jackson, Andrew L. Stone; Director of Photography: William C. Mellor; Editor: Doane Harrison; Art Directors: Franz Bachelin, Hans Dreier; Musical Score: John Leipold; Production Dates: late December 1937-early February 1938; Running Time: 88 minutes
Cast: Gene Raymond, Olympe Bradna, Glenda Farrell (Rita), Lewis Stone, Porter Hall, Douglass Dumbrille, Joseph Sawyer, Esther Dale, Charles Judels, Ferdinand Gottschalk, Charles Halton, Bert Roach, Rolfe Sedan, Horace Murphy, Ferdinand Schumann-Heink

Prison Break (July 15, 1938) Universal Pictures
Credits: Director: Arthur Lubin; Producer: Trem Carr; Associate Producer: Paul Malvern; Screenplay: Dorothy Reid; Story: Norton S. Parker; Director of Photography: Harry Neumann; Editor: Jack Ogilvie; Art Director: Charles Clague; Musical Score: Hayes Pagel, Frank Sanucci; Production Dates: May 23-mid-June 1938; Running Time: 72 minutes
Cast: Barton MacLane, Glenda Farrell (Jean Fenderson), Paul Hurst, Constance Moore, Edward Pawley, Edmund MacDonald, Ward Bond, Guy Usher, Victor Kilian, Frank Darien, George Cleveland, Johnny Russell, Thomas Louden, Paul Everton

The Road to Reno

The Road to Reno (August 1938) Universal Pictures
Credits: Director: S. Sylvan Simon; Producer: Jules Brulatour; Associate Producer: Edmund Grainger; Screenplay: F. Hugh Herbert, Charles Kenyon, Brian Marlow; Story: Roy Chanslor; Based on the novel by I.A.R. Wylie; Director of Photography: George Robinson; Editors: Paul Landres, Maurice Wright; Art Director: Jack Otterson; Musical Score: Charles Henderson; Production Dates: early June-late July 1938; Running Time: 72 minutes
Cast: Randolph Scott, Hope Hampton, Glenda Farrell (Sylvia Shane), Helen Broderick, Alan Marshal, David Oliver, Ted Osborne, Samuel S. Hinds, Charles Murphy, Spencer Charters, Dorothy Farley, Mira McKinney, Renie Riano, Lita Chevret, Willie Fung, Jack Clifford

Exposed (November 4, 1938) Universal Pictures
Credits: Director: Harold D. Schuster; Associate Producer: Max Golden; Screenplay: Franklin Coen, Charles Kaufman; Story: George Bilson; Director of Photography: Stanley Cortez; Editor: Maurice Wright; Art Director: Jack Otterson; Musical Score: Frank Skinner; Production Dates: September 9-21, 1938; Running Time: 63 minutes
Cast: Glenda Farrell (Claire "Click" Stewart), Otto Kruger, Herbert Mundin, Charles D. Brown, Richard Lane, Lorraine Krueger, Bernard Nedell, David Oliver, Frances Robinson, Eddie "Rochester" Anderson, Irving Bacon, Maurice

Cass, John Kelly, John Butler, James Blaine, Dorothy Arnold, Jenifer Gray, Matt McHugh, Ed Le Saint, John Harron, Robert Homans, Eddie Fetherston, Ed Mortimer, Armand "Curly" Wright, Al St. John, Ernie Adams, Lew Short, Charles Murphy, Lester Dorr, Milton Kibbee, Lynton Brent, William Alston, Jim Farley, Charles McMurphy, Billy Engle, John Barton, Tony Paton

Torchy Gets Her Man (November 12, 1938) Warner Bros. Pictures
Credits: Director: William Beaudine; Associate Producer: Brian Foy; Executive Producers: Hal B. Wallis, Jack L. Warner; Screenplay: Albert DeMond; Based on characters created by Frederick Nobel; Directors of Photography: Warren Lynch, Arthur L. Todd; Editor: Harold McLernon; Art Director: Charles Novi; Musical Score: Howard Jackson; Production Dates: mid-July-August 17, 1938; Running Time: 63 minutes
Cast: Glenda Farrell (Torchy Blane), Barton MacLane, Tom Kennedy, Willard Robertson, Thomas E. Jackson, Frank Reicher, John Ridgely, Joe Cunningham, Herbert Rawlinson, George Guhl, Frank Shannon, Edward Raquello, Greta Meyer, Ed Keane, Nat Carr, John Harron, Loia Cheaney, Cliff Saum, Jack Mower, Leo White, Stuart Holmes, Jack Goodrich, Paul Panzer, Al Lloyd, Jack Wise, Alice Connor, Vera Lewis, Sally Sage

Torchy Blane in Chinatown (February 4, 1939) Warner Bros.-First National Pictures
Credits: Director: William Beaudine; Associate Producer: Bryan Foy; Executive Producers: Hal B. Wallis, Jack L. Warner; Screenplay: George Bricker; Story: Murray Leinster; Based on characters created by Frederick Nebel; Director of Photography: Warren Lynch; Editor: Frederick Richards; Art Director: Charles Novi; Musical Score: Howard Jackson; Production Dates: began mid-August 1938; Running Time: 58 minutes
Cast: Glenda Farrell (Torchy Blane), Barton MacLane, Tom Kennedy, Henry O'Neill, Patric Knowles, James Stephenson, Janet Shaw, Frank Shannon, George Guhl, Anderson Lawler, Richard Bond, Eddy Chandler, Eddie Lee, Jack Mower, Cliff Saum, Charles Hickman, Bruce Mitchell, John Harron, Sol Gorss, Alice Connor, Tetsu Komai, Roger Gray, Gordon Hart, Eric Wilton, Lee Phelps, Vera Lewis, Leo White, Frank Mayo, John Ridgely, Ed Mortimer

Torchy Runs for Mayor (May 13, 1939) Warner Bros. Pictures
Credits: Director: Ray McCarey; Associate Producer: Bryan Foy; Executive Producers: Hal B. Wallis, Jack L. Warner; Screenplay: Earle Snell; Story Idea: Irving Rubine; Based on characters created by Frederick Nebel; Director of Photography: Warren Lynch; Editor: Everett Dodd; Art Director: Max Parker; Musical Score: Howard Jackson; Production Dates: began mid-February 1939; Running Time: 60 minutes

Cast: Glenda Farrell (Torchy Blane), Barton MacLane, Tom Kennedy, John Miljan, Frank Shannon, Joe Cunningham, George Guhl, Joe Downing, Irving Bacon, John Butler, Charles Richman, John Harron, Walter Fenner, Millard Vincent, Joe Devlin, Kenneth Harlan, Larry Williams, Jack Daley, Wedgwood Nowell, Fern Barry, Alice Connors, Jack Mower, Jack Goodrich, John Ridgely, Chester Gan, Tommy Bupp, James Conlin, Claude Wisberg, Stuart Holmes, Eddie Graham, Hal Craig, Dave Roberts, Jeffrey Sayre, Sidney Bracy, Kit Guard, Glen Cavender

Johnny Eager (January 17, 1942) Metro-Goldwyn-Mayer Pictures
Credits: Director: Mervyn LeRoy; Producers: John W. Considine, Jr., Mervyn LeRoy; Screenplay: John Lee Mahin, James Edward Grant; Story: James Edward Grant; Director of Photography: Harold Rosson; Editor: Albert Akst; Art Director: Cedric Gibbons; Musical Score: Daniele Amfitheatrof; Production Dates: September 2-October 28, 1941; Running Time: 107 minutes
Cast: Robert Taylor, Lana Turner, Edward Arnold, Van Heflin, Robert Sterling, Patricia Dane, Glenda Farrell (Mae Blythe), Henry O'Neill, Diana Lewis, Barry Nelson, Charles Dingle, Paul Stewart, Cy Kendall, Don Costello, Lou Lubin, Joe Downing, Connie Gilchrist, Robin Raymond, Leona Maricle, Byron Shores, Robin Raymond, Cliff Danielson, Leona Maricle, Nestor Paiva, Emory Parnell, Douglass Newland, Gladys Blake, Janet Shaw, Beryl Wallace, Georgia Cooper, Richard Kipling, Sheldon Bennett, Anthony Warde, Elliott Sullivan, Pat West, Jack Carr, Art Miles, Gohr Van Vleck, Joe Whitehead, Alice Keating, John Dilson, Charles Thomas, Art Belasco, Larry Clifford, Harrison Greene, James C. Morton, Alex Pollard, Mike Pat Donovan, Alonzo Price, Edward Earle, Hooper Atchley, Joyce Bryant, Stanley Price

Twin Beds (April 24, 1942) Edward Small Productions-United Artists Pictures
Credits: Director: Tim Whelan; Producer: Edward Small; Screenplay: Kenneth Earl, Curtis Kenyon, Edwin Moran; Based on the play by Salisbury Fields and Margaret Mayo; Director of Photography: Hal Mohr; Editor: Francis D. Lyon; Art Director: John DuCasse Schulze; Musical Score: Dmitri Tiomkin; Production Dates: late September-late October 1941; Running Time: 85 minutes
Cast: George Brent, Joan Bennett, Mischa Auer, Una Merkel, Glenda Farrell (Sonya Cherupin), Ernest Truex, Margaret Hamilton, Charles Coleman, Charles Arnt, Thurston Hall, Cecil Cunningham, George Carleton, Toto, a dog

The Talk of the Town (August 20, 1942) Columbia Pictures
Credits: Director and Producer: George Stevens; Screenplay: Dale Van Em-

The Talk of the Town

ery, Irwin Shaw, Sidney Buchman; Story: Sidney Harmon; Director of Photography: Ted Tetzlaff; Editor: Otto Meyer; Art Director: Lionel Banks; Musical Director: Morris Stoloff; Production Dates: January 19-April 25, 1942; Running Time: 118 minutes

Cast: Cary Grant, Jean Arthur, Ronald Colman, Edgar Buchanan, Glenda Farrell (Regina Bush), Charles Dingle, Emma Dunn, Rex Ingram, Leonid Kinskey, Tom Tyler, Don Beddoe, George Watts, Clyde Fillmore, Frank M. Thomas, William "Billy" Benedict, Lloyd Bridges, Max Wagner, Ralph Peters, Pat McVey, Eddie Laughton, Harold "Stubby" Kruger, Maynard Holmes, Jack Carr, Ralph Dunn, Bill Lally, Edward Hearn, Roberta Smith, Dorothy Babb, Al Ferguson, Lee Phelps, Eddie Coke, Jack Shay, Eddie Bruce, Joe McGuinn, Lee "Lasses" White, William Gould, Ferike Boros, Jack Gardner, Dewey Robinson, Lew Davis, Gino Corrado, Mabel Todd, Dan Seymour, Frank Sully, Lee Prather, Clarence Muse, Leslie Brooks, Alan Bridge, Joe Cunningham, Jack Lowe, Robert Walker, John Tyrrell, George Hickman, Frank Mills, Blanche Payson, Bud Geary, Georgia Backus, Lelah Tyler, Holger Bendixen, Joe Garcia, Jay Guedalia, Oscar Hendrian, Dave Harper, Dick Jensen, Robert Keats, Herman Marks, Charles Perry, Al Rhein, Al Seymour, Charles St. George, Victor Travers, Ralph Volkie

259

City Without Men: **Leslie Brooks, Glenda, Linda Darnell, Doris Dudley and Margaret Hamilton**

City Without Men (January 14, 1943 Columbia Pictures
Credits: Director: Sidney Salkow; Producer: Budd Schulberg; Executive Producer: Samuel Bronston; Screenplay: W.L. River, Donald Davis, George Sklar; Story: Martin Berkeley, Budd Schulberg; Director of Photography: Phillip Tannura; Editor: Al Clark; Art Directors: Lionel Banks, Cary Odell; Musical Score: David Raksin; Production Dates: August 20-September 26, 1942; Running Time: 75 minutes
Cast: Linda Darnell, Edgar Buchanan, Michael Duane, Sara Allgood, Glenda Farrell (Billie La Rue), Leslie Brooks, Doris Dudley, Margaret Hamilton, Constance Worth, Rosemary DeCamp, Sheldon Leonard, Don DeFore, George Chandler, Tom Dugan, Arthur Hoerl, Joseph Crehan, Oscar O'Shea, Clyde Fillmore, Robert Homans, James Flavin, Lloyd Bridges, Richard Loo, Kam Tong, Dewey Robinson

A Night for Crime (February 18, 1943) Producers Releasing Corporation
Credits: Director: Alexis Thurn-Taxis; Producer: Lester Cutler; Associate Producer: Chris Beute; Screenplay: Arthur St. Claire, Sherman Lowe, John Vlahos; Story: Jimmy Starr; Director of Photography: Marcel Le Picard; Editor:

Frederick Bain; Musical Score: Leo Erdody; Production Dates: June 27-early July 1942; Running Time: 68 minutes

Cast: Glenda Farrell (Susan Cooper), Lyle Talbot, Ralph Sanford, Lina Basquette, Lynn Starr, Donald Kirke, Forrest Taylor, Rick Vallin, Marjorie Manners, Edna Mae Harris, Jimmy Starr, Erskine Johnson, Edwin Schallert, Harry Crocker, Ruby Dandridge, Joseph DeVillard, Niels Bagge, Florence O'Brien, Robert Frazer

Klondike Kate (December 16, 1943) Columbia Pictures

Credits: Director: William Castle; Producer: Irving Briskin; Screenplay: Houston Branch, M. Coates Webster; Story: William A. Pierce; Director of Photography: John Stumar; Editor: Mel Thorsen; Art Director: Lionel Banks; Songs: Paul Francis Webster, Harry Revel; Musical Score: Albert Glasser; Production Dates: September 21-October 13, 1943; Running Time: 64 minutes

Cast: Ann Savage, Tom Neal, Glenda Farrell (Molly), Constance Worth, Sheldon Leonard, Lester Allen, George Cleveland, George McKay, Dan Seymour, Harry Cording, Hank Bell, Edward Earle, Edward Keane, Tommy Kingston, Lee "Lasses" White, Dick Alexander, Madge Journeay, Pat Donnelly, Loretta Barnett, Gwen Seager, Janet Green, Susan Rosser, Lucille Allen, Shirley Shear, Harry Bradley, Minerva Urecal

Ever Since Venus (September 14, 1944) Larry Darmour Productions-Columbia Pictures

Credits: Director: Arthur Dreifuss; Producer: Rudolph Flothow; Screenplay: McElbert Moore, Arthur Dreifus, Connie Lee, Victor McLeod; Director of Photography: Benjamin H. Kline; Editor: Otto Meyer; Art Directors: Lionel Banks, Cary Odell; Musical Score: Edward H. Plumb; Production Dates: May 19-June 4, 1944; Running Time: 74 minutes

Cast: Ina Ray Hutton, Hugh Herbert, Ann Savage, Billy Gilbert, Glenda Farrell (Babs Cartwright), Ross Hunter, Alan Mowbray, Marjorie Gateson, Thurston Hall, Fritz Feld, Dudley Dickerson, Stuart Foster, Bill Shawn, Doreen Mulvey, Carol Adams, Kernan Cripps, Eddie Borden, Muni Seroff, Paul Conrad, Ralph Dunn, Bertha Priestley, P.J. Kelly, Charles Jordan, Isabel Withers, Pat Hogan, Mary Gordon, Jack Carr, Byron Foulger, Chester Clute, Harry Depp, Jack Rice, Ann Loos

Heading for Heaven (December 6, 1947) Ace Pictures-Producers Releasing Corporation

Credits: Director: Lewis D. Collins; Producer: George Moskov; Executive Producer: Jack Schwarz; Screenplay: Lewis D. Collins, Oscar Mugge; Based on a play by Daniel Brown and Charles Webb; Director of Photography: George Robinson; Editor: Martin G. Cohn; Musical Score: Hal Borne; Production Dates: late July-early August 1947; Running Time: 65 minutes

Cast: Stuart Erwin, Glenda Farrell (Nora Elkins), Russ Vincent, Irene Ryan, Milburn Stone, George O'Hanlon, Janis Wilson, Ralph Hodges, Dick Elliott, Charles Williams, Selmer Jackson, Harry Tyler, Ben Welden, Betty West, John Elliott, Jack Del Rio

I Love Trouble (January 15, 1948) Columbia Pictures
Credits: Director and Producer: S. Sylvan Simon; Screenplay: Roy Huggins, based on his novel *The Double Take*; Director of Photography: Charles Lawton, Jr.; Editor: Al Clark; Art Directors: Stephen Goosson, A. Leslie Thomas; Musical Direction: Morris Stoloff; Production Dates: May 14-June 19, 1947; Running Time: 93 minutes
Cast: Franchot Tone, Janet Blair, Janis Carter, Adele Jurgens, Glenda Farrell (Hazel Bixby), Steven Geray, Tom Powers, Lynn Merrick, John Ireland, Donald Curtis, Eduardo Ciannelli, Robert Barrat, Raymond Burr, Eddie Marr, Arthur Space, Sid Tomack, Douglas D. Coppin, George Bell, Isabel Withers, Nan Holliday, John Hart, Harry Tyler, Martha Montgomery, William Stubbs, Lane Chandler, Gene Stutenroth, Vesey O'Davoren, Gary Owen, Roseanne Murray, Claire Carleton, Louise Franklin, Karen X. Gaylord, Paul E. Burns

Mary Lou (January 23, 1948) Columbia Pictures
Credits: Director: Arthur Dreifuss; Producer: Sam Katzman; Story and Screenplay: M. Coates Webster; Director of Photography: Ira H. Morgan; Editor: Viola Lawrence; Art Director: Paul Palmentola; Musical Score: Joseph Dubin; Production Dates: September 5-13, 1947; Running Time: 65 minutes
Cast: Robert Lowery, Joan Barton, Glenda Farrell (Winnie Winford), Abigail Adams, Frank Jenks, Emmett Vogan, Thelma White, Pierre Watkin, Charles Jordan, Leslie Turner, Chester Clute, Frankie Carle

Lulu Belle (August 15, 1948) Benedict Bogeaus Productions-Columbia Pictures
Credits: Director: Leslie Fenton; Producer: Benedict Bogeaus; Associate Producer: Arthur M. Landau; Screenplay: Everett Freeman, Karl Kamb; Based on the play by Charles MacArthur and Edward Sheldon; Director of Photography: Ernest Laszlo; Editor: James Smith; Art Director: Duncan Cramer; Musical Score: Henry Russell; Production Dates: October 27-December 13, 1947; Running Time: 86 minutes
Cast: Dorothy Lamour, George Montgomery, Albert Dekker, Otto Kruger, Glenda Farrell (Molly Benson), Greg McClure, Charlotte Wynters, Addison Richards, William Haade, Ben Erway, Clancy Cooper, John Indrisano, Bud Wiser, George Lewis, Harry Hays Morgan, Jack Norman, Martha Holliday

Apache War Smoke (September 25, 1952) Metro-Goldwyn-Mayer Pictures
Credits: Director: Harold F. Kress; Producer: Hayes Goetz; Screenplay: Jerry Davis; Based on a story by Ernest Haycox; Director of Photography: John Alton; Editor: Newell P. Kimlin; Art Directors: Cedric Gibbons, Arthur Lonergan; Musical Direction: Alberto Colombo; Production Dates: late May-June 11, 1952; Running Time: 67 minutes
Cast: Gilbert Roland, Glenda Farrell (Fanny Webson), Robert Horton, Barbara Ruick, Gene Lockhart, Harry Morgan, Patricia Tiernan, Hank Worden, Myron Healy, Emmett Lynn, Argentina Brunetti, Robert Blake, Douglass Dumbrille, Chubby Johnson, Charlita, Carlos Vera, Connie Vera, Iron Eyes Cody

Girls in the Night (January 15, 1953) Universal-International Pictures
Credits: Director: Jack Arnold; Producer: Albert J. Cohen; Story and Screenplay: Ray Buffum; Director of Photography: Carl E. Guthrie; Editor: Paul Weatherwax; Art Directors: Robert F. Boyle, Alexander Golitzen; Musical Score: Henry Mancini, Herman Stein; Production Dates: late September-early November 1952; Running Time: 83 minutes
Cast: Harvey Lembeck, Joyce Holden, Glenda Farrell (Alice Haynes), Leonard Freeman, Patricia Hardy, Jaclynne Greene, Don Gordon, Anthony Ross, Emile Meyer, Susan Odin, Tommy Farrell, Paul E. Burns, John Eldredge, Alan Dexter, Charles Cane, Valerie Jackson, Harry Tyler, Russ Conway, Tom Dugan, Billy Wayne, Mario Siletti, Frank Richards, Ruth Perrott, James Hyland, Isabel Withers, Dick Rich, Robert R. Stephenson, John Ayers, Pearl Early, Beverly Long, Frank Marlowe, Danny Welton, Janet Stewart, Martin Dean, Winnie Chandler, Connie Warner, Thiela Darin, Jeanette Quinn, Gerry Pattison, Dolores Fuller, Norma Jean Nilsson, Leon Burbank, Marilyn Caroll, Patrick Miller, Jimmy Hawkins, Mike Donovan, Charles Sherlock, Donald Gordon, Don Pietro, Gary Stewart, Doug Carter, Jack Reynolds, Ralph Votrian, Henry Blair, Erwin Berwick, A.D. Sewall, Phil Bloom, Joe Wallis

Secret of the Incas (June 6, 1954) Paramount Pictures
Credits: Director: Jerry Hopper; Producer: Mel Epstein; Screenplay: Ranald MacDougall, Sydney Boehm; Story: Sidney Boehm; Director of Photography: Lionel Lindon; Editor: Eda Warren; Art Directors: Tambi Larsen, Hal Pereira; Musical Score: David Buttolph; Production Dates: mid-October-late November 1953; Running Time: 100 minutes
Cast: Charlton Heston, Robert Young, Nicole Maurey, Thomas Mitchell, Glenda Farrell (Mrs. Winston), Michael Pate, Leon Askin, William Henry, Kurt Katch, Edward Colmans, Yma Sumac, Booth Colman, Marion Ross, Harry Stanton, Alvy Moore, Grandon Rhodes, Robert Tafur, Martin Garralaga, Geraldine Hall, Rosa Rey, John Marshall, Dimas Sotello, Anthony Numkena

Susan Slept Here (July 29, 1954) RKO Radio Pictures
Credits: Director: Frank Tashlin; Producer: Harriet Parsons; Screenplay: Alex Gottlieb; Based on the play by Steve Fisher and Alex Gottlieb; Director of Photography: Nicholas Musuraca; Editor: Harry Marker; Art Directors: Carroll Clark, Albert S. D'Agostino; Musical Score: Leigh Harline; Production Dates: mid-December 1953-late January 1954; Running Time: 98 minutes
Cast: Dick Powell, Debbie Reynolds, Anne Francis, Glenda Farrell (Maude Snodgrass), Alvy Moore, Horace McMahon, Herb Vigran, Les Tremayne, Mara Lane, Rita Johnson, Maidie Norman, Ellen Corby, Louella Parsons, Red Skelton, Sue Carlton, Benny Rubin, Barbara Darrow, Oliver Blake, Lela Bliss, Michael Jeffrey, Evan Loew, Ken Carpenter

The Girl in the Red Velvet Swing (October 19, 1955) 20th Century-Fox Pictures
Credits: Director: Richard Fleischer; Producer: Charles Brackett; Screenplay: Walter Reisch, Charles Brackett; Director of Photography: Milton R. Krasner; Editor: William Mace; Art Directors: Maurice Ransford, Lyle R. Wheeler; Musical Score: Lionel Newman; Production Dates: June 1-early August 1955; Running Time: 109 minutes
Cast: Ray Milland, Joan Collins, Farley Granger, Luther Adler, Cornelia Otis Skinner, Glenda Farrell (Mrs. Nesbit), Frances Fuller, Phillip Reed, Gale Robbins, James Lorimer, John Hoyt, Robert F. Simon, Harvey Stephens, Emile Meyer, Richard Travis, Harry Seymour, Ainslie Pryor, Rosemary Ace, Marjorie Hellen, Diane DuBois, Suzanne Alexander, Peggy Connelly, Jean McCallen, Kay Hammond, Karolee Kelly, Jack Raine, Helen Van Tuyl, Paul Glass, Paul Power, Fred Essler, Ivan Triesault, Raymond Bailey, Charles Tannen, Edmund Cobb, James Conaty, Harry Carter, Robert Adler, Ruta Lee, Barbara Wilson, Marlene Felton, Marlene Felton, Marlene Reilly, Betty Caulfield, Oliver Cross, Theresa Lyons, Harold Miller, Samuel Colt, Midge Dare, Jerry Martin, Max Wagner, Steve Darrell, Henry Kulky, Edith Evanson, William Forrest, Leslie Parrish, Gil Perkins

Middle of the Night (June 17, 1959) Sudan Productions-Columbia Pictures
Credits: Director: Delbert Mann; Producer: George Justin; Screenplay: Paddy Chayefsky, based on his play; Director of Photography: Joseph C. Brun; Editor: Carl Lerner; Art Director: Edward Haworth; Musical Score: George Bassman; Production Dates: January 5-February 16, 1959; Running Time: 118 minutes
Cast: Fredric March, Kim Novak, Glenda Farrell (Mrs. Mueller), Albert Dekker, Martin Balsam, Lee Grant, Lee Phillips, Edith Meiser, Joan Copeland, Betty Walker, Lou Gilbert, Rudy Bond, Effie Afton, Jan Norris, David Ford, Audrey Peters, Dora Weissman, Lee Richardson, Anna Berger, Alfred Leberfeld, Nelson Olmstead, Walter Matthews

Kissin' Cousins (March 6, 1964) Metro-Goldwyn-Mayer Pictures
Credits: Director: Gene Nelson; Producer: Sam Katzman; Screenplay: Gerald Drayson Adams, Gene Nelson; Story: Gerald Drayson Adams; Director of Photography: Ellis W. Carter; Editor: Ben Lewis; Art Directors: George W. Davis, Eddie Imazu; Musical Score: Fred Karger; Running Time: 96 minutes
Cast: Elvis Presley, Arthur O'Connell, Glenda Farrell (Ma Tatum), Jack Albertson, Pamela Austin, Cynthia Pepper, Yvonne Craig, Donald Woods, Tommy Farrell, Beverly Powers, Hortense Petra, Bobby Stone, Teri Garr, Maureen Reagan, The Jordanaires

The Disorderly Orderly (December 16, 1964) Jerry Lewis Productions-Paramount Pictures
Credits: Director: Frank Tashlin; Producer: Paul Jones; Executive Producer: Jerry Lewis; Associate Producer: Arthur P. Schmidt; Screenplay: Frank Tashlin; Story: Norb Liebmann, Ed Haas; Director of Photography: W. Wallace Kelley; Editors: Russel Wiles, John Woodcock; Art Directors: Tambi Larsen, Hal Pereira; Musical Score: Joseph J. Lilley; Running Time: 90 minutes
Cast: Jerry Lewis, Glenda Farrell (Dr. Jean Howard), Susan Oliver, Karen Sharpe, Kathleen Freeman, Everett Sloane, Del Moore, Alice Pearce, Milton Frome, John Macchia, Jack E. Leonard, Barbara Nichols, Muriel Landers, Frank J. Scannell, Murray Alper, Frankie Darro, Richard Deacon, Tommy Farrell, Mike Mazurki, Kent McCord, William Wellman, Jr., Benny Rubin, Mike Ross, Herbie Faye

Tiger by the Tail (January 1970) United Pictures-American International Pictures
Credits: Director: R.G. Springsteen; Producer: Francis D. Lyon; Executive Producer: Earle Lyon; Assistant Producer: William Welch; Screenplay: Charles A. Wallace; Director of Photography: Alan Stensvold; Editor: Terry Morse; Musical Score: Joe Greene; Running Time: 99 minutes
Cast: Christopher George, Tippi Hedren, Dean Jagger, Charo, Glenda Farrell (Sarah Harvey), Lloyd Bochner, Skip Homeier, R.G. Armstrong, John Dehner, Alan Hale, Jr., Burt Mustin, Dennis Patrick, Martin Ashe, Frank Babich, Marilyn Devin, Ray Martell, Fernando Pereira, Olga Velez, Della Young, Tricia Young, The Mescalero Apache Horn Dancers, Meredith Neal and the Boot Heel Boys

Appendix B
Short Films

From 1930 to 1939, Glenda appeared in the following short subjects.

"The Lucky Break" (May 1930) Warner Bros. Pictures
Credits: Director: Arthur Hurley; Screenplay: Homer Mason, Stanley Rauh; Running Time: 21 minutes
Cast: Harry Fox, Glenda Farrell, Walter Regan, Leonard Jerome, Charles Hopkins, Edward Butler, Arthur Shaw

How to Break 90 #2: **"Position and Back Swing"** (June 10, 1933) Warner Bros. Pictures
Credits: Director: George Marshall; Screenplay: O.B. Keeler; Director of Photography: Alfred L. Todd; Editor: Rex Steele; Running Time: 10 minutes
Cast: Bobby Jones, Glenda Farrell (Golfer's Wife), Guy Kibbee

"Things You Never See on the Screen" (1935) Warner Bros. Pictures [produced for Warners employees]
Credits: Running Time: 10 minutes
Cast: Robert Armstrong, Johnny Arthur, Busby Berkeley, Joan Blondell, George Brent, James Cagney, Anne Canova, Judy Canova, Zeke Canova, Leo Carrillo, Irene Dunne, Glenda Farrell (Herself, outtake from *Traveling Saleslady*), Kay Francis, William Gargan, Hugh Herbert, Harry Holman, Edward Everett Horton, Allen Jenkins, Mervyn LeRoy, Grant Mitchell, Jean Muir, Pat O'Brien, Dick Powell, Bert Roach, C. Aubrey Smith, Barbara Stanwyck, Rudy Vallee, Warren William, Donald Woods

"Sunday Night at the Trocadero" (October 2, 1937) Metro-Goldwyn-Mayer Pictures
Credits: Director: George Sidney; Producer: Louis Lewyn; Screenplay: John W. Krafft; Running Time: 21 minutes
Cast: Reginald Denny, George Hamilton, Louis and Celeste, Medina and Mimosa, Peter Lind Hayes, The Three Brian Sisters, Gaylord Carter, International Models, Dick Foran, John Howard, Margot Grahame, Chester Morris, Robert Benchley, Sally Blane, Norman Foster, Connee Boswell, Groucho Marx, Ruth Johnson, Frank Morgan, Bert Wheeler, Eric Blore, June Collyer, Stuart Erwin, Toby Wing, Russell Gleason, Cynthia Lindsay, Glenda Farrell (Herself), Frank McHugh, Benny Rubin

Glenda in an outtake from *Breakdowns of 1937*, a blooper reel from Warner Bros.' biggest stars made for employees (available on YouTube).

"Breakdowns of 1937" (1937) Warner Bros. Pictures [produced for Warners employees]

Credits: Running Time: 7 minutes

Cast: Humphrey Bogart, Alice Brady, George Brent, Jane Bryan, Ricardo Cortez, Bette Davis, Claire Dodd, Glenda Farrell (Herself, outtakes from *Smart Blonde*), Errol Flynn, Dick Foran, Kay Francis, Alan Hale, Hugh Herbert, William Hopper, Ian Hunter, Allen Jenkins, Boris Karloff, Patsy Kelly, Margaret Lindsay, Barton MacLane, Alan Mowbray, Pat O'Brien, Dick Powell, Claude Rains

"For Auld Lang Syne" (April 29, 1938) Warner Bros. Pictures

Credits: Running Time: 7 minutes

Cast: John Barrymore, Freddie Bartholomew, Humphrey Bogart, James Cagney, Donald Crisp, Lily Damita, Bette Davis, Glenda Farrell (Herself), Louise Fazenda, Errol Flynn, Benny Goodman, Lionel Hampton, Hugh Herbert, George Jessel, Gene Krupa, Mayo Methot, Paul Muni, Harmon Nelson, Dick Powell, Basil Rathbone, Adrian Rollini, Rudy Vallee, Hal B. Wallis, Marie Wilson, Benny Goodman Orchestra, Texas Rangers

"Breakdowns of 1938" (1938) Warner Bros. Pictures [produced for Warners employees]

Credits: Executive Producer: Jack L. Warner; Running Time: 13 minutes

Cast: Eddie Acuff, Katharine Alexander, Fay Bainter, Robert Barrat, Ralph Bellamy, Humphrey Bogart, George Brent, Sheila Bromley, Claudette Colbert, Walter Connolly, Richard Cromwell, Bette Davis, Glenda Farrell (Herself, outtakes from *Fly Away Baby*), Louise Fazenda, Errol Flynn, Henry Fonda, Dick Foran, Kay Francis, Marjorie Gateson, Gregory Gay, Edmund Goulding, Eddie Graham, Bonita Granville, Fernand Gravey, William Haade, Raymond Hatton, Hugh Herbert, Ian Hunter, Isabel Jeans, Allen Jenkins, Patsy Kelly, Tom Kennedy, Anita Kerry, Patric Knowles, Margaret Lindsay, John Litel, Al Lloyd, Carole Lombard, Anita Louise, Wilfred Lucas, Mary Maguire, Michael Mark, Robert J. Mauch, Frank McHugh, Paul Muni, Pat O'Brien, Hugh O'Connell, Eugene Pallette, Nat Pendleton, Mary Philips, Dick Powell, Claude Rains, Marcia Ralston, Marjorie Rambeau, Basil Rathbone, Ronald Reagan, Addison Richards, Beverly Roberts, Rosalind Russell, Daniel Boone Savage, Ann Sheridan, Penny Singleton, Verree Teasdale, Rudy Vallee, Emmett Vogan, Patricia Walthall, Ben Welden, Sammy White, Walter Young

"Breakdowns of 1939" (1939) Warner Bros. Pictures [produced for Warners employees]

Credits: Running Time: 14 minutes

Cast: Brian Aherne, Leon Ames, Joan Blondell, Humphrey Bogart, Jane Bryan, James Cagney, Joe Cunningham, William B. Davidson, Bette Davis, Gloria Dickson, Glenda Farrell (Herself, outtakes from *Torchy Gets Her Man*), Stanley Fields, Errol Flynn, Kay Francis, John Garfield, William Gargan, Leo Gorcey, Billy Halop, Allen Jenkins, Bobby Jordan, Victor Jory, Tom Kennedy, Walter Kingsford, Patric Knowles, Priscilla Lane, Rosemary Lane, John Litel, Morton Lowry, Barton MacLane, Dickie Moore, Wayne Morris, Pat O'Brien, Herbert Rawlinson, Ronald Reagan, Edward G. Robinson, May Robson, "Slapsie" Maxie Rosenbloom, Russell Simpson, Claire Trevor, Jane Wyman

Appendix C
Television Programs

From 1949 to 1969, Glenda appeared in the following television programs: broadcast live and, later, shot on film for airing at a later date. Whenever available, Glenda's character names are also included.

The Chevrolet Tele-Theatre: **"The Mirror and the Manicure"** (January 3, 1949)
Credits: Network: NBC; Running Time: 30 minutes
Cast: Glenda Farrell, Guy Kibbee

Studio One: **"June Moon"** (June 22, 1949)
Credits: Director: Walter Hart; Producer: Worthington Miner; Teleplay: Gerald Goode; Based on a story by George S. Kaufman and Ring Lardner; Network: CBS; Running Time: 60 minutes.
Cast: Glenda Farrell (Lucille), Jean Carson, Eva Marie Saint, Jack Lemmon, Betty Furness, Edward Andrews.

The Silver Theatre: **"Gaudy Lady"** (February 13, 1950)
Credits: Network: CBS; Running Time: 30 minutes
Cast: Conrad Nagel, Glenda Farrell

Versatile Varieties (April 7, 1950)
Credits: Network: NBC; Running Time: 30 minutes
Cast: Glenda Farrell

Your Show of Shows (December 2, 1950)
Credits: Writers: Mel Brooks, Lucille Kallen, Danny Simon, Neil Simon, Mel Tolkin; Set Decorator: Frederick Fox; Choral Director: Clay Warrick; Network: NBC; Running Time: 90 minutes
Cast: Sid Caesar, Imogene Coca, Marguerite Piazza, Carl Reiner, Howard Morris, Glenda Farrell (Herself), Tom Avera

The Prudential Family Playhouse: **"Ruggles of Red Gap"** (February 27, 1951)
Credits: Based on the play by Harry Leon Wilson; Network: CBS; Running Time: 60 minutes
Cast: Glenda Farrell (Effie Flound), Walter Abel, Eva Condon, Henry Jones, John Martin, Harold McGee, Richard McMurray, Ethel Remey, Cyril Ritchard, Philip Tonge

Faith Baldwin Romance Theatre: **"Fountain of Youth"** (March 3, 1951)
Credits: Network: ABC; Running Time: 30 minutes
Cast: Glenda Farrell

Starlight Theatre: **"The Come-Back"** (May 31, 1951)
Credits: Director: Curt Conway; Teleplay: Eric Hatch; Network: CBS; Running Time: 30 minutes
Cast: Glenda Farrell (Dorine), Nils Asther, Melville Cooper, Jack Albertson, Gregg Sherwood, Hope Miller, Peter Frye, Jean Stapleton; **Announcer**: Durward Kirby

Armstrong Circle Theatre: **"The Darkroom"** (April 15, 1952)
Credits: Director: Gary Simpson; Teleplay: Kay Arthur; Network: NBC; Running Time: 60 minutes
Cast: Louise Allbritton, Glenda Farrell, Walter Matthau. John Newland

Tales of Tomorrow: **"The Build-Box"** (February 6, 1953)
Credits: Network: ABC; Running Time: 30 minutes
Cast: Glenda Farrell

Armstrong Circle Theatre: **"The Straight and Narrow"** (April 14, 1953)
Credits: Teleplay: Hamilton Benz; Network: NBC; Running Time: 60 minutes
Cast: Staats Cotsworth, Glenda Farrell (Serena Price), Walter Matthau

Justice: **"House of Hatred"** (February 17, 1955)
Credits: Network: NBC; Running Time: 30 minutes
Cast: Glenda Farrell, Frank McHugh

The Elgin Hour: **"Crime in the Streets"** (March 8, 1955)
Credits: Director: Sidney Lumet; Teleplay: Reginald Rose; Network: ABC; Running Time: 60 minutes
Cast: John Cassavetes, Ivan Cury, Glenda Farrell (Mrs. Dane), Will Kuluva, Van Dyke Parks, Robert Preston, Mark Rydell, David Winters, Jerry Wynne

Studio One: **"Miss Turner's Decision"** (March 21, 1955)
Credits: Teleplay: Howard Rodman; Network: CBS; Running Time: 60 minutes.
Cast: Edward Andrews, Glenda Farrell (Irene), Nina Foch, Betty Furness, Cliff Hall

Goodyear Playhouse: **"The Expendable House"** (October 9, 1955)
Credits: Director: Daniel Petrie; Teleplay: Reginald Rose; Network: NBC; Running Time: 60 minutes

Cast: John Cassavetes, Glenda Farrell, Paul Hartman, Pat Hingle, Jack Klugman, Gena Rowlands

Kraft Television Theatre: **"Home is the Hero"** (January 25, 1956)
Credits: Network: NBC; Running Time: 60 minutes
Cast: Brian Donlevy, Glenda Farrell, J. Pat O'Malley, Anthony Perkins

Kraft Television Theatre: **"The Man on Roller Skates"** (February 15, 1956)
Credits: Network: NBC; Running Time: 60 minutes
Cast: Steve Allen, Glenda Farrell (Alma Wilkes), Brenda Forbes, Vinton Hayworth, Henry Jones, Murray Matheson, John McGiver, Polly Rowles

Front Row Center: **"Uncle Barney"** (February 26, 1956)
Credits: Director: Ralph Nelson; Teleplay: Ben Starr; Network: CBS; Running Time: 60 minutes
Cast: Jim Backus, Nan Boardman, Ronnie Burns, Jacqueline de Wit, Glenda Farrell (May Cooper), Eilene Janssen, Irene Ryan, Tom Tully

The Alcoa Hour: **"Doll Face"** (March 18, 1956)
Credits: Director: Sidney Lumet; Teleplay: Jerome Ross; Network: NBC; Running Time: 60 minutes
Cast: Patricia Englund, Glenda Farrell (Eloise Schroeder), Jeff Harris, Gene Lyons, Nancy Malone, Frank McHugh, Addison Powell

Kraft Television Theatre: **"The Last Showdown"** (April 11, 1956)
Credits: Network: NBC; Running Time: 60 minutes
Cast: Edward Arnold, Glenda Farrell (Stella Harvey), Victor Jory, Elizabeth Montgomery, Gerald Parker, Louise Platt

The Kaiser Aluminum Hour: **"Cracker Money"** (December 4, 1956)
Credits: Teleplay: Steve Gethers; Network: NBC; Running Time: 60 minutes
Cast: Glenda Farrell, Louis Jean Heydt, Carol Lynley

The 20th Century-Fox Hour: **"The Marriage Broker"** (June 12, 1957)
Credits: Director: Lewis Allen; Producer: Peter Packer; Teleplay: Charles Brackett, Richard L. Breen, Joseph Calvelli, Walter Reisch; Director of Photography: Lloyd Ahern; Art Direction: Louis H. Creber, Lyle R. Wheeler; Network: CBS; Running Time: 60 minutes
Cast: Parley Baer, William Bishop, Veda Ann Borg, Ellen Corby, Lloyd Corrigan, Glenda Farrell (Mae Swasey), Kipp Hamilton, Liz Hunter, Joanna Lee, Harry Morgan, Lee Patrick, Roy Roberts, Helen Walker, Jesse White

Kraft Television Theatre: **"The Old Ticket"** (September 11, 1957)
Credits: Network: NBC; Running Time: 60 minutes
Cast: Larry Blyden, Eddie Bracken, Glenda Farrell, Paul Hartman, Sam Levene

Sheriff of Cochise: **"Federal Witness"** (December 13, 1957)
Credits: Director: Paul Guilfoyle; Producer: Mort Briskin; Teleplay: Don Martin; Director of Photography: Joe Novak; Editor: Harry Harris; Art Direction: Ralph Berger, Charles F. Pyke; Production Company: Desilu/National Telefilm Associates; Network: syndicated; Running Time: 60 minutes
Cast: John Bromfield, Sidney Blackmer, Glenda Farrell (Sarah Avery), Joe De Santis, George Gilbreth, Roy Barcroft, Chris Alcaide, Dean Fredericks, Joe Kirk, Russ Bender, Len Lesser, David Fresco, Richard Reeves, Roy Engel, Mark Scott

Kraft Television Theatre: **"Polka"** (December 18, 1957)
Credits: Network: NBC; Running Time: 60 minutes
Cast: Glenda Farrell, James Gregory, Clayton Hall, Kimetha Laurie, Torin Thatcher, Shelley Winters

Studio One: **"The Other Place"** (January 13, 1958)
Credits: Director: Jack Smight; Teleplay: Theodore Apstein; Based on the story by J.B. Priestley; Network: CBS; Running Time: 60 minutes
Cast: Phyllis Avery, Richard Carlson, Marilyn Erskine, Glenda Farrell (Mrs. Endsley), Betty Furness, Sir Cedric Hardwicke

Studio One: **"The Edge of Truth"** (April 28, 1958)
Credits: Teleplay: Adrian Spies; Network: CBS; Running Time: 60 minutes
Cast: Paul Douglas, Glenda Farrell (Claire), Scott Forbes, Betty Furness, John Lupton, Barbara Pepper, Dolores Sutton

Cimarron City: **"A Respectable Girl"** (December 6, 1958)
Credits: Director: James Neilson; Teleplay: Leo Townsend; Network: NBC; Running Time: 60 minutes
Cast: George Montgomery, Audrey Totter, Dorothy Malone, John Smith, Glenda Farrell (Maggie Arkins), Harold J. Stone, John Beradino, Walter Sande, Hal Baylor, Stuart Randall, Selmer Jackson, Wally Brown, Tom Fadden, James Griffith, Georgianna Carter

The Further Adventures of Ellery Queen: **"Confession of Murder"** (April 17, 1959)
Credits: Teleplay: Frederic Dannay, Manfred Lee; Network: NBC; Running Time: 60 minutes

Cast: Lee Philips, Scott Marlowe, Glenda Farrell, Wayne Morris, Kay Medford

General Electric Theater: **"Night Club"** (October 11, 1959)
Credits: Director: Mitchell Leisen; Teleplay: Katherine Brush; Story: Hagar Wilde; Network: CBS; Running Time: 30 minutes
Cast: Glenda Farrell (Mrs. Brady), Barbara Hale, Jeanne Cooper, Bea Benadaret, Joi Lansing, Amanda Blake, June Lockhart, Kathleen Freeman, Rosemary DeCamp, Sue Randall, Lori Nelson, Hope Emerson, Mari Aldon, Hillary Brooke

The Bells of St. Mary's (1959)
Credits: Director: Tom Donovan; Producers: Jacqueline Babbin, David Susskind; Teleplay: Irving Gaynor Neiman; Network: CBS; Running Time: 90 minutes
Cast: Claudette Colbert, Marc Connelly, Glenda Farrell, Nancy Marchand, Barbara Myers, Robert Preston, Charles Ruggles

Buick-Electra Playhouse: **"The Killers"** (November 19, 1959)
Credits: Director: Tom Donovan; Producer: Gordon Duff; Teleplay: A.E. Hotchner; Based on the story by Ernest Hemingway; Network: CBS; Running Time: 90 minutes
Cast: Diane Baker, Dane Clark, Glenda Farrell, Ned Glass, Louis Jean Heydt, Ingemar Johansson, Frank McHugh, Robert Middleton, Frederick O'Neal, Dean Stockwell, Ray Walston

Wagon Train: **"The Jess MacAbee Story"** (November 25, 1959)
Credits: Director: David Butler; Producer: Howard Christie; Teleplay: Jean Holloway; Story: Howard Christie, James A. Parker; Network: NBC; Running Time: 60 minutes
Cast: Robert Horton, Andy Devine, Glenda Farrell (Belle MacAbee), Tammy Marihugh, Marlene Willis, Carol Byron, Karen Green, Terry Burnham, Bill St. John, Ray Teal

The U.S. Steel Hour: **"Queen of the Orange Bowl"** (January 13, 1960)
Credits: Director: Paul Bogart; Teleplay: Robert Van Scoyk; Story: Roger Squire; Network: CBS; Running Time: 60 minutes
Cast: Johnny Carson, Robert Elston, Glenda Farrell (Mrs. Rausch), Anne Francis, Nancy Kovack, Al Lewis, Frank McHugh, Elizabeth Wilson

Play of the Week: **"A Palm Tree in a Rose Garden"** (April 4, 1960)
Credits: Teleplay: Meade Roberts; Network: NET

Cast: Barbara Barrie, Barbara Baxley, Glenda Farrell (Rose Frobisher), Robert Webber

The Islanders: **"The Widow from Richmond"** (December 18, 1960)
Credits: Network: ABC; Running Time: 60 minutes
Cast: Diane Brewster, Frank DeKova, Robert Ellenstein, Glenda Farrell (Mrs. Dan King), Suzanne Lloyd, James Philbrook, William Reynolds, Ron Soble

Story of Love: **"A String of Beads"** (February 7, 1961)
Credits: Musical Score: Wladimir Selinsky; Network: NBC; Running Time: 60 minutes
Cast: Jane Fonda, Chester Morris, Glenda Farrell, George Grizzard, Louisa Horton

Westinghouse Playhouse: **"A Tale of Two Mothers"** (February 17, 1961)
Credits: Teleplay: Ranald MacDougall; Network: NBC; Running Time: 30 minutes
Cast: Nanette Fabray, Wendell Corey, Bobby Diamond, Jacklyn O'Donnell, Doris Kemper, Glenda Farrell (Laura), Kathryn Card, Carl Benton Reid

The U.S. Steel Hour: **"Summer Rhapsody"** (May 3, 1961)
Credits: Network: CBS; Running Time: 60 minutes
Cast: Glenda Farrell, Abigail Kellogg, Clint Kimbrough, Tom Tully

The U.S. Steel Hour: **"The Woman Across the Hall"** (August 23, 1961)
Credits: Director: Bruce Minnix; Teleplay: Robert Wallstein; Network: CBS; Running Time: 60 minutes
Cast: Andre Baruch, Alan Bunce, Louis Edmonds, Glenda Farrell (Edna Huntington), Philip Faversham, Ruth Ford, James Neumarker

Special for Women: The Glamour Trap (November 16, 1961)
Credits: Director: Lela Swift; Teleplay: George Lefferts; Network: NBC
Cast: Barbara Dana, Glenda Farrell (Beauty Operator), Meg Mundy, Lenka Peterson, Marian Seldes

Frontier Circus: **"Mighty Like Rogues"** (April 5, 1962)
Credits: Director: Alan Crosland, Jr.; Teleplay: Frank Price; Story: Lawrence Kimble; Director of Photography: Ray Flin; Editor: Lee Huntington; Art Direction: John Meehan; Network: CBS; Running Time: 60 minutes
Cast: Chill Wills, John Derek, Richard Jaeckel, Glenda Farrell (Ma Jukes), Jena Engstrom, J. Pat O'Malley, Rene Godfrey, Roger Mobley, Ruth Carlson, Carl Carlsson, Joby Baker

The Defenders: **"The Naked Heiress"** (April 7, 1962)
Credits: Director: Jack Smight, Teleplay: Alan Boretz; Network: CBS; Running Time: 60 minutes
Cast: E.G. Marshall, Robert Reed, Glenda Farrell (Edna Holley), Robert Goodier, Salome Jens, Conrad Nagel

The U.S. Steel Hour: **"The Inner Panic"** (September 19, 1962)
Credits: Director: Walter Gorman; Teleplay: Albert Meglin; Network: CBS; Running Time: 60 minutes
Cast: Glenda Farrell, Teri Keene, Bill McNally, Gary Morgan, Simon Oakland, Cynthia Pepper, Tommy Sands, George Segal, Martin Sheen, Truman Smith, Ernie Stone, Charles Taylor

Route 66: **"Man Out of Time"** (October 5, 1962)
Credits: Director: David Lowell Rich; Producer: Mort Abrahams; Executive Producer: Herbert B. Leonard; Teleplay: Larry Marcus; Director of Photography: Jack A. Marta; Editor: Jack Gleason; Musical Score: Nelson Riddle; Art Direction: John T. McCormack; Network: CBS; Running Time: 60 minutes
Cast: Martin Milner, George Maharis, Luther Adler, Frank McHugh, Bruce Gordon, Glenda Farrell (Laverne), Jack Hollander, Ted Gunther, Harold Gary, Tom Carlin

Ben Casey: **"A Cardinal Act of Mercy," Parts 1 and 2** (January 14 and 21, 1963)
Credits: Director: Sidney Pollack; Producer: Matthew Rapf; Teleplay: Norman Katkov; Title Music: David Raksin; Network: ABC; Running Time: 120 minutes
Cast: Vince Edwards, Sam Jaffe, Gary Crosby, Timmy Everett, Glenda Farrell (Martha Morrison), Miranda Jones, Lillian Powell, Napoleon Simpson, Kim Stanley

The U.S. Steel Hour: **"Moment of Rage"** (March 6, 1963)
Credits: Network: CBS; Running Time: 60 minutes
Cast: Charles Aidman, Marc Connelly, Valerie Cossart, Glenda Farrell (Grace Smith), Kathryn Hays, David O'Brien, Eleanor Wilson

Rawhide: **"Incident at Farragut Pass"** (October 31, 1963)
Credits: Director: Thomas Carr; Producer: Vincent M. Fennelly; Associate Producer: Paul King; Teleplay: Jack Turley; Director of Photography: Jack Swain; Editor: Roland Gross; Art Direction: John B. Goodman; Network: CBS; Running Time: 60 minutes

Cast: Eric Fleming, Clint Eastwood, Paul Brinegar, James Murdock, Steve Raines, Rocky Shahan, Robert Cabal, Frankie Avalon, Glenda Farrell (Mrs. Elizabeth Farragut), Tommy Farrell, John Pickard, William Henry, Ralph Reed, Dee Pollack, Tom Kennedy

Dr. Kildare: **"The Exploiters"** (October 31, 1963)
Credits: Network: NBC; Running Time: 60 minutes
Cast: Richard Chamberlain, Raymond Massey, Crahan Denton, Glenda Farrell (Vera Dennis), Tommy Farrell, Judson Laire, Nancy Malone, Johnny Washbrook

The Fugitive: **"Fatso"** (November 19, 1963)
Credits: Director: Ida Lupino; Producer: Alan A. Armer; Executive Producer: Quinn Martin; Teleplay: Robert Piroch; Director of Photography: Fred Mandl; Editor: Walter Hannemann; Art Direction: Serge Krizman; Network: ABC; Running Time: 60 minutes
Cast: David Janssen, Jack Weston, Burt Brinckerhoff, Glenda Farrell (Mrs. Maggie Lambert), Barry Morse, Vaughn Taylor, Paul Langton, Harry Beckman, Paul Birch, Gary Walberg, King Calder; **Narrators**: William Conrad, Dick Wesson

Bonanza: **"The Pure Truth"** (March 8, 1964)
Credits: Director: Don McDougall; Producer: David Dortort; Teleplay: Lois Hire; Director of Photography: Haskell Boggs; Editor: Everett Douglas; Art Direction: A. Earl Hedrick, Hal Pereira; Network: NBC; Running Time: 60 minutes
Cast: Lorne Greene, Pernell Roberts, Dan Blocker, Michael Landon, Glenda Farrell (Lulabelle "Looney" Watkins), Stanley Adams, Lloyd Corrigan, Jay Lanin, Ray Teal, Raymond Guth, Olan Soule, Maudie Prickett, Gene Coogan, Betty Endicott, Herman Hack, Al Haskell, Phil Schumacher

Felony Squad: **"The Deadly Innocents"** (October 3, 1968)
Credits: Director: George McCowan; Teleplay: Jack Turley; Network: ABC; Running Time: 30 minutes
Cast: Howard Duff, Ben Alexander, Dennis Cole, Brooke Bundy, Irene Cagen, Jeff Donnell, Glenda Farrell (Jeanette Anderson), Donald Woods

Bewitched: **"The Battle of Burning Oak"** (March 13, 1969)
Credits: Director: R. Robert Rosenbaum; Producer: William Asher; Executive Producer: Harry Ackerman; Teleplay: Leo and Pauline Townsend; Network: ABC; Running Time: 30 minutes

Cast: Elizabeth Montgomery, Dick York, Agnes Moorehead, Edward Andrews, Glenda Farrell (Hortense Rockford), June Vincent, Doreen McLean, Mauritz Hugo, Harry Stanton, Harriet E. MacGibbon, David White

Appendix D
Broadway Performances

From the time she was seven years old, Glenda appeared in scores of stage productions. This listing covers all the shows that were staged in theaters in the Broadway district of New York. Glenda's character names are also included.

Divided Honors (September 30-November 1929) Forrest Theatre
Credits: Director: William B. Friedlander; Producer: K.A.L.; Playwright: Winnie Baldwin; Number of Performances: 40
Cast: Richard Bowler, Jeanne De Me, Glenda Farrell (Vina Chase), Doris Freeman, Philip Heege, Edgar Henning, Jane Kim, Guido Nadzo

Recapture (January 29-February 1930) Eltinge 42nd Street Theatre
Credits: Director: Don Mullally; Producer: A.H. Woods; Playwright: Preston Sturges; Number of Performances: 24
Cast: Ann Andrews, Meyer Berenson, Stuart Casey, Melvyn Douglas, Glenda Farrell (Gwendoliere Williams), Celia Loftus, Louza Riane, Joseph Roeder, Gustave Rolland, Hugh Sinclair

Love, Honor and Betray (March 12-April 1930) Eltinge 42nd Street Theatre
Credits: Director: Don Mullally; Producer: A.H. Woods; Playwrights: Fanny Hatton, Frederic Hatton; Adapted from the French of Andre Antoine; Number of Performances: 45
Cast: Alice Brady, George Brent, Glenda Farrell (The Young Girl), Clark Gable, Wilton Lackaye, Mark Smith, Robert Williams

On the Spot (October 29, 1930-March 1931) Forrest Theatre
Credits: Directors: Lee Ephraim, Carol Reed; Producers: Lee Schubert, J.J. Schubert; In Association with Edgar Wallace and Lee Ephraim; Playwright: Edgar Wallace; Number of Performances: 167
Cast: John Adair, Glenda Farrell (Marie Pouliski), John Gallaudet, George Drury Hart, John M. Kline, George Spelvin, Mike Sullivan, Suezo Tckero, Arthur R. Vinton, Alan Ward, John Wheeler, Crane Wilbur, Jeanne Winters, Anna May Wong, Stanley Wood

Life Begins (March 28-April 1932) Selwyn Theatre
Credits: Director and Producer: Joseph Santley; Playwright: Mary Macdougal Axelson; Number of Performances: 8
Cast: Mary May Bell, Helen Brooks, Alan Bunce, Lucile Charles, Clayton Collyer, Mildred Dunnock, Glenda Farrell (Florette Darian), Edwin Fleming,

Glenda with Alan Dinehart and Lyle Talbot

Jean Fullarton, Darley Fuller, Winifred Harris, Eleanor Hicks, Ellen Lowe, Douglas MacPherson, Joseph Marra, Lewis Martin, William McFadden, Edward Pawley, Antoinette Rachte, Dean Raymond, Earl Redding, Joanna Roos, Ruthelma Stevens, Elaine Troy, Elizabeth Von Nardroff, Frank Wilcox, Valerie Ziegler

Separate Rooms (March 23, 1940-September 6, 1941) Maxine Elliott's, Mansfield and Plymouth Theatres
Credits: Director: William B. Friedlander; Producer: Bobby Crawford; Playwrights: Joseph Carole, Alan Dinehart; In collaboration with Alex Gottlieb and Edmond Joseph; General Manager: Ben Stein; Stage Manager: Alan Dinehart; General Press Representative: C.P. Greneker; Number of Performances: 613
Cast: Alan Dinehart, Glenda Farrell (Pamela Barry), Lyle Talbot, Mozelle Brittonne, Edmund Dorsey, Austin Fairman, Madora Keene, James Robbins, Jack Smart

The Life of Reilly (April 29-May 2, 1942) Broadhurst Theatre
Credits: Director: Roy Hargrave; Producers: Day Tuttle, Harald Bromley; Playwright: William Roos; Scenic Design: Samuel Leve; Number of Performances: 5

THE PLAYBILL

FOR THE BROADHURST THEATRE

Playbill from *Life of Reilly*

Cast: Charita Bauer, Theodora Bender, John Call, Guerita Donnelly, Glenda Farrell (Jackie Moultrie), Peter Hobbs, Len Hollister, George Mathews, Frances Nielsen, John Shellie, Howard Smith, Loring Smith, Norman Tokar, Polly Walters

The Overtons (February 6-July 7, 1945) Booth, Forrest and National Theatres
Credits: Director: Elisabeth Bergner; Producer: Paul Czinner; Playwright: Vincent Lawrence; Scenic Design: Edward Gilbert; Costume Design: Hattie Carnegie; Number of Performances: 175
Cast: Glenda Farrell (Judith Bancroft), Arlene Francis, Walter Greaza, Don Kohler, Charles Lang, Mary Lawrence, Jack Whiting

Mrs. Gibbons' Boys (May 4-7, 1949) Music Box Theatre
Credits: Director and Producer: George Abbott; Playwrights: Will Glickman, Joseph Stein; Scenic and Lighting Design: John Root; Costume Design: John Robert Lloyd; Number of Performances: 5
Cast: Edward Andrews, Lois Bolton, Francis Compton, Royal Dano, William David, Glenda Farrell (Myra Ward), Tom Lewis, Helen Mayon, Richard Taber, Ray Walston

Home is the Hero (September 22-October 16, 1954) Booth Theatre
Credits: Director and Producer: Worthington Miner; Playwright: Walter Macken; Production Designer: Marvin Reiss; Stage Manager: Elliot Martin; Number of Performances: 30
Cast: Glenda Farrell (Daylia), Frances Fuller, Peggy Ann Garner, Donald Harron, Loretta Leversee, Walter Macken, J. Pat Malley, Christopher Plummer, Art Smith, Ann Thomas

Masquerade (March 16, 1959) John Golden Theatre
Credits: Director: Jed Horner; Producers: Richard W. Krakauer, Louis D'Almeida; Playwright: Sigmund Miller; Incidental Music: Sol Kaplan; Scenic and Lighting Design: Paul Morrison; Costume Design: Robert Mackintosh; General Manager: Herman Bernstein; Company Manager: Edward Choate; Production Stage Manager: Herman Shapiro; Stage Manager: William Callan; Press Representatives: Karl Bernstein, Ben Kornzweig, Robert E. Feinberg; Number of Performances: 1
Cast: Jack Cannon, Donald Cook, Glenda Farrell (Isabel Chamberlain), Anne Ives, Cloris Leachman, Gene Lyons, Marc Richman; Understudies: William Callan, Jack Cannon, Gertrude Corey, Constance Simmons

Forty Carats (December 26, 1968-November 7, 1970) Morosco Theatre
Credits: Director: Abe Burrows; Producer: David Merrick; Associate Producer: Samuel Liff; Playwrights: Pierre Barillet, Jean-Pierre Gredy; Adapted by Jay Allen; Scenic Design: Will Steven Armstrong; Costume Design: William McHone; Lighting Design: Martin Aronstein; Hair Design: Ernest Adler; Assistant to Mr. Aronstein: Lawrence Metzler; Assistant to Mr. Adler: Ray Iagnocco; General Manager: Jack Schlissel; Company Manager: Richard Highley; Assistant to Mr. Schlissel: Joel Thurm; Production Stage Manager: James Burrows; Stage Manager: Jeff Chambers; Assistant Stage Managers: Michael Nouri, Susan King; Number of Performances: 780
Cast: Julie Harris, Franklin Cover, Glenda Farrell (Maud Hayes), Murray Hamilton, Polly Rowles, Marco St. John, Gretchen Corbett, John Cecil Holm, Nancy Marchand, Michael Nouri, Iva Withers; Understudies: David Baker, Jeff Chambers, Susan King, Cele McLaughlin, Michael Nouri

Appendix E
Glenda's Favorites

Following are biographical sketches of Glenda's best friends and colleagues who worked with her in the Warner Bros. "stock company" during the 1930s.

Joan Blondell (August 30, 1906–December 25, 1979)

Born into a vaudeville family in New York City, Rose Joan Blondell began her acting career at the age of four months, lying in a cradle, during a stage performance of *The Greatest Love*. After her itinerant parents settled in Texas, Joan won the 1926 Miss Dallas pageant and placed fourth in the Miss America contest held in Atlantic City. She attended teacher's college at what is now the University of North Texas in Denton, and she eventually moved to New York where, in 1930, she and James Cagney were "discovered" by Al Jolson in the play *Penny Arcade*.

Signing a contract with Warner Bros., Blondell appeared opposite Cagney in *Sinner's Holiday* (1930), the film version of *Penny Arcade*, *Other Men's Women* (1931), *The Public Enemy* (1931), *Blonde Crazy* (1931), *The Crowd Roars* (1932), *Footlight Parade* (1933) and *He Was Her Man* (1934). Other

***Kansas City Princess*: Joan Blondell and Glenda**

than her seven films with Cagney and nine with Glenda, she also appeared in Warner Bros.' *Union Depot* (1931), with Douglas Fairbanks, Jr., *Lawyer Man* (1932), with William Powell, *Gold Diggers of 1933* (1933), with Warren William, *Dames* (1934) with Dick Powell, *Bullets or Ballots* (1936), with Edward G. Robinson and Humphrey Bogart and *The Perfect Specimen* (1937), with Errol Flynn.

Her work at other studios includes 20th Century-Fox's *A Tree Grows in Brooklyn* (1945), *Nightmare Alley* (1947) and *Will Success Spoil Rock Hunter?* (1957). One of her later film roles, in MGM's Steve McQueen drama *The Cincinnati Kid* (1965), reunited her with Edward G. Robinson. She also worked frequently on television.

Blondell was married three times, to cinematographer George Barnes (1933-1936), actor Dick Powell (1936-1944) and producer Mike Todd (1947-1950). She passed away, aged 73, from leukemia in Santa Monica, California. Her star on the Hollywood Walk of Fame is located at 6311 Hollywood Boulevard.

Mary Brian (February 17, 1906–December 30, 2002)

Born in Corsicana, Texas, Mary Byrdie Dantzler moved to Long Beach, California while a teenager. At 18, she was discovered while competing in a bathing beauty contest and landed a screen test at Paramount, where she was placed under contract. For the next eight years, she starred in over 40 films, including *Peter Pan* (1924), with Betty Bronson, *Beau Geste* (1926), with Ronald Colman, *Varsity* (1928), with Buddy Rogers and *The Virginian* (1929), with Gary Cooper. She easily made the transition from silent to sound pictures.

During her years as a freelance player, Brian appeared in Warner Bros.' *It's Tough to be Famous* (1932), with Douglas Fairbanks, Jr., *Blessed Event* (1932), with Lee Tracy and Dick Powell, *Hard to Handle* (1933), with James Cagney and *Girl Missing* (1933), with Glenda. After retiring in 1954, she pursued her interest in portrait painting.

Brian was married twice, to magazine illustrator Jon Whitcomb (May 4–August 8, 1941) and film editor George Tomasini (1947–1964; his death). She died, aged 92, of heart failure in Del Mar, California. Her star on the Hollywood Walk of Fame is located at 1559 Vine Street.

Ruth Donnelly (May 17, 1896–November 17, 1982)

Born in Trenton, New Jersey, the brilliant comic actress Ruth Donnelly made her stage debut at age 17 in the chorus of the touring show *The Quaker Girl* (1913). Admired by George M. Cohan, she appeared in several of his Broadway productions, including *Going Up* (1917), *A Prince There Was* (1918) and *The Meanest Man in the World* (1920).

Havana Widows: Joan Blondell, Frank McHugh, Guy Kibbee, Lon Talbot, Ruth Donnelly and Glenda.

After relocating to Hollywood in 1931, Donnelly played wisecracking wives, mothers and friends of the heroine in many Warner Bros. films, including five with Glenda. She bounced her witty repartee off James Cagney in *Hard to Handle* (1933) and Edward G. Robinson in *A Slight Case of Murder* (1938), and has the distinction of playing Guy Kibbee's wife in several pictures, including Columbia's *Mr. Smith Goes to Washington* (1939).

Her later films include Universal's *My Little Chickadee* (1940), starring W.C. Fields, RKO-Radio's *The Bells of St. Mary's* (1945), costarring Bing Crosby and Ingrid Bergman, 20th Century-Fox's *The Snake Pit* (1948), starring Olivia de Havilland, and *Where the Sidewalk Ends* (1950), with Dana Andrews and Gene Tierney. She made her final filmed appearance in an episode of the television show *The Doctors and the Nurses* in 1965.

Donnelly returned to Broadway one last time, as a replacement for actress Patsy Kelly, in Busby Berkeley and Burt Shevelove's *No, No, Nanette* (1971-1973), with Jack Gilford and Ruby Keeler. She was married to airline executive Basil de Guichard (1932-1958). Following his death, she lived at Manhattan's Wellington Hotel. She died, aged 86, in New York City.

Hugh Herbert (August 10, 1884–March 12, 1952)

Born in Binghamton, New York, vaudeville comedian and writer Hugh Herbert appeared on Broadway in *Polly of Hollywood* and in Warner Bros.' film *Husbands for Rent* in 1927. While under contract to the studio, he appeared in *Footlight Parade* (1933), *College Coach* (1934), with Pat O'Brien, *Wonder Bar* (1934), with Al Jolson, *Dames* (1934), *A Midsummer Night's Dream* (1935), with James Cagney and *The Perfect Specimen* (1937). He co-starred with Glenda eight times at Warners and once for Columbia (*Ever Since Eve*).

Herbert was adept at playing eccentric and absentminded, often wealthy or scholarly characters. Known for stammering to himself and using a trademark "woo, woo" (or "hoo, hoo") laugh (which grew more frequent in later years), he also appeared in *The Black Cat* (1941), with Basil Rathbone and Bela Lugosi, and *Hellzapoppin'* (1941) at Universal, *Mrs. Wiggs of the Cabbage Patch* (1942), with Fay Bainter at Paramount, *Kismet* (1944), with Marlene Dietrich at MGM, and *A Song is Born* (1948), with Danny Kaye for Samuel Goldwyn-RKO Radio. He gave his final feature film performance in Republic's *Havana Rose* (1951), starring Estelita Rodriguez.

Herbert was married twice, to Anita Pam (dates unavailable) and Rose Epstein (1932-1949). He died, aged 67, of a heart attack in North Hollywood. His star on the Hollywood Walk of Fame is located at 6251 Hollywood Boulevard.

Allen Jenkins (April 9, 1900–July 20, 1974)

David Allen Curtis Jenkins was born in Staten Island, New York. (His birth name was not "Alfred McGonegal," as previously reported.) Following studying at the American Academy of Dramatic Arts, he made his stage debut alongside James Cagney in the off-Broadway musical *Pitter-Patter*. From 1923, he played roles in Broadway productions, including *The Front Page* (1928), *Five Star Final* (1930) and *Blessed Event* (1932), when he was "discovered" by Darryl F. Zanuck.

While under contract to Warner Bros., he usually played a variation on the same character, a Brooklyn-accented wise guy, in both comedies and dramas. He has the distinction of playing sidekick to *all* the Warners' tough guys, Edward G. Robinson, James Cagney and Humphrey Bogart, in numerous films. His other studio credits include nine titles with Glenda, *Blessed Event* (1932), *Blondie Johnson* (1933), with Joan Blondell and Chester Morris, *The Mind Reader* (1933), with Warren William, *The Singing Kid* (1936), with Al Jolson and *Footsteps in the Dark* (1941), with Errol Flynn.

Jenkins' work at other studios includes Columbia's *Whirlpool* (1934), with Jack Holt and Jean Arthur, Samuel Goldwyn's *Dead End* (1937), with Bogart, Universal's *Destry Rides Again* (1939), with James Stewart and Marlene Dietrich and RKO-Radio's *Falcon* detective series starring George Sanders.

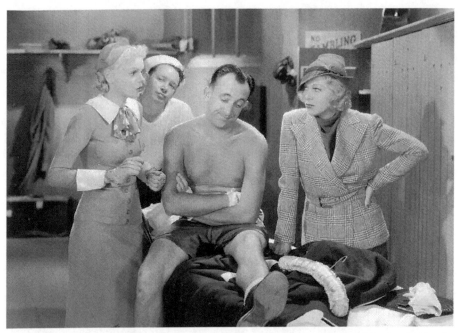

Kansas City Princess: Marie Wilson, Eddie Acuff (back), Allen Jenkins and Glenda

Jenkins was a prolific presence on television. One of his later film roles, in Warner Bros.' *Rat Pack* musical *Robin and the 7 Hoods* (1964), required him to reprise his gangster's sidekick from the 1930s.

Jenkins was married to Mary Landee (dates unavailable). Troubled by alcoholism, he spoke about the malady in the United States House and Senate, and helped found the first Alcoholics Anonymous programs in California women's prisons. He died, aged 74, from complications after lung cancer surgery in Santa Monica, California.

Guy Kibbee (March 6, 1882–May 24, 1956)

Born in El Paso, Texas, Guy Bridges Kibbee began his acting career while performing aboard Mississippi riverboats. Following two Broadway shows, he moved to Los Angeles in late 1930. Small roles in several Hollywood films led to a contract with Warner Bros. the following year. He was equally adept at comedy and drama, and appeared in a wide variety of films.

Kibbee's Warner Bros. credits include five films with James Cagney, *Two Seconds* (1932), with Edward G. Robinson, *42nd Street* (1933), with Warner Baxter, *The Life of Jimmy Dolan* (1933), with Douglas Fairbanks, Jr., *Babbitt* (1934), with Aline MacMahon and *Captain Blood* (1935), with Errol Flynn. He worked in three Warners films with Glenda, as well as one for Columbia (*Lady for a Day*).

His films for other studios include Columbia's *Mr. Smith Goes to Washington* (1939), with James Stewart, United Artists' *Our Town* (1940), with William Holden, and two John Ford Westerns starring John Wayne: RKO-Radio's *Fort Apache* and MGM's *3 Godfathers* (both 1948), which proved to be his final feature films.

Kibbee was married twice, to Helen Shea (1918-1923) and Esther Reed (1925-1956; his death). He died, aged 74, of complications from Parkinson's disease in East Islip, Long Island, New York. Warner Bros. player Milton Kibbee (1896-1970), his younger brother, appears in small roles in 15 of Glenda's films for the studio.

Aline MacMahon (May 3, 1899–October 12, 1991)

Born in McKeesport, Pennsylvania, Aline Laveen MacMahon was raised in New York City. She attended Brooklyn's Erasmus Hall High School and Barnard College before making her Broadway debut in *The Madras House* (1921). She worked steadily in the theater, including roles in *Artists and Models* (1925), *Maya* (1928) and *Winter Bound* (1929).

MacMahon's first film was Warner Bros.' *Five Star Final* (1931), starring Edward G. Robinson. While under contract to the studio, she appeared in two films with Glenda, as well as *The Mouthpiece* (1932), with Warren William, *Week-End Marriage* (1932), with Loretta Young, *Silver Dollar* (1932), with Edward G. Robinson, *Heroes for Sale* (1933), with Richard Barthelmess, and *The World Changes* (1933), with Paul Muni.

Beginning in 1939, MacMahon alternated between Hollywood and Broadway assignments. She received a Best Supporting Actress Oscar nomination for MGM's *Dragon Seed* (1944). She later appeared in MGM's *The Search* (1948), with Montgomery Clift, and Columbia's *The Man from Laramie* (1955), with James Stewart. She also sporadically worked on television, and played her last stage role in 1975.

MacMahon was married to architect and city planner Clarence Stein (1928-1975; his death). She passed away at age 92 of pneumonia, in New York City.

Frank McHugh (May 23, 1898–September 11, 1981)

Francis Curray McHugh was born into a theatrical family in Homestead, Allegheny County, Pennsylvania. He began performing in his parents' stock company as a young child, joining his older brother Matt (1894-1971) and younger sister Kitty (1902-1954). Frank later appeared on Broadway in *Fog*, *Tenth Avenue* and *Excess Baggage* (all 1927), as well as *Conflict* and *Show Girl* (both 1929).

Signed by Warner Bros. in 1930, McHugh worked with nearly every star, including his close friend, James Cagney, with whom he appeared in 11 films. A prodigiously talented comedian (with his own trademark laugh), he could play drama equally well (*The Roaring Twenties* [1939]). His Warner Bros. work also includes seven films with Glenda, *The Widow from Chicago* (1930), with Edward G. Robinson, *The Strange Love of Molly Louvain* (1932), with Ann Dvorak, *Ex-Lady* (1933), with Bette Davis and *Dodge City* (1939), with Errol Flynn.

McHugh's films at other studios include *The Front Page* (1931), with Pat O'Brien, for Caddo-United Artists, *I Love You Again* (1940), costarring William Powell and Myrna Loy, for MGM and *Going My Way* (1944), with Bing Crosby, for Paramount. He continued to work in films and frequently on television until 1969.

McHugh was married to Dorothy Spencer (1933-1981; his death). He passed away, aged 83, in Greenwich, Connecticut. His siblings, Matt and Kitty, also played dozens of roles in Hollywood films, including many for Warner Bros.

Lyle Talbot (February 8, 1902–March 2, 1996)

Born Lysle Henderson in Pittsburgh, Pennsylvania, Lyle Talbot grew up in Brainerd, Nebraska and left home at 17 to become a magician's assistant. After playing in tent shows and his own stock company, he was given a screen test at Warner Bros. in 1931, impressing both Darryl F. Zanuck and William Wellman.

Talbot appeared with Glenda, whom he also saw on a social basis, in six Warner Bros. films and one for PRC (*A Night for Crime*). His Warner Bros. credits also include *Love is a Racket* (1932), with Douglas Fairbanks, Jr. and Ann Dvorak, *20,000 Years in Sing Sing* (1933), with Spencer Tracy and Bette Davis and *Oil for the Lamps of China* (1936), with Pat O'Brien.

One of the founders of the Screen Actors Guild, Talbot became deeply involved in labor activism, which eventually led to Warner Bros. ending his contract. For a time, he took whatever roles came his way, including many Poverty Row productions, the most infamous being Edward D. Wood's awe-inspiringly awful *Glen or Glenda?* (1953), *Jail Bait* (1954) and *Plan 9 from Outer Space* (1959), the final film starring Bela Lugosi.

But Talbot's versatility weathered the storm, and he remained active, in films, on television and on the stage, retiring in 1987 at the age of 85. He was married four times, to Marguerite Cramer (1937-1940), actress Abigail Adams (January 22-September 11, 1942), Keven McClure (1946-1947) and Margaret Carol Epple (1948-1989), with whom he finally found wedded happiness. Prior to his death from natural causes in San Francisco at age 94, he was the last remaining founder of SAG.

Bibliography

Interviews

Farrell, Tommy. Interview with Dan Van Neste. *Classic Images*, Vol. 275, May 1998.

Harris, Julie. Interview with Scott Allen Nollen, May 1996.

Hoey, Michael A. Conversation with Scott Allen Nollen, 6 November 2013.

Letters and Telegrams

Borzage, Frank. Western Union telegram to Columbia Pictures, 21 September 1933.

Harris, Julie. Letter to Scott Allen Nollen, 5 May 1996.

Archives

University of Southern California, Los Angeles. The Papers of Edward G. Robinson.

University of Wisconsin, Madison. Wisconsin Center for Film and Theatre Research. Warner Bros. Files.

Memoirs

Burns, Robert E. *I Am a Fugitive from a Georgia Chain Gang!* Athens: University of Georgia Press, 1997.

Burns, Vincent G. *Out of These Chains*. Los Angeles: New World Books, 1942.

Robinson, Edward G., with Leonard Spigelglass. *All My Yesterdays: An Autobiography*. New York: Hawthorn Books, Inc., 1973.

Studio and Theatre Promotional Material

Blondes at Work press book. Warner Bros. Pictures, 1938.

Forty Carats Playbill. Morosco Theatre, Volume 5, Issue 12, December 1968.

The Girl in the Red Velvet Swing press book. 20th Century-Fox Film Corporation, 1955.

Biographies

Druxman, Michael B. *Paul Muni: His Life and Films*. New York: A.S. Barnes and Company, 1974.

Gansburg, Alan L. *Little Caesar: A Biography of Edward G. Robinson*. Lanham, Maryland: The Scarecrow Press, Inc., 2004.

Guralnick, Peter. *Careless Love: The Unmaking of Elvis Presley*. New York: Little, Brown and Company, 1999.

Nash, Alanna. *The Colonel: The Extraordinary Story of Colonel Tom Parker and Elvis Presley*. Chicago: Chicago Review Press, Inc., 2003.

Periodicals

Biery, Ruth, "The Mystery of Glenda Farrell's Missing Necklace," *Motion Picture*, August 1935.

Blondell, Joan, "My Pal, Glenda," *Hollywood*, January 1936.

Davis, Richard S., "Glenda Farrell Stars at Pabst," *Milwaukee Journal*, 12 September 1939.

Dowling, Mark, "Strictly Personal," *Movie Classic*, March 1934.

"Dr. Henry Ross, 89, Eisenhower's Chief of Health in War," 28 June 1991.

English, Richard, "Why Risk Love for a Wedding Ring?" *Hollywood*, August 1934.

Exhibitors Herald-World, 1930.

Exhibitors Herald and Moving Picture World, 1928.

Farrell, Tommy, "My Mom," *Photoplay*, Vol. XLVII, No. 6, May 1935.

Film Daily, 1928-1959.

Fletcher, Adele, "Weird Things Happen to the Stars," *Photoplay*, Vol. LI, No. 1, January 1937.

"Glenda Farrell Finally Given Leading Role," *Regina Leader-Post*, 17 November 1934.

"Glenda Farrell Gets Tough Role," *St. Petersburg Times*, 24 October 1943.

"Glenda Would Eat Candy If She Could," *Pittsburgh Press*, 27 December 1943.

Haynes, Harmony, "Should a Girl Marry Her Boss?" *Hollywood*, October 1935.

Herzog, "Buck," "Blond Glenda Farrell Likes Hollywood, But Is Glad to Get Away to Play Stock," *Milwaukee Sentinel*, 7 September 1939.

Hollis, Karen, "They Say in New York," *Picture Play*, October 1934.

Hollywood, 1934-1943.

Hollywood Filmograph, 1930-1934.

"Hollywood Has Gone to the Cats," *Hollywood*, July 1936.

Hollywood Reporter, 1932-1959

"Homes of the Stars," *Movie Classic*, Vol. 11, No. 6, February 1937.

International Photographer, 1931-1941

Jackson, Robert, "Legs! Do They Have to Show Them?" *Movie Classic*, July 1933.

Lee, Sonia, "Which Stars Will Survive Color?" *Movie Classic*, April 1935.

LeRoy, Mervyn, as told to Frederic Lewis, "A Director's Bird's-Eye View of the Stars," *New Movie Magazine*, June 1933.

Lusk, Norbert, "The Screen in Review," *Picture Play*, November 1932; January 1933; June 1935.

Morley, Dickson, "Discontented Toughy," *Picture Play*, April 1933.

Motion Picture, 1919-1941.

Motion Picture Daily, 1931-1934

Motion Picture Herald, 1931-1959

Motion Picture News, 1930.

Motion Picture Review Digest, 1936-1939.

Movie Classic, 1931-1937.

Movies, Vol. 4, No. 2, 1 June 1933.

The New Movie Magazine, 1931-1935.

New York Times, 1929-1971.

Oliver, Jane, "Silence is a Blight," *Hollywood Screen Life*, Vol. 28, No. 1, January 1939.

Palmer, Gordon, "They Discovered Friendship through Heartbreak," *Photoplay*, Vol. LI, No. 6, June 1937.

Picture Play, 1931-1938.

"Practical Suggestions for Good Looks," *Photoplay*, October 1934.

Radio Mirror, 1931-1939.

Rankin, Ruth, "How to Win Enemies," *Hollywood*, April 1938.

Reed, Dena, "Shady Lady's Son," *Picture Play*, August 1933.

Sylvia, "'Beware the Danger Line, Glenda,' Warns Sylvia," *Photoplay*, Vol. XLV, No. 6, May 1934.

Thomas, Bob, "Glenda Farrell Returns to Films after Five Years," *Pittsburgh Post-Gazette*, 19 June 1952.

Time, 30 May 1988.

Universal Weekly, 21 March 1936.

Van Neste, Dan, "Glenda Farrell: Diamond in the Rough," *Classic Images*, Vol. 275, May 1998.

Variety, 1926-1955

Williams, Whitney, "How Lines are Learned," *Picture Play*, March 1935.

Youngstown Vindicator, 3 September 1946.

Books on Cinema and Television

Balio Tino, ed. *I Am a Fugitive from a Chain Gang*. Madison: University of Wisconsin Press, 1981.

Bubbeo, Daniel. *The Women of Warner Brothers: The Lives and Careers of 15 Leading Ladies*. Jefferson, North Carolina: McFarland and Company, 2001.

Buhle, Paul, and Dave Wagner. *Radical Hollywood: The Untold Story Behind America's Favorite Movies*. New York: The New Press, 2002.

Gianakos, Larry James. *Studio One Anthology*. 6-DVD set. KOCH Entertainment, 2008.

Gifford, Denis. *A Pictorial History of Horror Movies*. London: The Hamlyn Publishing Group Limited, 1973.

Hirshhorn, Clive. *The Warner Bros. Story*. New York: Crown, 1979.

Nollen, Scott Allen. *Warners Wiseguys: All 112 Films That Robinson, Cagne-and Bogart Made for the Studio.* Jefferson, North Carolina: McFarland and Company, 2007.

Schatz, Thomas. *The Genius of the System: Hollywood Filmmaking in the Studio Era.* New York: Pantheon Books, 1988.

Documentary Films

"*Little Caesar*: End of Rico, Beginning of the Antihero." *Little Caesar* DVD. Turner Entertainment Co., 2005.

If you enjoyed this book,
write for a free catalog of
Midnight Marquee Press titles
or visit our website at
http://www.midmar.com

Midnight Marquee Press, Inc.
9721 Britinay Lane
Baltimore, MD 21234
410-665-1198
mmarquee@aol.com

Made in the USA
Middletown, DE
11 July 2016